Christine Manfield is one of Australia's most celebrated chefs – a perfectionist inspired by strong flavours, and a writer whose successful books *Dessert Divas*, *Tasting India*, *Fire*, *Spice*, *Stir*, *Christine Manfield Originals* and *Christine Manfield Desserts* have spiced up the lives of keen cooks everywhere.

An inveterate traveller, Christine regularly works alongside respected chefs around the world and hosts gastronomic tours to exotic destinations including India, Morocco, Spain and Bhutan. Having eaten her way around India for more than two decades, and more recently Bhutan, she is a passionate and erudite guide to the food of these endlessly fascinating lands.

A PERSONAL

GUIDE TO

INDIA

& BHUTAN

CHRISTINE
MANFIELD

LANTERN

an imprint of
PENGUIN BOOKS

CONTENTS

INTRODUCTION

'INDIA IS NOT A DESTINATION, IT IS AN EXPERIENCE.'
This is a favourite quote from my friend and colleague Navina Jafa, a Delhi-based cultural historian, and it sums up my attitude to India perfectly.

India defies description. Each journey is a discovery; every corner is mysterious and relatively un-interpreted. The sheer panorama can take your breath away, its energy palpable and infectious. It pays to delve into the very heart and soul of the country to experience the unexpected. At its best, India is a heady mix of adventure, exotic flavours, delightful surprises and intoxicating memories. It offers a cornucopia of colours, textures and tastes.

India's rich tapestry is evident in its people, its religion and its food. With its complex religious and ethnic fabric, India is a country that boasts 'Unity in Diversity' and this is apparent in so many parts of the country – from Nagaland in the north-east across to Kerala in the south-west and Kashmir in the north-west. You'll be humbled by the kindness and friendliness of strangers and the warmth and grace of the people as you are made to feel welcome and treated as an honoured, highly esteemed guest.

India's food is anything but homogenous and I urge you to use this guide as a starting point for your own gastronomic adventures. Indians are renowned for their generosity and hospitality, and the delights of travelling in India are infinite. You could be invited to share home-cooked food at the family table in a private house, savour delectable snacks from a street vendor, or experience the thrill of an early-morning train ride. This is a favourite adventure of mine; a journey that lasts for around five hours is perfect to soak up the lively atmosphere and passing landscape. At every stop, food vendors stalk the aisles, bustling through crowded carriages, hawking their wares from samosas, chaat snacks, sweets and pastries to chai and coffee – it's a cacophony of sound. The type of food on offer changes according to the region and may vary from one stop to the next. Every journey is like a microcosm of Indian life – and the old adage that the journey is as important as the destination was never truer. Indian chefs and home cooks are exploring new culinary frontiers and offering more diverse experiences, while their restaurant culture is flourishing, so there is much to explore and experience.

This book makes an ideal companion to *Tasting India*; it's a guide from my first-hand experiences. I have visited and personally recommend every place in this book. I want this book to make you, the reader, aware of India and awaken your desire to visit this incredible country, while fostering a respect for its traditions. It is written with a modern and current perspective that includes my favourite tips on where to find the best street food as well as suggestions for diverse regional dishes to sample during your travels. Adopt my philosophy, 'Life begins at the end of your comfort zone.' ✿

TRAVEL TIPS

Food safety

To eat any of the foods you have longed for or heard about at their very source is a rite of passage, a homecoming for me; an opportunity to worship the diversity of flavours I so adore. Street food is one of the best ways to discover the essence of India, so don't miss out because of some ill-conceived fear that you will get food poisoning. Apply the same safety rules as you would anywhere in the world and trust your instincts. A general rule of thumb is to drink bottled water and don't eat cut fruit from a street vendor; buying whole fruit that you can peel is perfectly fine. Bottled water is used for all food preparation in restaurants. Street vendors who use bottled water will have a sign to say so. I keep away from anything that is water-based when eating street food as the water source can be unreliable. This includes sugar cane juice (great when made with bottled water in a restaurant but it can cause a chronic reaction if not), and tamarind water in puri snacks – just have the snacks dry, minus the tamarind, unless of course you are eating them from a reliable source.

Safety for female travellers

I strongly recommend you plan for reliable ground support through your travel agent, and ask for a car with an English-speaking driver for the duration of your stay, especially if you are doing any distance trips.

Book a local guide for each city or place you are visiting; this can be arranged through a reputable travel agent or ground operator in India. Walking around and sightseeing with an expert local (man or woman) acts like an invisible shield of protection, with the added advantage of gaining better insight into the culture along the way.

If you go shopping or to dinner, book a hotel car; the driver will give you his mobile number to call when you are ready to be picked up – it takes all the stress out of finding a reliable taxi.

There are many travel agencies and urban initiatives now that support women and solo travellers, such as taxi services for women only in Bombay, Delhi and other big urban centres, with female drivers. (www.womenstaxi.org)

As you will mostly encounter men in the public domain, foreign women are more often than not a cause for curiosity. Deal with any unwanted conversations by being firm without being rude. The best response to petty annoyances is to ignore them.

Be street-savvy and keep your wits about you (this applies to any country you visit) – it helps to have some idea of where you are going and to appear confident on the streets. Rely on your inner sense of feeling safe. Don't walk alone at night – take the usual precautions you would anywhere. Travel with a small group tour if you don't feel confident venturing out on your own.

You will equally encounter so many acts of kindness and generosity and meet wonderful people.

Tipping

Tipping for service is discretionary and not mandatory, but local custom assumes a small gratuity or token of appreciation when a bellboy carries your bags to your hotel room or to check in, or on to a train carriage – the standard practice is 30 to 50 rupee per bag. Some larger hotels, independent boutique properties and camps have

a tipping policy in place where you can leave something upon departure which is pooled and distributed among the staff. Service is often added on to a bill in a restaurant, so check first and if not, then anything up to 10 per cent is appreciated. If you have a car and driver, a guide or other personal services, then check with your travel agent about the appropriate procedure when you are booking the service.

Beggars

In areas popular with tourists, beggars of all types – street kids, disabled and disenfranchised or homeless adults – may approach travellers asking for money or sweets. Giving money to allay feelings of guilt only exacerbates and perpetuates the problem and dampens your spirit. It would be wiser to give fresh food or clean water as an immediate quick fix.

It's about trying to break the cycle of poverty and corruption, so that children aren't forced to beg to supplement a meagre family income or to be enslaved to a mafia boss who controls it all – they could go to school and be educated.

Perhaps carry something unique from your own country, such as photo postcards, stickers, pens, pencils or picture books; donate to a school library or invest in a philanthropic cause that touches your heart – there are plenty to choose from that do fantastic work in India. Spend time talking to locals at every opportunity and contribute in a positive way; something that is meaningful and respectful.

Getting a visa

Finally India has liberalised its visa regime and introduced Visa on Arrival enabled by ETA (Electronic Travel Authorisation) for forty-three countries including Australia. It's a four-step process (navigation and set-up is not that straightforward) – attach a scanned photograph with a white background and a scanned copy of your passport photo page with your online application. Visas can be applied for no fewer than five days and no more than thirty days prior to arrival. www.indianvisaonline.gov.in

Alternatively, you can fill out a visa application form online, print it out and take it into the Indian Passport and Visa Office in Australia for processing, which takes about three working days. A tourist visa is valid for six months and you can request a single or double entry when applying. www.vfsglobal.com/india/australia

BHUTAN

It was my love for the Himalayas that drew me to the remote kingdom of Bhutan, a natural extension to my mountain travels through India. Sandwiched between north-east India and Tibet, Bhutan's appeal lies in its difference from any other place on earth. ❀

A visit to this ancient kingdom is a pilgrimage, and each time I can't help but be touched by the peaceful Zen energy of this Buddhist land. Monasteries and temples cling to the sides of impossibly high cliffs across the country; how they were built in the first place defies belief. Chortens (or stupas), Buddhist burial mounds that are used as places of meditation, are scattered across the landscape. There is magic in the air everywhere.

Bhutan is distinguished by having the economic slogan of Gross National Happiness (GNH), coined by a visionary king (the fourth Druk Gyalpo, which means 'Dragon King') in the early Eighties. This means that the country's performance is measured on the wellbeing of all Bhutanese. Happiness is thought more important and valuable than 'product'. This is a revolutionary concept that has sparked the imaginations of modern philosophers, economists and thinkers, because there is an emphasis and real value placed on the wisdom of elders, and on peaceful co-existence rather than youth, beauty, strength and outer prosperity. With an economic policy that would no longer consider consumerism more important than social progress, a new doctrine was introduced that would reduce pollution, mental illness, depression, obesity, suicide, drug use and general unhappiness or malaise, with a higher value placed on age, wisdom, peaceful coexistence and inner

prosperity and spiritual enlightenment. It's a revelation that reminded me of the wise words of Robert Kennedy in 1968: '[Gross national product] measures neither our wit nor our courage, neither our wisdom nor our learning, neither our compassion nor our devotion to our country. It measures everything, in short, except that which makes life worthwhile.'

Bhutan is the last surviving kingdom in the Himalayas and since 2008, a constitutional monarchy. Learn the local greeting of kuzu-zang-bo-la – 'hello' in the national language of Dzongkha – and watch the delighted reactions of the Bhutanese. Take time to stop and chat to people; the Bhutanese are famous for their warm hospitality and kindness, and travelling there is made all the richer by interacting with the people and engaging in conversation. People are proud, generous and acutely conscious of the need to preserve their unique cultural traditions and physical environment. The government actively discourages mass tourism by imposing a daily mandatory tax of around $200 or so per person for visitors that includes a driver and guide, food and accommodation. You don't just arrive and go romping off without guidance. Bhutan promotes responsible, sustainable, carefully managed tourism, nurturing its pristine environment and remaining culturally intact. Taxes collected are used wisely, particularly for health services and the

education of children and women in remote rural areas. The country has looked closely at its immediate neighbours and seen the devastating destruction caused by mass tourism, has taken lessons from this and employed a different strategy. The doors have recently opened to visitors, who come in small but increasing numbers. You have the feeling of being somewhere untouched, of another world; of a magical place coming out of seclusion.

It's utterly delightful to traverse the country and not see a single billboard; no advertising, no tacky western food chains anywhere. It's a place that commands respect for its traditions and lifestyle. It will be interesting to see how the country responds to television and the internet, which have recently become available, with their powerful, pervasive and invasive influences. Its capital Thimphu is fast changing; buildings are being erected at a rate of knots, with hotels, apartments and shops under construction. Paro remains reminiscent of a Wild West frontier town, and travellers are venturing further east beyond Bumthang to Trashigang, while the remote north remains the sole territory of yak herders and the dedicated trekker.

Bhutanese love to eat the same thing every day, so to avoid monotony and discover real regional diversity, it pays to become friendly with local foodies, who can introduce you to a much broader selection of flavoursome food. The best Bhutanese food is cooked at home, where an amazing array of dishes can be presented on the table if you're as lucky as I have been. The produce everywhere is organic, spanking fresh and seasonal; the weekly markets across the country are a revelation. It's possible to taste myriad chillies from mild to searing hot, organic asparagus, wild mushrooms, nettles, fiddlehead ferns, the indigenous red rice (actually a pale pink colour), bony little river trout fished from the mountain streams, the local cheese that is used in just about every dish, yak meat, peaches, apricots, apples and strawberries, depending on the season.

From my extensive travel and in-depth research across India and Bhutan, I have realised that I have an insatiable appetite and a deep, passionate love for India and the Himalayan region that includes Bhutan.

These are not countries that you put on your shortlist to be seen, skimmed over and ticked off – that misses the point entirely. My advice is to stay in places that make you feel pampered, that offer genuine and often luxurious hospitality, so my suggestions of where to sleep are unashamedly at the higher end of the spectrum and not designed for the budget traveller. I urge you to explore the regional diversity and many experiences on offer, to make the most of the suggested essential sights and put food in its context to give an invaluable, deeper meaning to the travel experience.

TRAVEL TIPS

Rather than an ad hoc approach, I suggest you invest in direct, meaningful philanthropy by donating to a local accredited NGO charity such as RENEW renewbhutan.org. The Australian Himalayan Foundation works closely with RENEW to support education for girls in remote communities of Bhutan and was established in 2004 by Her Majesty (Queen Mother) Ashi Sangay Choden Wangchuck. It's an initiative that aims to increase awareness and improve the lives of the Bhutanese people by identifying and filling critical gaps and one that I have lent my support to since first visiting the kingdom.

BOMBAY (MUMBAI)

City

THE CITY OF DREAMS AND OPPORTUNITY! INDIA IS a land of paradoxes, contradictions and contrasts, highs and lows, beauty and despair, joy and sadness, wealth and poverty, and Mumbai has all of these. It is the most frenetic city in India, without a doubt – an exciting, exhilarating, edgy urban jungle, a kaleidoscope of riotous colour and energy that leaves a lasting impression, and a true melting pot where you can't help but feel alive – the mesmerising, seductive and cosmopolitan heartbeat of modern India. Bombay's name was officially changed to Mumbai in the 1990s, but everyone still refers to it as Bombay, so I will stick with the locals and use this name here. Both are acceptable and interchanged without fuss. Everyone, whether local or visitor, wants a piece of Bombay's fame and fortune. It's one of India's key tourist destinations, big on personality and style, exhilarating at every turn, its food a showcase of regional diversity. ✿

ESSENTIAL SIGHTS

Walk through the Colaba, Fort and Ballard Estate districts and eyeball the wonderful colonial edifices and neoclassical architecture. Stop off at one of the street vendors along Khao Galli, a terrific food street, at lunch between 1 and 3 p.m.; look out for *kheecha* (seasoned rice flour flatbread cooked over hot coals) and perennial staples – *vada pav* (soft white bread roll with spiced potato and tamarind chutney filling – a Maharastrian staple) and *bhel puri* (a snack of puffed rice, diced potato and onion, tangy tamarind, chilli, *moong dal* and coriander chutney).

Explore the Crawford Market for amazing fresh produce, get your spices from the Spice King (shop number 133 in the fourth lane) or head to Mirchi Galli (Chilli Lane) in the Lalbaug district for the abundant displays of dried chillies, and the snack shops next door where everything is made by hand. Don't miss the early-morning flower market in Dadar (just before sunrise) near the heritage area of Shivaji Park where many Maharashtrian vego cafes and food vendors have set up to feed workers and shoppers.

Stand outside Marine Lines station a little after 11 a.m. to watch the distribution of tiffin lunch boxes as the tiffin wallahs get off the trains and deliver over two million lunches each day. It's miraculous to see: food is cooked in home kitchens, collected and delivered to the right person at the right office every day. An urban marvel that is ingenious and brilliantly organised.

To experience excellent, authentic home cooking at a shared table in a private

residence with true local character, check out www.mealtango.com. It is a brilliant initiative started up by Saket Khanna – you choose online from the various options and regional cuisines available, from Assam, Kerala, Rajasthan, Maharasthra and more. I had lunch with a Maharasthran family who educated me into the subtleties of the various sub-genres and clans within the community – food that you would only ever find in the home, not at restaurants. It was a revelation and something I can highly recommend. It's like tapping straight into the spirit of the city, shared with generous and engaging hosts.

Visit the sacred Banganga Tank, an ancient water tank that forms part of the Walkeshwar Temple Complex in the Malabar Hill area, revered by Hindus. The origin of the tank is shrouded in Hindu myth, connected to the god Rama. The site has a reputation for medicinal properties and is used as a place of purification. Hindus on pilgrimages to the Walkeshwar Temple Complex ritually wash in the Banganga Tank before entering the temple. The site has become a cultural centre as well as a place of spiritual pilgrimage. One of the oldest surviving structures in Bombay, it is a national heritage site protected by the government.

Hang out at Chowpatty Beach in south Bombay or Juhu Beach in north Bombay and sample myriad snacks from the street food vendors and watch the sun sink into the sea. The action becomes lively after dark when locals flock to the beach to relax and catch up with friends and family.

Bandra in north Bombay has a local food scene that is vibrant, diverse and fun. In the early morning, head to the Bazar Road market; in the evening, take a stroll through Union Park where the young guns hang out, the long street lined with fast food joints and street cafes with an eclectic mix of Middle Eastern, Greek, Italian, Indian and Tibetan, then stop off at candlelit Olive Bar and Kitchen for a well-deserved cocktail or glass of wine. Of all the bars here, it has the most happening, friendly vibe.

Rummage around Chor Bazaar (Thieves' Market), a maze of streets dedicated to antiques, anything vintage, Bollywood posters and furniture.

Spend a morning walking through Dharavi, the largest slum in Mumbai and India. There are a staggering 2000 slums in Bombay alone – and gain insight into the cheek by jowl contrasts that are among the city's most compelling spectacles. You can't do this on your own, so contact We the Local – a group of students who live with their families in the slum and offer wonderful insights in to the daily lives and routine of this city within a city, offering a responsible travel initiative. My guide Ankit tells me Dharavi is three square kilometres, with a density of 530 000 people per square kilometre. In Bombay the figure is 35 000 per square kilometre, just to give you some perspective. Colour Box is an art space featuring art by slum residents made with recycled materials, so check for regular exhibitions. The Dharavi art biennale was launched in February 2015, an inspirational initiative by SNEHA, a Mumbai-based, not-for-profit organisation that targets health, nutrition and domestic violence by combining art and science, to highlight the contribution of the people of Dharavi to

India's economic and cultural life, and to share information on urban health. www.dharavibiennale.com

At sunrise, visit Sassoon Dock wholesale fish market in Colaba – just make sure you go with a local resident. If you're brave and can cope with intense crowds, cajoling, pushing and shoving, it's worth it to watch the fishermen unload their boats on to the dock where the fish is dispensed to other markets and shops across the city.

Join a local food walk and discover first-hand some of the interesting parts of the city; this also gives you a chance to hang out with fellow food lovers.

Taste the city's best *lassi* (Indian yoghurt drink) at Lassiwalla (Shop 312, outside Dadar station); this district is the heartland of Maharashtrian culture, reflected in the many food places that define the area.

Become addicted to *bhel puri* – a savoury *chaat* (snack) of puffed rice, potato, tangy tamarind sauce and herbs, thought to have originated on the beaches of Bombay. If you are there during monsoon season, try some of their monsoon treats, when dishes become hot and spicy as an antidote to the steamy wet weather and dull grey skies. Every region of India celebrates the monsoon with some distinctive food to help boost immunity, keep infections at bay and aid digestion. In Bombay, snacks such as sprouted lentils mixed with a spicy *masala* and served with *pav* (a soft white bun), or *batata kachori* (mashed potato mixed with grated coconut, green chilli, coriander, cashews and raisins, rolled into balls and flattened to make a round patty, then deep-fried), served with a sweet potato and tamarind chutney, are firm favourites.

A handy address for solo female travellers and well worth supporting: the all-women taxi service in Bombay. www.priyadarshinitaxi.com.

If you have time on your hands and want to explore the state further inland, book yourself on to the **Deccan Odyssey** for a dose of luxury train travel that offers a one-week round trip from Mumbai to Sindhudurg, Goa, Chandrapur, the spectacular Ajanta Caves and Nashik (the up-and-coming wine region of India). www.deccan-odyssey-india.com.

Catch a suburban local train (out of peak hour) in the middle of the day – ride a few stops and experience how millions of people commute on a daily basis. I suggest you splash out and buy a first-class ticket; the extra few rupees are definitely worth it.

Extra resources for feel-good philanthropic travel: www.grassroutesjourneys.com www.gophilanthropic.com

EAT: SOUTH BOMBAY

Ankur Bar and Restaurant

Meadows House, M.P. Shetty Marg,
Tamarind Lane, Fort
Tel: 2265 4194

A local haunt once patronised by the city's poets and writers, Ankur remains a safe bet for lunch with a menu featuring coastal seafood favourites. Try the prawn *gassi* (a rich, spicy coconut gravy), the fish (*kane*) *koliwada*, *paneer makkhani* or the vegetable Hyderabadi *biryani*.

Apoorva

Vasta House, S.A. Breelvi Rd,
Fort (near Horniman Circle)
Tel: 2287 0335

As in many of the city's restaurants, the menu appears unwieldy. Cut to the chase – their speciality is coastal cuisine, so stick to that. I like their king crab Hariyali *masala* (a green masala gravy with herbs, spinach, ginger garlic paste and aromatic spices), prawn *sukka* (dry fried with spices) and Mangalorean fish curry, a mildly spiced gravy with chopped coriander and mint.

Ayub's

43 Forbes St (Dr V.B. Ghandi Marg),
behind Rhythm House, Kala Ghoda, Fort
Tel: 098 21 199147

This place has become one of the most happening spots in town during the evening, especially late when locals stop off for a kebab on their way home after a night in a bar or club. It's always packed, so expect to queue, especially on weekends. Hang in or next to your car, as the locals do – this is called bonnet service, or 'eat on the street'. Try the egg *paratha* roll or *paneer* roll if you're vego; my favourites are the chicken *tikka kathi* kebab roll and *boti* (mutton) kebab, big on spicy flavour with delicious chutneys. Finger-licking good and cheap as chips, and the vibrant street theatre is free of charge.

Bademiya

Tulloch Rd, Apollo Bunder, off M.B. Marg,
Colaba (laneway behind Taj Mahal Hotel)
Tel: 2284 8038 (to call for take-away)

Street food vendor showcasing various kebabs, grilled meats and kebab *roti* rolls with a buzzy atmosphere. Sadly, the live theatre provided by eating on the street has given way to stricter regulations – gone are the tables and chairs on the pavement. You now sit inside a nondescript cement bunker type room off the street, so a little of that former magic has disappeared and the whole experience has become sanitised. The guy making *roomali roti* over a red-hot convex metal plate has been stationed behind the counter, no longer on the street where you could once walk right up and stand next to him. The breads are sensational and cooked to order. Locals drive by to collect take-away or sit on their car bonnets for a makeshift dinner table.

Batchelor's

Marine Drive, opposite Chowpatty Beach
Tel: 2368 1408

Roadside stall on opposite side of road to the beach (and opposite Thakkers) selling divine ice cream, a local landmark. Green chilli and ginger are my two favourite flavours: perfect afternoon snacks. It gets very busy during the evening when hordes descend. They also make fresh juices with seasonal fruits.

By the Way Cafe

Pandita Ramabai Rd, Gamdevi
(next door to police station)
Tel: 2380 3532 | www.sevasadan.org

Run by the Seva Sadan Society for the empowerment of underprivileged girls and women. Support this worthwhile cause and stop by for a sandwich or some *dal* with rice when you visit Mahatma Gandhi's house, just around the corner. Honest and simple.

Cafe Military

Ali Chamber, Tamarind Ln, Fort
Tel: 2265 4181

Another Irani Parsi cafe, this humble corner cafe also serves beer. The standout dish is their brilliant *kheema ghotala* – minced lamb cooked with eggs and spices. Like many Irani places, they have a daily changing menu with a different specialty dish each day.

Cafe Samovar

Jehangir Art Gallery, Kala Ghoda
Tel: 2204 7276

An ideal place to stop for coffee, a drink or a snack. Try the flaky *parathas* stuffed with spiced potato and soak up the buzzy original atmosphere.

Cafe Zoe

Tody/Mathurada Mill Compound,
N.M. Joshi Marg, Lower Parel
Tel: 2490 2065

A place that operates on sustainable principles and does a brisk trade from morning breakfast late into the night when the space morphs into a club (party bar) after dinner and the pace picks up – popular with locals who live or work in the area, which is full of corporate offices. This cafe, in a converted mill (as are many businesses around here), has a contemporary feel and post-industrial ambience, and is a generous open space with lots of light. The breakfasts are okay; the service can be a little tardy but their salads and sandwiches make good comfort food and the strawberry smoothie is delicious.

Chetana

34 K Dubash Marg (opposite Jahagir
Art Gallery), Kala Ghoda, Fort
Tel: 2284 4968

A good place to try authentic Maharashtrian food. Come for lunch and order one of their *thalis* (they have different ones for each region). The small stuffed eggplants that are cooked with coconut and peanuts (or cashews), the *moong dal* and their rice flour *rotis* are among my favourite dishes here.

Ideal Corner

12F/G, Hornby View, Gunbow St, Fort
Tel: 022 2262 1930

I love the rich, spice-laden *dhansak* here (a slow-braised lamb, vegetable and lentil stew); arguably the most famous of the Parsi dishes that are served like clockwork every Friday at this popular city cafe. It's a dish packed with wholesome flavour and motherly love. The menu features a special dish for each day of the week, and their version of *akuri* (Parsi-style scrambled eggs) is a good breakfast choice.

Konkan Cafe

Taj President Hotel, Cuffe Parade, Colaba
Tel: 6665 0808

Chef Ananda Solomon's regional food, which follows the principles of slow cooking, is a showcase of India's best from the Konkan coast of Maharashtra to Goa and Karnataka, flavours that are refreshingly authentic and honest with wonderful complex layers of texture, astute seasoning and beautifully cooked seafood, even if the surrounds are somewhat kitsch. His menus are based on three seasons: monsoon, winter and summer. They do some wonderful dishes with *bombil* (Bombay duck), a local fish only found in this city, and whatever you do, don't miss the stuffed eggplants (*Bharleli Vanghi*), crab pepper fry, Konkan Masala clams, and the dry-fried Malvani prawns (*Taleli Sungte*). The kitchen also makes a fantastic *jalebi* that's not to be missed.

Kyani and Co. Bakery

Jer Mahal Building, 657, Kalbadevi,
JSS Rd, Tak Wadi, Lohar Chawl, Marine Lines
(near Metro Theatre)
Tel: 022 2201 1492

A typical Irani heritage cafe with age-old charm and an extensive menu: an institution with the locals. Try the *parsi akuri* – a wonderful spicy scrambled egg dish, or the mutton crisp pastries, which look like sausage rolls. You get two for 18 rupees and they are delicious. Make sure to also try their berry *pulao* (a typical Persian rice dish) and their very popular *kheema ghotala* – minced lamb cooked with masala and eggs. Leave space for the caramel custard or a raspberry soda.

Leopold Cafe

Colaba Causeway
(at corner of Nawroji F Rd), Colaba
Tel: 2202 0131

A local landmark for more than a hundred years, now a rite of passage for any visitor to Mumbai. This is one of those places that you simply have to visit. Go to soak up the frenetic, noisy atmosphere. Made more famous by its mention in Gregory David Roberts' extraordinary novel *Shantaram*, what was once a home for writers is now a travellers' staple and draws a more western crowd. Stop for a refreshing lemonade or for a crème caramel after dinner elsewhere. The menu is pretty pedestrian, so a drink will suffice.

Mahesh Lunch Home

8B Cawasji Patel St, Fort
Tel: 2287 0938

My favourite place for fish and seafood in Bombay, with an extensive menu that features Mangalorean and Konkan favourites, their crab dishes are the speciality of the house – crab tandoori, crab meat tossed in garlic pepper butter and the crab *sukha* (dry-fried with *masala* spices) are the stars, as is the fish *masala* fry. The fish is fresh off the day boats so trust their suggestions and be sure to order some *neer dosa*, soft rice flour crepes. Try *sol kadi*, a digestive drink made with thin coconut milk and *kokum* syrup, seasoned with ginger powder, black rock salt and coriander leaves. It's very refreshing and clean tasting.

Neel on the Turf

Keshav Rao Khadye Marg,
Mahalaxmi Racecourse
Tel: 6157 7777

A fine dining restaurant with silver service waiters, a grand room with tables framed by large windows. The menu features a variety of Lucknowi and Peshawari dishes, where flavours are refined, rich, spicy and perfectly cooked. The fish is tender, the kebabs melt-in-the-mouth, the condiments (chutneys and pickles) show real attention to detail and they make the best *jalebi* I have eaten in Bombay – ethereally light batter, not too sweet.

Sardar Pav Bhaji

Taredo Rd, Janata Nagar, Taredo (just up from the corner of Bellasis Rd)

The most typical Bombay staple from street vendors across town, *pau bhaji* or *vada pav* – potato curry in soft white bun – is India's version to a hamburger, only tons better. A breakfast favourite at one of the city's must-visits.

Shree Thakker Bhojanalay

1st Floor, 31 Dadiseth Agiary Marg
(opposite GT High School, off Kalbadevi Rd),
Bhuleshwar
Tel: 2201 1232 or 2206 9916

The ideal approach is to walk through the laneways and congested streets of the wholesale cloth market, jewellery market and past the kitchen utensil market to arrive at this hidden gem. The vegetarian lunch *thali* is one of the best in town, the menu items change regularly but you can expect corn *dhokla*, *aloo rasawala*, a vegetable *pulao* and more. The variety of flatbreads they serve is second to none and they love it when you ask for seconds. The room is modest, with the ambience of an informal workers' canteen. The staff are friendly and welcoming. One of the city's essential food experiences.

Soam

Ground floor, Sadguru Sadan,
Grant Road (opposite Babulnath Temple),
Girgaum (near Kemps Cnr)
Tel: 2369 8080

A vegetarian menu that showcases a broad range of Gujarati and Marwari specialties.

Start with the *chaat*: *bhel puri*, *sev puri*, *pani puri* (round hollow puris filled with tamarind water, chutney, chilli, chaat masala, potato, onion and chickpeas), *dahi puri* (yoghurt) and *dahi papdi chaat* (fried puri disks topped with potato, sprouts, chutney, yoghurt and *sev*) are a must, then try a few *farsan* (snacks) – *palak* (spinach) and cheese samosas, *dhokla* (steamed rice and white lentil cakes) and *makai wadi* (fried corn cakes), or the *jain paanki* – chickpea batter spread between two banana leaves and steamed. For mains – order two dishes, and that will be enough to share between six after tasting all those snacks. The sweet and salty *lassi* (yoghurt drink) is heaven, and try the mango when it's in season, as well as the fresh sugar cane juice. The decor is modern and chic. There are no bookings, so be prepared to queue as this is one of Mumbai's most popular lunch places.

The Table

Ground floor, Kalash Peshi Building
Chhatrapati Shivaji Maharaj Marg, Apollo
Bunder Marg, Colaba (opposite Dhanraj
Mahal and below Suba Palace Hotel)
Tel: 2282 5000

This is the place to head when you need a fix of contemporary European food. The chef is from San Francisco, and the menu is Western with global flavours. The desserts alone are worthy of a visit. Start with a perfectly balanced beetroot risotto or the slow-roasted lamb shank, and make sure you order the salted caramel and popcorn sundae for dessert; it's to die for. They have a smart wine list and the bar makes a decent cocktail.

Taj Ice Cream

40 Sayed Abu Mohammed Rd,
Bhendi Bazaar, Buleshwar
Tel: 2346 1257

Also in the Bhori Muslim enclave, this fifth-generation family business has been serving hand-churned ice creams to locals for many decades, using seasonal fruits such as custard apple, gooseberry, strawberry and mango. Get chatting with the owners, they are charming.

Thackers Club

116–118 1st Marine St, Chowpatty
Tel: 2205 3582

Head upstairs to the large room with swift service where they serve a set-price Gujarati vegetarian *thali*. Best at lunch, it's great value and the flavours are distinct and authentic. The *dal* and vegetable dishes vary according to the season. It's like your very own never-ending buffet, with an array of dishes set on a *thali* plate – the waiters keep topping up till you say no more.

Trishna

7 Sai Baba Marg, Kala Ghoda, Fort
Tel: 2270 1623

Sophisticated fine dining restaurant for the city's A-list, considered some of the best seafood in the city and packed with the moneyed business set at lunch. It's the place of choice for the city's movers and shakers. Reservations are essential, and make sure you request a table in the front (main) dining room – not the side room, as it feels a little like Siberia. My favourite dishes include prawns *koliwada* (tiny local prawns fried in a crisp batter seasoned and coloured with deep red Kashmiri chilli powder), their signature butter pepper garlic crab, pomfret green masala and *reshmi* chicken (tender chunks of chicken cooked in a ginger garlic coriander paste with yoghurt and ground almonds or cashews).

Vali Bhai Payawala

45 Gujar St (near Zainabia Hall),
Bohri Mohalla
Tel: 2345 9994

Head into the heart of the Bhori Muslim community amid the throngs of people who flock here each evening. Located under the JJ flyover near the Chor Bazaar (Thieves Market), it comes alive at night. Head in to find this modest eating house that specialises in *bara handi*, where twelve *handi* pots are set into a flat tile bench, with each containing different cuts of meat and offal – ranging from trotters (*chote ka paya*) to bone marrow, tail (*pichota*) and liver, each in a spicy, oil-rich gravy and served with *naan*. Also worth tasting is a dish of potatoes cooked with Kashmiri chilli, *kokum*, curry leaves, mustard and coriander seeds – it's tart and tangy, and a good foil for the richness of the meat. There are many

places that serve this; what distinguishes one from the other is the quality and depth of flavour of the broth. Other places sell delicious-looking chicken kebabs, *biryani* and other sizzling snacks that cook on the hot grill.

Volga Paan House

Ground Floor, Islam Building (opposite Akbarallys), Nanabhai Ln, Kala Ghoda, Churchgate
Tel: 022 2288 1442

This is a *paan* institution owned by the Singh brothers, who have been turning out fresh *panto* for devotees in the city for many decades. *Paan* is a betel leaf filled with various ingredients, among them betel nut, lime paste, spices and sometimes tobacco – an acquired taste. Have it delivered to your car as you drive by; now that's service.

Yadzani Irani Café

11 Cawasji Patel St, Fort
(opposite Flora Fountain)
Tel: 2287 0739

This family-owned Irani bakery and tea shop housed in an old Japanese bank does a roaring trade from early morning throughout the day. The various breads and pastries are baked in a huge wood-fired oven at the back of the shop. Their *brun maska* (crusty bread roll with butter) and Irani chai are their benchmarks – they are what you come for; and are bloody delicious. It's also worth trying their freshly baked apple pie, or take one away with you along with a loaf of their seven-grain bread. Many locals say you are not a true resident of Bombay until you've visited Yadzani.

EAT: NORTH BOMBAY

Bong Bong

5 Silver Croft, CHS, corner 16th
and 33rd Rd, Bandra West
Tel: 6555 5567

A tiny space (next door to Khane Khas) that seats a mere fourteen people with a counter at the front that makes assorted rolls for a quick-fix snack on the go – try the *paneer bhurji roll* or the *egg mutton roll*. The food is contemporary Bengali and the hits on the menu include mango pickle steamed fish, baby eggplant in mustard coriander sauce, prawns in Bengal mustard sauce and the railway mutton curry. Whatever you do, make sure you try the weird-sounding but heavenly 'plastic chutney': thin slices of green papaya cooked in sugar, lime and chilli with raisins – truly memorable.

BusaGo

St John Rd, Pali Hill, Bandra West
(next door to Suzette)
Tel: 6127 8897

A smart little Asian cafe (sister to Busaba) that makes the best *kaukswe* in town. This is a nourishing Burmese staple with Indian spicing; rice noodles and chicken (and sometimes egg) are added to an aromatic coconut broth, with fresh, crunchy condiments such as fried shallots, coriander, prawn pickle, chilli and sprouts added for extra flavour and texture. It's the ultimate comfort food. If you want a sandwich with a difference, try one of their *banh mi* (Asian flavours in a French-style baguette) that have been the rage for some time now. Needless to say, the 'CSI: Mumbai' has a distinctive Indian flavour.

Candies

5AA Pali Hill, Bandra West
(next to Learners Academy School)
Tel: 2642 4124

The narrow street entrance belies the size of this place, which is a favourite hangout for the young locals. The vibe is relaxed and hip, and there are different levels; head towards the back and upstairs to the rooftop terrace. The unwieldy menu embraces Western and Indian comfort food favourites, appealing to its broad clientele. I stick with either a chicken tikka roll or the lightly spiced Afghani chicken, cooked in the tandoor. I steer clear of the garish desserts and cakes, where someone has certainly been let loose with artificial colouring.

Elco

2A Elco Market, 46 Hill Road, Bandra West
Tel: 6515 7171

A *pani puri* centre, with delicious vegetarian *chaat* snacks. Whatever you do, don't miss the *pani puri* – round, hollow *puri*, fried crisp and filled with a mixture of mint-flavoured water, tamarind chutney, chilli, *chaat masala*, potato, onion and chickpeas. Each one is handmade to order and is a sensational burst of flavour and texture – the best snack imaginable. One of my favourite places to eat *chaat* in Bombay.

Ganesh Bhavan

2 Juhu Beach, Juhu Tara Rd
(opposite the Ramada Plaza Palm
Grove Hotel)

Juhu Beach at sunset is action packed,
full of locals out to socialise, and the food
vendors do a roaring trade. This place
serves south Indian food, and their *dosas*
(flat crisp crepe made from a batter of fermented rice and lentils) and *dal vada* (fried
lentil and chilli patties) are knock-outs.
Food is cooked to order and the tastes transport you south to Kerala. At other vendors,
try the *pav bhaji* (bread roll with vegetable
and tomato stew) or the *ragda pattice* –
potato patties with gram gravy, onion
and crispy *sev* sprinkled over the top.

Gypsy Corner

Opposite Shiv Sena Bhawan, Keluskar Rd,
Dadar Shivaji Park
Tel: 2446 7518

The Dadar district is home to Maharashtrian vegetarian food and this place is
authentic and good. Come at lunch, put
your name on the list if the tables are full,
expect to queue but the wait is never too
long as the pace is fast. Start with *piyush*,
a light liquid *shrikhand* – yoghurt drink flavoured with saffron. Try *puris* made with
amaranth flour; the *puri* with *dalimbi usal*
(pomegranate and sprouts) is divine. The
bharli wangi (stuffed baby eggplant in a thick
peanut gravy) is a standout; I also recommend *thalipith*, a flatbread made with grains
and lentils; *misal* – a sprout curry that varies
in its spiciness with potatoes, tomato and
coriander and fried bits on top (also a
popular street snack); *puran poli*, a flatbread
stuffed with lentils and jaggery; and *modak*,

a sweet steamed dumpling similar to a *momo* with a coconut, jaggery and cardamom stuffing. Every dish we tasted was utterly delicious. When you leave, check out the sweets and snacks at Shree Samarth or stock up on a few pickles and *masala* pastes from *Santosh Masale* across the road.

Highway Gomantak

44/2179 Ghandi Nagar (facing highway), Bandra East
Tel: 2640 9692

Bandra East is far less cosmopolitan and more humble than the west side and this place displays that contrast perfectly. A modest, bustling canteen serving traditional Maharashtran seafood from the Konkan coast and packed with family groups and workers during the day (best at lunch). Turn up and join the queue; the wait is never that long. Order one of the fish *thalis*; try the ladyfish if it's on the menu, and ask for *tandalachi bhakari* (a flatbread made with rice flour) and a plate of fried *bombil* (Bombay duck) with chutney and you're sorted.

Khane Khas

Shop 4, Silver Croft Building, 16th Rd at 33rd Rd (on corner), Bandra West
Tel: 2600 6970

If you are in Bandra, this place is a must, located in a central precinct that hosts many different eating places within a few steps of each other. Here, the food is Punjabi and sets the standard for north Indian specialties: the tandoori chicken is succulent and the kebabs cooked over hot coals are memorable, as was the *suka* mutton (meat cooked with turmeric, onions and green chilli) with buttery *kulcha* (Punjabi bread cooked in the tandoor). Finish with the

moreish *rabdi* for dessert – reduced milk flavoured with cardamom, saffron, almonds and pistachio, and you'll leave with a big smile on your face.

Madras Cafe

Shop 38B, Circle House, Maheshwari Udhyan, Bhaudaji Rd, Matunga East
Tel: 2401 4419

Ten minutes north of Dadar under the flyover, this modest place has the best South Indian Tamil food in the city, featuring classics such as *masala dosa*, *idli*, *sambar*, *rasam vada* (crisp lentil dumplings in spicy pepper broth) and *dahi vada*. Communal tables set the tone here and make sure you try both the *upma pudi* (semolina porridge with chutney) and *idli pudi* (steamed savoury cake made with ground rice and *urad* lentils) made with ghee with chutney on top.

Masala Library

Ground floor, First International Finance Centre, G Block, Bandra Kurla Complex (BKC), Bandra
Tel: 6642 4142

Opened in late 2013, this glamorous restaurant attests to the city's thirst for serious fine dining, showcasing contemporary Indian food using modern culinary techniques at its most promising. Situated in the new BKC business hub, which feels more Dubai than Bombay, this is a destination restaurant where it pays to put your faith in the chef's tasting menu. Owned by famous Indian restaurateur Jiggs Kalra, the focus however is definitely on the young chef brigade (who trained under Manish Mehrotra at Indian Accent in Delhi), their work bearing the indelible influence of their mentor. I found the bite-sized appetiser snacks to be the most thrilling bursts of flavour and texture on the menu. The inside-out *vada pav* is a clever interpretation of the staple street snack; the curry leaf and pepper prawns with curd rice and banana chips is delicious, and the tiny lamb cutlet glazed with maple syrup, tamarind and *kokum* is inspired. On the a la carte menu, don't miss the *papad* sampler (listed on the vegetarian starters page), a clever showcase of various *papads* with pickles and chutneys. Little surprises such frozen *mishti doi* that gets the nitrogen treatment, *khandvi* (*paan*-flavoured candy floss, made to order at a waiter's station) and *kulfi* (ice cream) lollipops appear during the meal regardless of how you order.

Pali Bhavan

10 Aadarsh Nagar, Pali Naka, Bandra West
Tel: 2651 9400

Stylised street food, with traditional recipes crafted in a contemporary way. Great ambience and a modern sensibility; must-haves include *bharleli Vaangi* (stuffed baby eggplant), *vada pao* (cocktail-sized soft buns with spicy potato and *ghati masala*), pumpkin *kofta* curry (pumpkin and cottage cheese in a delicious saffron gravy), and their *chutneywala paneer tikka* (chargrilled, spiced cottage cheese with tamarind and mango chutney) is unbeatable. Whatever you do, don't miss the *paan ki kulfi* – ice-cream flavoured with *metha paan* wrapped in betel leaf, served as bite-size triangles – clever and delicious, cleansing flavours of fennel, mint and rosewater.

Pal's Fish Corner

8 Kailash Shopping Centre, 16th Rd,
Bandra West
Tel: 2600 2995

Stop off at this modest cafe for their *fish koliwada*, the best in north Bombay: the fish is succulent and the spicy coating is feathery light and not soggy.

Peshawri

ITC Grand Maratha Sheraton Hotel (near the international airport), Sahar Rd, Andheri
Tel: 2830 3030

If you have time to kill before a late-evening airport departure, this makes an ideal stop. Punjabi-style kebabs, tandoori and grilled meats, divine rotis and *dal makhani* are some of the highlights from their menu featuring the specialities of the north-west frontier region.

Prithvi Café

20 Janki Kutir, Juhu Church Rd,
Vile Parle West
Tel: 2614 9546

About ten minutes from Juhu Beach heading north, walk down a quiet lane to discover this outdoor courtyard cafe. Part of a popular community theatre with a bohemian ambience, this place is well supported by the arts community, who also come for play readings and theatre. It's a lovely place to sit under the canopy of trees away from the busy congested streets and soak up the lively atmosphere. They have made their name serving excellent Irish coffee, but I prefer to order some *chai* and a chocolate brownie, or a *paratha* if I want something savoury.

Punjabi Sweet House and Restaurant

Dheeraj Arcade, 84 Pali Naka, Bandra West
Tel: 2655 3866

There's a mindboggling array of food on display. At the front, facing the street, the guy is busy making *chaat* snacks to eat on the spot or take away. The *dahi batata chaat* (*puri* stuffed with lentils, spiced potato and tamarind and smothered in yoghurt) is pure heaven. You get a plate of six for a mere 70 rupees ($1.40). The menu extends to *parathas*, *pakoras* and more, but it's the snacks that bring me here. They also sell many different kinds of *farsan* snacks and delectable sweets like *jalebi* and *gulab jamun* as take-away, perfect for munching on later.

Suzette

St John Rd, Pali Hill, Bandra West
Tel: 2641 1431

Open for breakfast, lunch and dinner – one of the best places to start the day with made-to-order fruit and vegetable juices, organic produce, salads, sandwiches and crepes made with buckwheat flour. Customers are made to feel very at home here: great ambience, a cool crowd and switched-on staff.

Wild Side Café

53 Chimbai Rd, Bandra West (next door to Yoga House)
Tel: 2641 0030

This family-owned place specialises in steaks and burgers, with a barbecue menu every Wednesday. Let the super-friendly matriarch Mrs Serpis fuss over you and assist you with your decisions; you will leave feeling part of the family.

Yoga House

Nargis Villa (opposite ICICI ATM),
Sherly Kajan Rd, Pali Hill
Tel: 22 6554 5001

A small space serving organic, healthy vegetarian food and fresh juices – I love their 'happy juice' made with pineapple, sweet lime and orange, or fresh pomegranate when it's in season, and the green detox juices make me feel right at home. Come at 7 a.m. and kickstart the day with a yoga session, stay for a healthy breakfast (think house-made granola with honey and blackberries or whatever fresh fruit is in season) and leave feeling rejuvenated after spending time in this peaceful environment – a rare treat in busy Bombay. Fresh organic salads with crunchy raw textures make the ideal healthy, light lunch. Closed Mondays.

SLEEP

Abode Boutique Hotel

Level 1, Landsowne House, M.B. Marg, Colaba
www.abodeboutiquehotels.com

This bijou property in the heart of Colaba makes a terrific base to explore south Mumbai. It opened in January 2014 and has proven to be a most welcome addition to the city's hotel culture. It's chic and stylish; opt for either a luxury or super luxury room. It's worth the extra few dollars to have a sitting area and bigger bathroom. The beds are heavenly, there are lovely little extra touches that give it a personal charm, and the staff are engaging and helpful. It feels like a home away from home.

Taj Lands End Hotel

Bandra West
www.tajhotels.com

A luxury hotel, popular with business travellers, with a prime sea-facing location right next to the historic Bandra Fort at the tip of Lands End and overlooking the impressive Sea Link bridge. It's the ideal location for exploring north Bombay, which reduces time in traffic; it's close to the airport and to many well-heeled suburbs and business districts. Service is courteous and helpful. Be sure to request a sea-facing room on the higher floors for the best views.

Taj Mahal Palace Hotel

Colaba
www.tajhotels.com

The luxury flagship of the Taj hotel group, the grand imperial style of this place is matched by its exemplary service. Since it opened in 1903, the Taj Mahal Palace, Mumbai has created its own unique history. The hotel is an architectural marvel and brings together Moorish, Oriental and Florentine styles. Offering panoramic views of the Arabian Sea and the Gateway of India, the hotel is a gracious landmark of the city. For a quintessential Mumbai experience, it is mandatory to stay here at least once to experience its glamour and style. My preference is to go directly to the Heritage (or Palace) Wing rather than the more modern (and less impressive) Tower wing. Request a room or a suite on the Taj Club floors in the Heritage wing for a truly memorable Mumbai experience. Have breakfast or high tea in the Sea Lounge on the first floor of the Heritage Wing; the choice is as opulent as the setting.

SHOP

Bazar Road Market

Bandra West

A daily street market in north Bombay with spanking fresh produce. Mornings are best, before 11 a.m. This is where the locals come to shop for fish, meat, veg, spices, pickles and more.

Brijwasi

Narayan Building, Colaba Causeway, Colaba
Tel: 2282 0963

Sweet shop with silver-wrapped sugar treats, including a range of Bengali sweets.

The Farmers Market

Main Gate, Maharashtra Nature Park, Bandra-Sion Link Rd (opposite Dharavi Bus Depot), Dharavi

Beautiful all-organic produce that connects the city with Maharashtrian farmers promoting natural, organic, sustainable and earth-friendly initiatives. Opens on Sunday mornings at 10 from October through March (closed during the monsoon season). There's also a great cafe that serves organic food, so come with an appetite.

Jaffson Pickles and Masalas

103/2 Rahat Manzil, Bazar Rd, Bandra
West (on your right as you walk into the
market from St Peters Rd)
Tel: 2640 8684

Owner Naeem Jaffer is passionate and
knowledgeable about his authentic spice
masala blends and homemade pickles, and
is happy to engage with you on the specifics
of using spice blends in your cooking.

Mohan Lal Mithai Wala

Shop 399/401, MS Ali Rd, Grant Rd East
(near Sheetal shop and the Gandhi Museum)

Bombay's definitive halwa shop, where
locals flock for their sweet treats. Try
the ice *halwa* – thin sheets of a sugary
confection flavoured with pistachio,
almonds or saffron.

Nature's Basket

Hill Road, Ranwar, Bandra West
www.naturesbasket.co.in

India's leading gourmet food store, which
stocks foods from India and the world –
cheeses, olives, groceries, organic foods,
olive oils, cured meats, pasta, noodles and
so much more. A one-stop shop for food
lovers. Catering to locals and expats, it's
a great store to explore, and also provides
online shopping and home delivery.

Parsi Dairy Farm

261 Shamaldas Gandhi Marg (Princess St),
Marine Lines
Tel: 2201 3633

Popular shop selling all manner of dairy
products: milk and cream, sweet *dahi*,
paneer, *kulfi*, *mawa* cakes, pure ghee, traditional sweets and the most delicious *lassi*.
They also home deliver. Look for the bright
blue signage across the front of the shop.

Sweet Bengal

Kenwood Building, Ambedkar Rd,
Bandra West (near Pali Village)
Tel: 6124 5846

One of the better sweet shops in the city,
serving up mouth-watering *ladoo*, *sandesh*,
creamy *mishti dhoi*, *roshagulla* and even
savoury *samosa* and *kachori*. During the
cooler months (Dec–Feb) they sell seasonal
sweets flavoured with date jaggery.

The Tea Centre

Resham Bhawan, 78 Veer Nariman Rd,
Churchgate
Tel: 2281 9142

They offer a wide range of teas and can
also do tastings. The place has become
somewhat shabby over the years but is still
worth visiting. There's a shop attached for
take-away purchases.

DELHI

City

DELHI, THE IMMORTAL CITY AND CAPITAL OF INDIA, is a metropolis of more than 19 million citizens, defined by impressive architecture – old and new – and wide boulevards, different to every other Indian city. The imagery is spectacular! The city boasts colonial gems, citadels, temples and ruins – constant reminders of its turbulent imperial past. Being the capital, Delhi has many fine dining restaurants that showcase different cuisines from around the world. Much has changed on the restaurant scene in the past twenty years. Delhi has such a rich and diverse food culture – it's nine cities layered on top of each other. The richness of its past and its modern influences have shaped what it has to offer. Regardless of where you go, it takes only a nanosecond to realise that Delhi has extraordinary culinary traditions, and there is such variety to tempt your palate. It is considered the most happening food destination in India because of the sheer diversity on offer. ❀

ESSENTIAL SIGHTS

Spend a day in Old Delhi walking along Chandni Chowk, the main street. The street food is bountiful and worth sampling, so do stop for little bites along the way; it's one of the old city's essential experiences. Dive into the maze of alleyways and detour into Gali Parathe Wali, a narrow lane full of vendors making and selling *parathas*, made to order and served with dal and chutney, then head across to the other side of Jama Masjid Mosque to Gali Kebabian, off Urdu Bazar Road, for kebabs and biryani and all manner of Muslim food. It's best to take a rickshaw when travelling between both. Another essential taste is the *chole kulcha*, a Punjabi-style chickpea *dal* with rich buttery flatbread cooked in the tandoor.

As a contrast, engage a guide and take a late-night walk (around midnight) through the streets of Old Delhi – the food action never stops.

Walk through Khari Baoli in Chandni Chowk and soak up the atmosphere; this is the country's largest wholesale spice market, with a mindboggling display and frenetic action.

Explore the city's bazaars and markets – they are infinitely more interesting and colourful than the homogenous shopping malls that seem to be taking over the world.

Visit the historic sights of Red Fort, Janpath, India Gate, Parliament Building (Lutyens' architectural legacy in New Delhi), Humayan Tomb, the National Museum and Qutb Minar to gain an appreciation of the city's history.

Engage Dr Navina Jafa, one of the city's most authoritative cultural and heritage experts, who advises the government on all matters historical, to arrange a walk through the complex of Hazrat Nizamuddin, along with an introduction to Sufism and a visit to the Sufi Temple. She explains how the landscape has changed from a rural to an urban neighbourhood; her knowledge is formidable and her delivery mesmerising – you will be captivated, as I was. www.navinajafa.net

Experience a contrasting side to the city and spend a day exploring New Delhi. Take a drive through the diplomatic enclave, past the grand embassy mansions, wander through the laneways of Hauz Khas (now a happening hub) and visit small boutiques, art galleries (ones that specialise in Bollywood posters), antique shops and cafes through to the ancient ruins in the park to get some historical perspective. Best bets for food are Elma's Bakery (bread, cakes and pastries to take away) and a nourishing soup at Yeti Himalayan Kitchen (on the first floor).

Visit the bustling INA market, a large fresh produce market south of Lodi Gardens in the Safdarjung enclave towards Hauz Khas, where the locals come to shop for fruit and veg, fish, meat and condiments. Cross to the other side of the busy road and wander through Dilli Haat, where local handicrafts from different regions are set up like a village market.

Check out the Delhi Street Food Festival if you are in town during December around Christmas time. An annual feast that brings together hundreds of food vendors from all over India, it's like a massive open-air market at Jawaharlal Nehru Stadium – a food lover's paradise.

Visit Bengali Market, a cultural hub near Connaught Place for *chaat* snacks – among the oldest and most popular markets in New Delhi. Bengali Market also includes the neighbouring residential area, near Triveni Kala Sangam and Mandi House.

Explore the popular Shahpur Jat neighbourhood with its hip, eclectic boutiques, vintage wear, books and modern designers – then nourish your appetite at Pot Belly.

During Diwali, look out for wandering street carts that sell *daulat ki chaat* – a frothed buffalo milk concoction sweetened with sugar and rosewater – it's ethereally light in texture and disappears on the tongue – garnished with saffron, *khoya* (a fresh cheese like a heavily reduced milk), silver leaf and pistachio.

Many of the five-star hotels offer an extravagant champagne brunch buffet on Sundays (set price), a hugely popular pastime with locals, who head out for some leisurely weekend socialising. It's fun to join the mix and feel the vibe. My favourite spots are at the Imperial, the Leela and the Oberoi.

Gurudwara Bangla Sahib, the best-known Sikh temple in Delhi; lunch is served there every day (top).

EAT

Aap ki Khatir

B-781 Lodhi Rd, Hazrat Nizamuddin West
Tel (m): 09 891 989 786

A defining taste experience in Delhi right
near a city flyover in a busy Muslim enclave.
The rubber tyre shop by day transforms to
become a kerbside kebab barbecue as the
sun goes down, frequented by locals in the
know – and it pays to come with one. This
place is renowned for its kebabs and *biryani*.
The mutton *kakori* kebab is spicy and one
of the best in Delhi, so make sure you order
this and several other kebabs from this
popular street vendor. It's live street theatre
and you can eat kerbside or order take-away.

Andhra Pradesh Bhavan Canteen

1 Ashoka Rd (near Connaught Pl)
Tel: 2338 7499

This government-run workers' canteen
in the diplomatic sector of New Delhi
features the regional food of southern
Andhra Pradesh, and serves lunch daily.
The fiery flavours are abundant in the
house *thali* (120 rupees for all you can eat –
great value) or you can opt for their famed
Hyderabad *biryani*. It's packed with local
workers, so expect to queue. No bookings;
just turn up.

Ashok and Ashok

42 Subhas Chowk, Basti Harphool Singh,
Sadar Thana Road, Sadar Bazaar, Old Delhi

This is THE place to try chicken korma,
spiced with a magical *masala* blend, the
meat meltingly soft, enriched with ghee.
In hot demand with locals in the know.

Bukhara

ITC Maurya Hotel
Diplomatic Enclave, Sadar Patel Marg
Tel: 2611 2233

For kebabs in an upscale restaurant, this
place is the go if you don't fancy mixing it
with the locals at the street vendors. Serving
food typical of the North West Frontier
(Khyber region), the short menu features
shared dishes cooked in the tandoor. The
lamb kebabs are a must-have – the meat is
marinated in malt vinegar, cinnamon and
black cumin before being threaded on long
metal skewers and cooked in the tandoor.
The result is meltingly tender morsels, which
are accompanied to perfection with buttery
paratha and *dal bukhara*. Equally flavoursome
is the chicken tandoori with yoghurt, garlic
ginger paste, chilli and turmeric, and the
sikandari raan – whole lamb leg slow-cooked
in oil then finished in the tandoor – ideal
when there are a few of you to share. The
breads are to die for, especially the *laccha
paratha* (a flaky buttery, multi-layered north
Indian flatbread), so don't hold back.

Dum Pukht

ITC Maurya Hotel
Diplomatic Enclave, Sadar Patel Marg
Tel: 2611 2233

On a level below Bukhara at the same hotel,
the decor at this restaurant is ornate, in
keeping with Mughal tradition, and the
menu features the extravagant Adwadhi
cuisine of the Lucknowi Nawabs. Slow *dum
pukht* cooking (food is steamed in a tightly
sealed vessel – *dum* means 'to breathe in'
and *pukht* 'to cook') is a signature typical
of its Persian heritage, and the flavours
are refined and deliciously authentic.
I love their *jhinga dum nisha*, succulent
prawn kebabs spiced with *ajwain* and

saffron, the *dahi* (curd) kebabs, the cauliflower cooked in the *tandoor* and the *biryani gosht awadh* (mutton perfumed with rosewater and pandan and simmered with basmati rice, dum style) is flawless. Come with friends to share an extravagant feast.

Dzukou Tribal Kitchen

Block E22, 3rd Floor, Hauz Khas Market
Tel (m): 08 447 703 774

Walk up to the third floor to discover this small dining room offering typical food from the tribal people of Nagaland in north-east India, very different from all other food of India. Run by vivacious owner Karen Yepthomi, whose menu lists home-style dishes such as *momo* dumplings with either vegetable or chicken stuffing served with a fiery chilli relish, fried pork ribs, a seriously chilli-hot spiced beef salad and a pork *thali* (lots of porky things with rice on the one plate), or a smoked meat curry – all are serious comfort food. The food is pretty damn hot and spicy, just the way I like it, and the use of chilli is liberal. Nagaland is where the super-hot *raja mirchi* or 'ghost' chilli comes from – a little goes a very long way. Dried leaves and bamboo shoots, *anishi* (yam leaf paste), *angoshe* (a local black pepper), fermented beans and grains are staples in their rustic cooking. Also a popular place for hosting local blues bands and singers.

Elán

The Lodhi Hotel, Lodhi Rd, Lodhi Gardens
Tel: 4363 3333

The food at this fine dining hotel restaurant has cranked up several notches since executive chef Ritesh Negi took over the reins. His Indian dishes showcase a refined palate, a thorough understanding of authentic trad-

itional flavours with a modern sensibility. Grab a table in the outside courtyard (weather permitting) and snack on his sensational meat pickles while you ponder the menu, and be sure to try *dahi ki kebab* (vermicelli-coated curd kebabs stuffed with mango chutney), *palak ki chaat* (crisp fried spinach leaves with fennel chutney and pomegranate seeds), *bhuna methi murgh* (chicken cooked on the bone with fresh fenugreek leaves), *taar gosht* (baby lamb shank braised in a velvety stock, seasoned with aromatic garam masala, cloves, saffron and cardamom), duck *tawa masala* (duck dry-roasted with onions, ginger and star anise) and the wonderful breads – *methi paratha*, *kulcha*, *michi paratha* and *naan*. Don't miss *malai ghevar*: gossamer-fine sugar pastry filled with reduced cream and nuts – my favourite Indian dessert, done to perfection here.

Ghantewala Confectioners

1862A Chandni Chowk
(near Gurudwara Sis Ganj Sahib)

Lots of delicious Indian sweets, in particular their *sohan halwa* (Persian in origin, this is a dense, sweet confection made with nuts and sugar, shaped into a disc and flavoured with saffron and cardamom).

Gopal Chaat

Chandni Chowk, Old Delhi

Look out for this tiny stall at the entrance to Katra Neel at the Fatehpura end of Chandni Chowk that serves delicious chaat snacks and puris – I like their *papri chaat*, crisp fried dough wafers made from refined white flour and oil, served with potato, chick peas, chilli, yoghurt and tamarind chutney, topped with *chaat masala* (spice blend) and crisp *sev* (small crunchy pieces of fried noodles made from chickpea flour).

Haldiram's

Shop 1454, 2 Sheeshganj Gurudwara,
Chandni Chowk, Old Delhi
Tel: 2883 3008

This is the flagship of the well-known
national fast food chain and renowned for
its hygiene. Order from the counter and
stand streetside while munching on a spicy
kachori (a variation of *puri*), *puri* or *samosa*.
You can also sit inside, on the first floor
and order from their vegetarian menu,
but I prefer to keep it casual and watch the
passing street action. You can also stock
up from their extensive range of packets
of dried snacks – *namkeens* (savoury snacks),
sev, *puri*, chips, *bhujia*, *boondi* and Bombay
mix *masala*, *moong dal*, *papad*s and sweets
to take home with you. There are branches
across the city and the entire country; the
name is synonymous with reliable quality
fast food.

Indian Accent

Manor Hotel
77 Friends Colony (West)
Tel: 2692 2299
www.indianaccent.com

Chef Manish Mehrotra (formerly of
Tamarind London) leads the vanguard for
the best contemporary Indian food in Delhi
– and India, for that matter. The dinner

menu at this sophisticated restaurant is
a roll call of refined tastes, and highlights
include the potato *chaat*, *phulka* (puffed
wheat bread) stuffed with lamb curry and
topped with a crisp potato disc or beetroot
tikka with *wasabi* chutney; the *meetha achaar*
Chilean spare rib (pork) with sundried
mango and toasted nigella seeds is
memorable; and also not to be missed is the
basa fish steamed with spices and flavoured
with green mango juice and cumin or the
house *dal* (I reckon it's the best in the
country). Manish also hosts private cooking
classes at lunchtime in his intimate 'chef's
table' kitchen if you fancy picking up a few
secret tips. To discover familiar flavours
with a new twist, this is the place to be.

Jai Hind Paratha Bhawan

36 Gali Parathe Wali, Chandni Chowk,
Old Delhi

Discovering the hidden gems in Old Delhi
is a quintessential experience. In a laneway
lined with *paratha* shops, hence its name,
the most heavenly stuffed *paratha*s are
to be found at this family-run business,
something of an institution in the old
city. Look for a queue.

Kainoosh

122–124 DLF Emporio Promenade
Vasant Kunj
Tel (m): 09 560 175 533

Chef/owner and culinary maestro Marut
Sikka has been brave enough to establish one
of the city's best freestanding restaurants,
and his cooking is to be applauded. Think
defined authentic Indian flavours presented
in a contemporary style – small plates for
sharing – in modern, stylish surroundings.
The bespoke thali is the perfect way to
experience the excellent talents of this Indian

chef; I always let him advise me on the best combination of dishes. The private room seats ten and is an ideal place to have a sharing dinner with friends.

Karim's

16 Gali Kebabian, Gate 1, Jama Masjid

Walk down Matya Mahal (just off Kasturba Hospital Marg, behind the mosque) to reach this Muslim canteen that has fed the workers and locals of Old Delhi for the past century. Karim's is something of a landmark and offers an authentic Delhi experience. It's a little oasis hidden off a laneway lined with many other food shops offering similar fare (also worth trying is the nearby Al Jawahar, especially for their kebabs). The outdoor kitchen has the male cooks sitting cross-legged behind huge *handis* (cooking pots) dispensing various curries, including an intriguing and popular brain curry, and a long grill with glowing hot coals churning out delicious kebabs. They also serve *Nihari* – a rich lamb and marrow stew slow-cooked in a large clay pot over a low fire all night, so come at dawn for breakfast to indulge in one of the city's favourite food rituals. This is the place to come for a meat fix and indulge in one of Delhi's best-known and most popular food destinations.

Kathputli

35 Defence Colony Market, Defence Colony
Tel: 09 911 729 955

Great place to visit if you hunger for an authentic Rajasthani vegetarian *thali*, served on beautiful silver plates. The room has a casual, cool modern ambience and the service is friendly and helpful. Expect your plate to be piled with *mirchi pakora* (chilli fritters), *gatta curry*, *dal baati choorma*, *methi thelpa* (flatbread (wheat and gram flour) and chopped fenugreek leaves rolled into a cylinder after they are cooked) and *sookhi gobhi shaak* and more, each morsel packed with pronounced aromatic flavours.

Khan Chacha's

1st floor, 50 Middle Lane, Khan Market
Tel: 9810 804 114; 9811 152 722

This is THE place for kebabs in Delhi. The original hole-in-the-wall take-away closed in early 2010 (making front-page news) and relocated a few months later to a first-floor restaurant round the corner where you sit down to eat. It does a roaring trade in take-away too. Banda Hasan's two sons Mohammed and Javed have taken over the business and continue the tradition of sensational, cooked-to-order kebabs. Join the queue for chicken tikka kebab *roomali* rolls or mutton *seekh roomali* rolls. *Roomali* is the 'handkerchief' bread used to wrap the grilled meat with red onion slices and mint relish. I can't decide which tastes better, the chicken or the lamb, so what the heck, I get one of each! I now make a pilgrimage here every time I pass through Delhi. They have recently opened a second shop in Gurgaon to meet an ever-growing demand.

Latitude 28 Café

2nd level, Good Earth Store
Khan Market
Tel: 2462 1013

This stylish cafe offers a lovely calm respite from shopping and the hectic pace of street life or when you just need a break from Indian food. Owner Ritu Dalmia, a well-known food identity in Delhi, writes a good comfort menu and her hand is evident with dishes such as my favourite salad of quinoa, grilled chicken, tomato and avocado, as well as various bruschetta, sandwiches and other healthy salads. There are usually a couple of different house-baked cakes or tarts available each day if you need a sweet fix.

Moolchand Parathawala

Lajpat Nagar IV, opposite Moolchand metro station (under the flyover)

Roadside vendor selling mouth-watering *parathas* – the egg *paratha* is a must-have and a great late-night snack. Look for the high stack of *parathas* that disappears as the queues get longer – they cook at a furious pace to keep up with demand.

Moti Mahal

Plot No 20/48, Diplomatic Enclave,
Chanakyapuri
Tel: 09 811 680 519

Historically important, this was one of India's first good restaurants (the owner

basically introduced the Punjabi art of tandoori and butter chicken to Delhi in the 1950s) with reliably consistent food. Their barbecued meats baked in the *tandoor* (clay oven) never miss a beat and are great with *kali dal* (black lentils cooked in a spicy gravy with cream and butter, also known as *makhni dal*) and garlic naan as accompaniments – this is what they do best and it's elegant sufficiency.

Nathu Sweets

23–25 Bengali Market, Connaught Place
Tel: 2371 9784

A Delhi institution that specialises in Bengali sweets, this is an ideal place to stop for snacks when shopping in the area. Try the *puri*, *tava roti* and *lassi* and finish with a *rasgulla* or *gulab jamun*.

Old and Famous Jalebiwala

1795 Chandni Chowk (at corner of Dariba Street, or the Silver and Gold Lane), Old Delhi

When I explore the old city with noted historian Navina Jafa, she always insists we start with snacks here, one of her favourite food vendors, and it has become my first pit stop when visiting Old Delhi. They are known for two things: potato samosas and thick, syrupy sweet *jalebi* – the perfect combo, savoury and sweet. It sets the pace for more taste discoveries of the old city.

The Pot Belly

4th floor, 116C (behind UCO Bank), Shahpur Jat
Tel: 9811 122764

This quaint rooftop restaurant with a colourful, youthful ambience (above) serves Bihari food, a cuisine with a heritage of influences from the Mauryas, Bengal Nawabs, Buddhists, Jains, Turks and Mughals. Owned by the dynamic Puja, the menu features family recipes handed down over several generations from their home in Muzzafarpur (Bihar). The kitchen is overseen by her mother and the food is characterised by the use of simple ingredients to create dishes that unite smoky aromas with rich rustic flavours. Walk up the narrow staircase to the fourth floor and don't be afraid to ask for guidance with the menu; it's just like being in a family dining room. Everything I have tried from their menu tastes great, but do try the *pakora* basket (assorted vegetable fritters), *sarson machhli* (rohu fish simmered in mustard gravy), the spicy hot chicken (or mutton) *khanda masala* and the perfectly seasoned *baingan chokha* (smoked bringal / eggplant). Leave room for the pineapple upside-down cake if it's on the menu, it's bloody delicious. The *masala chai* is damn good too.

Prince Paan

M Block Market, Greater Kailash 1

If you happen to be staying in or near this residential district in South Delhi, then make sure you try their delicious *chaat* snacks – the *raj kachori* (fried balls of puffed wheat dough stuffed with vegetables), *aloo tikka* (fried patties garnished with curd and chutney) and *papdi chaat* (small pastry disks mixed with potato, chickpeas, chutney and curd and a sprinkle of ground chilli) are worth the effort and are amongst the best in the city.

Ram Swaroop Gopal Chaat

Sitaram Bazaar, Old Delhi

Try the *bedmi aloo* (potato cooked in its skin and seasoned with coriander, cumin, chilli and hing (asafoteida)) and the *halwa nagori*, a crispy fried puri made with semolina, flour and ghee: crumbly, crisp and not too sweet.

Sitaram Diwan Chand

2246 Chund Mandi (off Tilak Gali), Pahar Ganj (near the Imperial Cinema and in the same building as Hotel Chanakya)
Tel: 2358 6128

This part of Old Delhi is a maze and can be confronting, it's pretty grungy. Look out for a small shop with a few tables and chairs out the front, and a queue. It's one of Delhi's favourite fast-food shops specialising in the North Indian breakfast. The locals consider the *paneer bhatura* and the *chole bhatura* to be worth driving across town for.

SodaBottleOpenerWala

73 Khan Market
Tel: 011 4350 4778

On trend in Delhi right now and situated in the affluent district of Khan Market, this place has captured the attention of the hip, young cool crowd who are flocking to the quirky, colourful modern space themed to resemble a typical Irani cafe with food that pays respect to Parsi traditions, reinterpreted to suit modern palates. I loved their *khanda bhaji*: crispy onion fritters in chickpea batter, dusted with chilli powder and served with a wedge of lime and coriander mint chutney – a great starter snack. The berry mutton *pulao* (mutton chunks cooked with rice, caramelised onions, sour red berries and cashew nuts), a Parsi classic, is true to form, and if you are up for a sweet fix, try the *mawa* cake (made with evaporated milk) or their rendition of *lagan nu* custard (a rich baked egg and cream caramel custard always served at Parsi weddings). True to current trends, mocktails are served in glass soda bottle jars.

Swagath

14 Defence Colony Market
(near Lodi Gardens)
Tel: 2433 0939

The extensive menu features Mangalorian seafood and tandoori chicken dishes. The prawn or fish *gassi* (cooked in coconut milk spiced with red masala paste and tamarind), the *pomfret hariyali* (cooked in a gently spiced green masala gravy), the *paneer koliwada* (soft white cheese pieces fried in spicy batter) and the *murgh Afgani* (chicken marinated in yoghurt with cashew paste and baked in the tandoor oven) are what I order each time I visit. The *parathas* and *appams* are pretty special, too.

Threesixtyone

Plot No. 443, off Swarna Jayanti Marg,
Udyog Vihar, Gurgaon
Tel: 0124 245 1234

A state-of-the-art, modern Asian restaurant with a broad menu that caters to its diverse clientele, there's something here for everybody. I head immediately to the pages showcasing some of the smartest Chinese food in Delhi. Start with a cocktail or a glass of champagne in the outdoor lounge bar before proceeding indoors. The dim sum pastries (prawn *har gow* dumplings and mini steamed pork buns) rival anything you will get in China and my favourite dishes from their extensive menu are Chinese staples such as Peking Duck, *kung pao* (prawns stir-fried with peanuts), *shui zhu yang rou* (sizzling Sichuan spiced lamb with chilli bean sauce), garlic and chilli oil, the hot and numbing *chong qing lazi qi* (stir-fried chicken with Sichuan pepper) and slippery noodles tossed with tiny asparagus spears and egg. If you want something less fiery, I can also recommend the sushi, sashimi and teppanyaki dishes from their specialty Japanese menu.

Town Hall

60–61 Khan Market
Tel: 4359 7155

A recent newcomer, this warehouse space is sophisticated, chic and wonderfully urban with a lively switched-on vibe. Walk up to the first level from the lane, past the sushi bar counter with its glistening display of raw fish flown in from Tokyo's Tsukiji Fish Market. Chef Augusto Cabrera has put together a menu that is typically on trend in Delhi. Sashimi (and raw food in general) is a rare luxury in India, so this is the place to indulge your lust for sushi, sashimi or a hand

roll. There is dim sum, and I've even seen an enticing thin-crust pizza (from a wood-fired oven) that whizzed by to another table, so the menu is a little eclectic. I recommend you try the pomelo, pickled radish and green bean salad with chilli, peanuts and toasted nori seaweed – textural, fresh and zingy. The snappy bar makes really good cocktails too and a DJ plays in the evenings.

Varq

Taj Mahal Hotel, lower level
Tel: 11 6651 3151

Classic Indian dishes have been given a modern facelift with contemporary flavours by the company's executive chef, Hemnant

Oberoi, in opulent surroundings. Some dishes work better than others: the seafood in particular is cooked with a Western sensibility (ie not overcooked), the fish and prawns are succulent and the chicken kebabs are juicy, though I found some of the flavours to be a little muted for my liking, and wished the kitchen would be more brave in its spicing and embrace its rich heritage. Portions are small, a perfect way to experience several tastes and share with friends. Expensive – pitched to Westerners and cashed-up locals.

SLEEP

G54 Zaza Stay

G54 Nizzamuddin West (near Mathura Rd)
stay@zaza.co.in
www.zaza.co.in

Owner Christine Rei has been a Delhi resident for many years and she brings her elegant sensibility to this urban hideaway, a bijou guesthouse in the green centre of South Delhi. With only six rooms, it's like staying at a friend's house. Opt for one of the front rooms with an outdoor balcony.

The Imperial

Janpath, Connaught Place
www.theimperialindia.com

This grand dowager hotel is the epitome of glamorous Art Deco colonial style, class and attention to detail. Impeccable (if slightly formal) service adds to its credentials. It's a joy to just walk around the expansive hallways, lounge in the bars overlooking the garden, swim in the pool at sunset or just stay room bound for a day and be pampered. The more generously sized heritage suites are the better option; request one that overlooks the manicured gardens. A leisurely breakfast in the Verandah Lounge offers an extravagant breakfast buffet before heading out to explore the city sights.

The Lodhi

Lodhi Rd, Lodhi Colony
(opposite Delhi Golf Club)
www.thelodhi.com

Previously an Aman Resorts property, sold and rebranded in 2013, now independently managed, this remains the ultimate contemporary urban retreat and a sanctuary of luxurious calm in the city (left). Ideally situated opposite the Lodhi Gardens, the enormous suites are the epitome of chic and each has its own plunge pool and outdoor day bed on the terrace. The gym is the most sought after in town, and be sure to attend one of the morning yoga sessions with Naveen, a perfect start to the day. The breakfast menu will break down your willpower and they have two inhouse restaurants: Elan (with a terrific Indian menu) and On the Water (Asian and Western menu). Breads and pastries are baked daily at the Lodhi Bakery, where you can stop off for a coffee and snack or pick up take-away.

Manor Hotel

77 Friends Colony West
Tel: 11 2692 5151 | www.themanordelhi.com

Small boutique hotel, Art Deco in style located in a quiet residential area about thirty minutes' drive from the city centre, longer when traffic is heavy. Affordable rates; some rooms are better than others, and one minus is the lack of a swimming pool, so it's best avoided during summer. Inhouse dining at the Indian Accent Restaurant should be mandatory; it's highly regarded for its award-winning, delicious contemporary Indian food and adventurous menu.

Oberoi Gurgaon

Plot No. 443, off Swarna Jayanti Marg,
Udyog Vihar, Gurgaon
www.oberoihotelscom/oberoi_gurgaon

I stay at an airport hotel when I am in an overnight transit or need a room for a few hours to freshen up and relax before a late evening flight departure (saves time in traffic). The Oberoi (and Trident, see below) are welcome additions to the hotel scene in Gurgaon, a fast-growing prime business precinct right by the airport. This hotel is ultra modern and stylish with spacious rooms that focus on creature comforts. Their Asian restaurant Threesixtyone (see page 34) is without doubt the best Asian food in the city and worth a visit even if you're not staying inhouse. Kitchen stations are scattered throughout the space, each one specialising in a different cooking medium – teppanyaki, sushi bar, Chinese dim sum, a wok station and tandoor. Amaranta is their other fine dining restaurant, with a menu dedicated to India's coastal cuisine.

Trident Gurgaon

443 Udyog Vihar, Phase V, Gurgaon
www.tridenthotels.com

Next door neighbour to the Oberoi, also rated five-star but with more affordable rates (half the price) if your budget doesn't quite stretch to the dizzy heights of the Oberoi. The hotels are conveniently linked with a covered walkway; you can shop and eat next door, making it the best of both worlds. Rooms are stylish and set in wonderful landscaped gardens; opt for a deluxe pool view room. To get the day underway, they offer complimentary yoga classes in the morning; then head to breakfast at Cilantro, where the food (and choice) is excellent.

SHOP

Aap ki Pasand

Sterling House
15 Netaji Subhash Marg, Delhi Gate Rd
Tel: 2326 0373

A fantastic tea gallery in Old Delhi whose engaging owners are master tea blenders. I come here to buy some of the finest teas India has to offer and make time to sit amidst the calm to enjoy a first-flush Darjeeling tea served in fine china. Some people prefer the pomp and ceremony of high tea in a five-star hotel, but I much prefer to come here after a morning wandering through Chandni Chowk in Old Delhi for a much more authentic and informed experience.

Bangla Sweet House

Khan Market, New Delhi

Terrific pastries and Indian sweets. They make *jalebi* to order, which is magical.

Kaleva

109 Bangal Sahbi Rd, Connaught Place
Tel: 11 2336 5125

Savoury and sweet snacks to lust after; the ideal take-away. Try the *chaat* snacks, the samosas and the sweet *barfi*.

Mehar Chand and Sons

6535 Khari Baoli, Chandni Chowk, Old Delhi

Best place to buy spices; they will pack them for you to bring home.

The Taste

33 Main Market, Defence Colony
Tel: 2433 3733

Complete gourmet food store – this is where I come to shop if I am staying with friends and have access to a kitchen. There is a terrific selection of imported as well as local fresh produce, fish, meat and wine.

Yamu's Panchayat Paan Parlour

92 NDMC Market, Connaught Place,
New Delhi
Tel: 2341 4644

An extensive menu of *paan* sweets were being hand-rolled to order by a very stylish woman the day we visited. The sweets feature all manner of exotic and odd ingredients, an acquired taste that have the locals addicted, here they are packed like jewels for take-away with prices ranging from a mere 50 rupees to 1000 rupees.

Nizamuddin Dargah, the mausoleum of one of the most revered Sufi saints.

GOA

State

THE SMALLEST STATE IN INDIA, ON THE WEST COAST
facing the Arabian Sea and sandwiched between Maharashtra and Karnataka,
Goa charms with its food, beach culture, architecture, history and pure
vibrancy – there's a cosmopolitan ambience and international vibe. Goa's
history has ensured that its personality, a rich amalgam of Portuguese and
Indian influences, is unlike any other in India. Goa is an ancient crossroads,
where traders since the Greeks and Arabs to the colonial Dutch, English and
Portuguese have influenced its culture, architecture and cuisine. This alone
makes it a vital place to explore. Its multi-religious, multilingual blend of
modern and ancient have created a fascinating place.

Goa is noticeably Westernised, and has two distinct personalities – the Portuguese Indian and the traditional Hindu Indian – which are reflected in the food, culture, style of clothing and language (the local dialect is Konkani, an official national language). While the Portuguese left a legacy of vinegar, *amchur* (dried mango), *chourico* (pork sausage, below), eggs and nuts, the inland forests of Goa are authentic Hindu territory, with an entirely different vibe and the distinctive flavours of liberally used tamarind, *kokum* and asafoetida, curry leaves, jaggery and black mustard seed. Both styles of cuisine rely heavily on green chillies, coconut and fish.

Goa's food culture and traditions are also very different from the rest of the country – look out for their *chourico pulao*: rice cooked with local spicy chourico sausage during the monsoon season (May–July) or the traditional Ross Omelet, with green chilli, onion and tomato or a spicy chicken *xacuti* gravy. Hanging out in Goa is all about the beach, so plan to stay at one of the many beach shacks along the coast – there's more choice the further south you go, particularly after Cabo de Rama. 🌸

ESSENTIAL SIGHTS

The churches of **Velha** or Old Goa (the original Portuguese settlement) are now a listed UNESCO World Heritage site. **Church of Bom Jesus** contains the remains of Saint Francis Xavier and across the road, you'll see the **Se Cathedral Church**, which took eighty years to complete. The golden bell there is regarded as the sweetest-sounding in the world. Also visit the beautiful baroque interior of **St Cajetan Church**, close to Mandovi River.

Explore the elegant old **Fontainhas quarter** (Latin Quarter) in Panjim on a guided walking tour to absorb some of its Portuguese heritage. The walk offers photo opportunities of the cathedrals and the district's elegant old villas. Settlement dates back some 150 years and it is the most charming part of the town, with its narrow lanes, winding alleys and quaint Indo-Portuguese architecture.

Spend a morning wandering through the massive **Mapusa market** in North Goa, with its wonderful displays of spicy chourico sausages, spices and chillies, glistening vegetables and fruit, fish and meat. You'll find lots of preserved and dried fish at the markets, a staple when the waters are too rough for fishing. Bombay duck, mackerel and sardines are often air-dried, preserved and added to curries and rice for flavour.

Buy a spice paste from **Gurukrupa Masala** shop at the Panjim Municipal Market, near Gate 2 on the river side of the building.

Try a glass of *Feni*, a strong alcohol made with cashew liquor. Be warned, it's potent!

Visit **Braganza Heritage House** (above), a rambling, massive family mansion-estate from rubber plantations. A private tour can be arranged with one of the remaining family members who lives here to give you a sense of how the elitist, landed gentry lived during colonial times.

Explore the beaches of north and south Goa.

Stop at one of the roadside vendors for an *omelet poi*, a Goan favourite snack that's like an egg burger, but much better.

Head inland, away from the overpopulated tourist beaches, to discover original Goan charm and its Hindu heritage. Wander through a spice plantation and inhale the heady aromas. The **Tropical Spice Plantation** in Ponda (about twenty minutes' drive from Panjim) is owned by the Satakr family, who have generously hosted me in the past and cooked the most divine food using produce from their gardens. www.tropicalspiceplantation.com

Further south, inland from Agonda, near Netravali, is the **Tanshikar Spice Farm**; wander through the bamboo forest while they prepare your lunch. www.tanshikarspicefarm.com

EAT: NORTH GOA

Baba au Rhum

Arpora
Tel (m): 982 207 8759

Follow the signposts from Salima
Apartment on Calangute-Anjuna Road
and discover one of the best places for
breakfast French-style, with delicious
croissants, baguette, eggs, fresh juices
and good coffee – their *pain au chocolat* is
to die for. A great place to start the day,
or to stop off on your way to nearby
Mapusa market.

Bomras

247 Fort Aguada Road, Candolim
(near Fort Aguada Hotel)
Tel: 982 210 6236 | www.bomras.com

A fab and funky newcomer to the Goan
dining scene that opened in 2010. Owner/
chef Bawmra Jap is Burmese, and his
excellent food is essentially Burmese with
South-east Asian influences. Bomras is a
triumph with locals and those in the know,
with a terrific menu of inspired pure and
spicy flavours. He draws on his rich Kachin
heritage and the close connection India
and Burma have shared for aeons. Start
with a lip-smacking tamarind margarita.

The menu is a hit list of many favourites,
but I particularly love the spicy tuna *larb*,
the squid and spicy papaya salad, the crispy
pork with pomelo and pomegranate,
the chopped rockfish in banana leaf with
wakame and black fungus, the pickled
tea leaf salad and the sweet tamarind
duck curry. Leave space for the ginger
lemongrass crème brulee – light and
refreshing. This is beachside outdoor
garden dining at its best. The restaurant
is seasonal, open from November through
April, and closed during the steamy
monsoon summer months.

Café Chocolatti

409a Fort Aguada Road, Candolim
Tel (m): 932 611 2006

A great place to hang if you have an attack
of the munchies – offers a menu of snacks
like chocolate brownies, cakes and buttery
pastries. Chill out under a tree in this
gorgeous garden setting.

Elevar

Ashvem Beach, near Pernem
Tel: 098 235 31102

Swing by at dusk, grab one of the sea-facing
sofas and try one of the inventive cocktails
flavoured with *kokum*, basil or green chilli
from this modern, hip bar. If you stay for
a few drinks, then order the chicken *thali*
and make a night of it.

Gunpowder

6 Saunta Vaddo, Assagao, Bardez
Tel: 0832 2268091

This open-air peninsula kitchen started
its life as a modest canteen in Hauz Khas
village in Delhi several years back and
gained a huge following. Owner Satish

Warier relocated to Goa and serves deliciously authentic food of the south Indian peninsula, including masala dosa, vadas, egg appams and idlis. Tamarind rice is perfectly tangy and the spicy Kerala fish curry made with toddy is not to be missed. The courtyard garden setting in an old Portuguese house is a bonus.

Harmony Bistro

Opposite Sonesta Inn, Escrivao Waddo, Calangute Candolim Sinquerim Road, Arpora

This modest family-owned Nepalese bistro serves consistently reliable home-cooked food, and is a favourite with locals and visitors – whether it's fruit and toast or a stuffed flaky *paratha* at breakfast, sizzling fish tandoori and *roti* for lunch, a seafood feast or a pizza for dinner.

La Vie en Rose

Pequem Peddem, South Anjuna
Tel: 227 4848

When you fancy a change of pace, visit this local stalwart for its home-style French food. Sit at one of the few tables in the lovely garden setting and order a *croque monsieur*, a salad or quiche for lunch – you won't be disappointed.

Om Made Café

North Anjuna Beach
Tel (m): 982 385 0276

Overlooking the beach, this is a classic whitewashed beach cafe with a casual, laidback vibe. Come for breakfast and sample the interesting and wholesome menu, which showcases local and organic ingredients. I usually order a fresh juice and one of their egg dishes with bacon – readily available here thanks to the Portuguese

influence of all things porky. It's also a great place to sit and watch the sunset over the ocean.

Pousada by the Beach

Holiday Street, Gaura Vaddo, Calangute
Tel (m): 9922 279 265

Neville Proenca is one of Goa's most charming hosts. The food at the beach shack is utterly delicious: casual meals that display a modern sensibility with light, clean punchy flavours. Fish is cooked to perfection, and they do a terrific Goan-style meze plate, perfect after a swim in the ocean. Chef Kevin cooks one of the best prawn *balachao* (with a red masala paste) to be found in Goa, and make sure you leave room for the 'Allebelle' – coconut ice-cream pancake – you will thank me afterwards; it is sublime.

Shore Bar

Ajuna Beach

I love coming to this beach shack right on the water's edge for their fresh fish (cooked as you like) and a healthy salad – a great lunch option when hanging at the beach. They do a mean cocktail too to get you into the mood.

Souza Lobo

Calangute, North Goa
www.souzalobo.com

With its beachfront location, this has long been a Goan institution. Managed by Jude Lobo, the founder's great-grandson, it serves decent Goan food. Try the fish *cafreal* with steamed rice – the fish is cooked in a green paste of coriander and spices – or the delicious crab papad.

Thalassa

Small Vagator Beach
(near Anjuna Police Station)
Tel (m): 98 500 333 537

One of my favourite spots for a sunset drink in North Goa. With a brilliant clifftop location, the place is constantly jam-packed – ring ahead to book a table out on the terrace. There's a list of fabulous summery cocktails – they make a good mojito. Nibble on a plate of Greek-inspired Mediterranean snacks or a succulent lamb or chicken souvlaki wrap with tzatziki if you're hungry, but it's really the view and what's in your glass that you're here for. This is THE happening place in North Goa, as the crowds attest.

Villa Blanche Bistro

283 Badem Church Rd, Assagao
Tel (m): 9822 155 099

A favourite cafe with in-the-know locals, offering fresh-baked breads, waffles, cakes and more. The lemon tart and the chocolate cake are not to be missed. Sunday brunch is legendary and a definite to include when you visit if you want to experience real local action.

EAT: PANJIM

Anand Bar and Restaurant

MG Road, Santa Inez, Panjim
(near Vivanta by Taj Hotel)
Tel: 0832 222 9201

A modest place popular with the locals, with terrific seafood dishes on its menu. Go early to avoid missing out. Start with a plate of crispy fried *bhaji* or *samosa* snacks, then order either a fish curry rice or the fried mackerel and *dal*. Payment is by cash only.

A Tona Bar and Restaurant

House No. 167B, Reis Magos, Betim
Tel (mobile): 9326 122 282

Open for dinner only, this riverfront restaurant right on the Mandovi River, run by two sisters, Carina and Carla, was recommended by my local guide Jonas and serves authentic Goan Portuguese favourites with recipes from their grandmother's kitchen. Try the spicy, coconut-rich prawn curry or the *marisco pulao* (think seafood paella). Do try the chicken soup, which has *chourico*, the local Goan pork sausage, added to it.

Bhojan

Hotel Fidalgo (ground floor)
18th June Rd, Panjim
Tel: 0832 222 6291

Another place that's incredibly popular with the locals, serving sensational vegetarian Gujarati *thali* for a mere 200 rupees – the waiters keep topping up your dishes until you say stop. The food is regional, home-style and authentic, and the line-up includes rice, *dal*, curry, vegetables, sprouted beans, *farsan* (snacks), pickles and chutney, buttermilk, parathas and rotis.

Mum's Kitchen

854 Martins Building, DB St,
Miramar Beach, Panjim
www.mumskitchengoa.com

The menu is compiled by the 'Mothers of Goa' and has an emphasis on heritage recipes and home cooking; the flavours are truly authentic. The crab *xec-xec* alone is worth a visit, or if you're vegetarian, try the lentil curry, *varam*. The *kismur* – a relish of dried prawn, coconut and red chillies – is an essential condiment when you have fish curry rice.

Ritz Classic

1st Floor, Wagle Vision
18th June Road, Panjim
Tel: 664 4796

This is a local institution and it's always packed, so it's essential to book ahead. Come for the fish curry rice – a must for lunch – it's complete in itself and a bargain. The Goan fish curry, grilled pomfret or a butter garlic crab are also standouts on the menu. The decor is classic fifties, just like its name, and the service is efficient and friendly.

EAT: SOUTH GOA

Jila Bakery

Ambora (near the church),
about 7km from Margao
Tel: 0832 277 7224

We stopped off on the way to Braganza House for a feast of sweet pastries; the eclairs are a knock-out. You can ring and order in advance to avoid missing out.

La Plage

Ashvem Beach
Tel (m): 982 212 1712

On a beach with pristine sand for beautiful long walks, this stylish beach shack with tables and chairs in the sand is an epicentre for modern French dishes – try the sardines or the tuna – and delicious desserts, like the chocolate *thali*. It's so popular with the hip crowd, you need to book ahead.

Palacio Do Deao

Quepem (opposite the Holy Cross Church)
Tel: 266 4029
www.palaciododeao.com

A restored Portuguese mansion (above) that emanates elegance, style and rustic charm, and its owners Rueben and Celia are gorgeous, generous hosts. The place oozes charm and generosity. Lunch is served on the covered balcony overlooking the garden. For a more in-depth experience, arrange a cooking class with Celia before lunch; it's engaging, fun, interactive and worthwhile, with authentic home-style food.

Spice Studio

Alila Diwa Hotel, Majorda Village,
Adao Waddo
Tel: 0832 274 6800

A menu of fabulous authentic flavours of Goan and Indian regional specialities, making it possible to dine here more than once and have a completely different food experience each time. The dining room has a luxe contemporary design, a great aesthetic with attentive but not intrusive service and there are some good options on the wine list. The spicy *masala* pastes are made inhouse and infuse many of the dishes.

Zeebop by the Sea

Utorda Beach
Tel: 275 5333

A beach shack that is a great place for a sunset drink or two. It's a big place, a party venue, crowded with locals and visitors during peak times – one place where you can feel the vibe of Goa and hang out for the evening. Order snacks or share a plate of grilled spicy seafood and take it all in. Leave space for a sweet treat – *bebinca* or *dodol*. Like many of Goa's beach shacks, it's closed during the monsoon season.

SLEEP: NORTH GOA

Elsewhere

Mandrem Beach, North Goa
www.aseascape.com

Simple luxury at its best; a pure Goan experience. An exclusive property situated on a coastal strip separated from the mainland by a saltwater creek, Elsewhere is prized for its remote, idyllic and private location, away from the crowds and known for its discretion – specific directions are given by Denzil the owner once you have booked. There are four houses and three tents facing the beach or the creek. Closed during the monsoon season. Stay in one of four ancestral houses (choose a room with air con) that date back to the 1880s, or if you choose a tent, it is more glam camping in style! The restaurant tent on the beach serves tasty local food.

Fort Tiracol Heritage Hotel

Tiracol, Pernem, North Goa
www.forttiracol.com

At the northern tip of Goa, this seventeenth-century fort converted into an intimate heritage hotel with only seven rooms overlooks the Tiracol River and the Arabian Sea. The downside is there is no swimming pool and it's a ten-minute drive down to the beach (so it's best avoided when it's hot), but if it's peace and quiet you want, staying put with expansive, uninterrupted sea views where you can see dolphins frolicking in the river, then this is for you.

1) Church of Our Lady Immaculate Conception, Panjim 2) Bags of spices and lentils at Mapusa Market
3) Portuguese church on Mandovi River, Old Goa 4) Calangute Beach, North Goa

Nilaya Hermitage

Arpora Bhati, North Goa

www.nilya.com

A boutique ten-room hotel in the hills a few kilometres inland from Ajuna Beach, with contemporary-style rooms, each named after cosmic elements, and a great terrace with infinity pool for chilling out. Book a soothing treatment at their Ayurveda Centre after a day exploring or when you're just back from the beach – it's heaven.

Pousada Tauma

Porbavaddo, Calangute, Bardez
North Goa
Tel: 832 227 9061
www.pousada-tauma.com

A delightful, eco-friendly, small boutique hotel in North Goa. Book one of the villa rooms with private terrace (some rooms are very small), set amid beautifully manicured gardens and with a heavenly swimming pool. Owned by Neville Proenca, the charming hands-on owner and most gracious host, this retreat has been designed to use minimal resources and features traditional architecture. It offers a lovely respite from the frenzy of nearby tourist resorts and its restaurant Copper Bowl serves elegant European food and superlative Goan specialities.

Vivanta by Taj Holiday Village

Dando, Candolim
www.vivantabytaj.com/Holiday-Village-Goa

Individual Goan-Portuguese-style cottages are scattered through the expansive tropical gardens facing the ocean. It's an extremely popular resort, which is fine if you are with friends, but if you prefer solitude, then this is not for you (you can always check into sister property Taj Fort Aguada down the road on the headland). However, either way it is definitely worth having dinner at Beach House – the in-house restaurant. Grab a table out on the terrace overlooking the beach and order any of the terrific Goan dishes recommended by Rego, one of Goa's most noted chefs. I can recommend the kingfish *piri piri* and the tamarind tangy pork *sorpotel*, both local specialties.

SLEEP: SOUTH GOA

Agonda White Sand Beach Huts and Villas

Agonda Beach (near Palolem), South Goa
www.agondawhitesand.com

About ninety minutes' drive south of the airport, these wooden beachfront cottages set in a lush coconut plantation offer a glimpse of Goa's languid pace by the ocean. Rustic, stylish simplicity at its charming best. The produce for the menu is locally sourced and they cook fish straight off the boat. The whole fish cooked in the tandoor oven is damn fine, and I can never go past any of their curries with rice. Perfect vagabond living. They have more recently added three beautifully designed beachfront luxury villas to their property if you really want to splash out. Pure bliss.

Alila Diwa Goa

48/10 Village Majorda, Adao Waddo, Salcette
www.alilahotels.com/diwagoa

Situated in South Goa, twenty minutes
south of the airport and close to the
southern end of the beach. Overlooking
lush paddy fields with a backdrop of green
rice plantations, this is a welcome addition –
contemporary Goan-style with spacious
rooms and verandahs. Opt for the Villa
wing, set away from the main hotel at the
other end of the expansive garden; it's more
private, with its own pool and restaurant,
and offers better service. There's a shuttle
truck to the beach (ten minutes) if you
don't fancy the twenty-minute walk to the
expansive stretch of white sand – clean and
less crowded than the northern beaches.

The Leela

Mobor, Cavelossim Beach
www.theleela.com/goa

The first place I stayed in Goa a few decades
ago, when South Goa was opening up to
the big, international-brand hotels that
now dominate the beachfront. It's a big,
glamorous property, and the garden set
around the lagoons on the beachfront is
its best feature, with several food options.
Arrange a private candlelit dinner in the
garden or have a seafood BBQ dinner on
the beach at Susegado Restaurant.

Vivenda dos Palhaços

Majorda Beach
www.vivendagoa.com

A 100-year-old Hindu–Portuguese house
converted into a seven-room guest house in
a quiet village near Majorda, Goa's longest
beach. Contemporary, stylish and lovingly
restored, this is a slice of heaven. I like the
front rooms in the Portuguese section of
the house. There's also a fab swimming
pool in the garden. Ideally, go with a group
of friends and book out the whole place.

SHOP

Anjuna flea market

Wednesdays, October to May (closed
during summer).

Desmond Nazareth

Owner Desmond has created India's first
agave spirits in his micro-distillery, which
makes agave liqueurs and cocktail blends
under the DesmondJi Spirits label (www.
desmondji.com). You can also find his
cocktails at the popular Boutique House
Bar at the happening Arpora Saturday night
market from November through April.

Mapusa Market

Huge fresh produce market in Panjim,
open daily. Get yourself a Goan jute tote
bag from the Mapusa market stuffed full
of spices to take home.

Zantye's

Samrat Ashok Theatre,
18th June Road, Panjim
Tel: 0832 222 5144

Goa is renowned for its premium cashews
and this family-owned business sells the
best. Buy a packet of spice-salted cashews
or roasted cashews to take home – if they
last that long.

MADHYA PRADESH

State

THE LANDLOCKED CENTRAL STATE OF INDIA HAS many hidden gems; it's a region less travelled and offers an amazing diversity of options – a veritable paradise for foodies. This state easily rivals the majesty of Rajasthan's heritage properties with its forts and palaces and the tribal lands of lush forests and dry plains are the perfect habitat for the Bengal tiger and other wildlife. This stunning region of rural India is less touched by modern development than the rest of the country, and is still abundant in astounding natural beauty, stretching from the rugged ravines of Chambal to the borders of Maharashtra, Andhra Pradesh and Chhattisgarh. With its boundaries touching seven other states, Madhya Pradesh inherits some of the surrounding cultures and traditions, making it a vibrant state to explore.

Chaat snacks are hugely popular, and are a benchmark of the state's cuisine – *dahi bhalla, raj kachori, aloo kachori, samosa chaat*, each sprinkled with *namkeen* (small crunchy fried tidbits such as *sev, dhania chivda* or *dal moth*). The justifiably famous breakfast staple *poha jalebi* – rice flakes cooked with tempered mustard seeds, curry leaves, potato, green chilli and turmeric and topped with shredded coconut, pomegranate seeds, sliced red onion and lime and served with syrupy hot *jalebis* is a unique combination – sensational. ✦

ESSENTIAL SIGHTS

Visit the extraordinary and immaculately restored tenth-century Hindu temple complex of the Chandela Dynasty at Khajuraho, with its explicit, sensuous, erotic Kama Sutra stone carvings (opposite). These exquisite depictions of human life and emotions equate passion with spiritual union. There are gods and goddesses and even a few depictions of bestiality! Visit during the Khajuraho Dance Festival that runs for a week in late February; it's a bewitching extravaganza and a showcase for India's rich classical dance, with the beautiful temples as a backdrop.

The east and south of the state are tiger territory. There are various national parks where you can go on a tiger safari, and these are havens for the region's diverse wildlife. Fly into Khajuraho and drive to Panna or Bandhavgarh, or fly into Jabalpur or Nagpur and drive to Pench, or Khana to see the *barasingha deer* that has defied extinction. Each national park hosts luxury safari camps.

Fly into Indore and spend an hour or so exploring the sights of the town – the ornate Kanch Mandir Jain temple, the Raj Wada mansion in the centre of town and Lal Bagh Palace. Join the queue of locals at Johny's Hot Dogs for either an egg *benjo* (a spiced omelette in a white bun), a *bao bhaji* (vegetable hot dog) or a mutton hot dog, the tender meat sandwiched in a soft white bun, which can also have egg added, before driving south to Maheshwar, on the Narmada River, one of India's holiest waterways. This temple town is mentioned in the epics of Ramayana and Mahabharata and is known for its spiritual significance, drawing pilgrims and Hindu holy men to its ancient temples and ghats, a spectacle I witnessed one February during the Maha Shivarati Festival. Today, Maheshwar is also known for its distinctive hand-woven Maheshwari saris and beautiful textiles.

Spend a day exploring Mandu (between Indore and Maheshwar) in the heart of the Malwa region, home to extraordinarily intact medieval Afghan architectural ruins with forts and palaces, hamams and pavilions, an easy ninety-minute drive from Ahilya Fort. Perched along the Vindhya ranges, Mandu was originally the fort capital of the Parmar rulers of Malwa and was built as a city of pleasure for leisurely pursuits. Stop for a picnic lunch at the ruins of Chishtikhan's Palace, overlooking the valley below.

Another great way to explore the state is to drive from Khajuraho to the deserted, exotic medieval ruins of Orchha with its derelict sandstone palaces and havelis on the banks of the Betwa River then on to Bhopal and south to Indore; there are lots of architectural wonders along the way such as the beautiful Taj-ul-Masjid mosque and Jehan Numa Palace in Bhopal.

1) Potato patties at Johny's Hot Dogs, Indore
2) *Poha jalebi* – takeaway breakfast, Maheshwar
3) Kachori pastries frying in hot oil, Maheshwar
4) Wall of Jami Masjid mosque, Mandu
5) Ahilya Fort, Maheshwar

SLEEP & EAT: AHILYA FORT

Maheshwar

www.ahilyafort.com

This massive, eighteenth-century fort (above) that dominates the Narmada River at Maheshwar, a ninety-minute drive south of Indore and off the beaten track, makes for an appealing visit. Converted into a heritage hotel, it offers an intimate and genuine experience of India. Richard Holkar is the proprietor, and is a direct descendant of Queen Ahilya Bai, and the son of the last Maharajah of Indore (the dynasty's cultural imprint is visible everywhere in town). The property supports a local school project and the neighbouring Rewha women's textile workshop and cooperative, both just outside the main gate of the fort. Another terrific weaving cooperative in the village

centre is Women Weave, a charitable trust established by Sally Holker (Richard's ex-wife) for local women, whose beautiful contemporary fabrics are available for purchase from their shop (www.womenweave.org). It's essential to stay for at least a few days, forget the worries of the world and be pampered by the genuine hospitality and generosity on offer – my favourite room is Bul Bul, which looks out on to the quiet internal courtyard.

Known for its delicious home-style cooking, with produce picked each day from the thriving organic kitchen garden that comes complete with chooks, meals are served *table d'hote*, either at the main table or if you prefer, at your own private table. There is no fixed dining room; meals are truly a moveable feast! By special request, a private dinner can be arranged on Rupmati Island further along the river, with food cooked over hot coals – particularly magical during the full moon, sitting at a lavishly set table out in the open around a raging fire. Lunch is casual and features chilled soups and light Western fare like salads and pasta. The evening dinner highlights Indian recipes from Richard's cookbook *Cooking of the Maharajahs* (he is a keen cook and food enthusiast and oversees the daily menus whether he is in residence or not). There's a lovely swimming pool in the garden for relaxing,

or you can take a walk through the village – early morning is best – and taste *poha jalebi* and some of the local street food from one of the roadside stalls. Take a boat ride out to the phallic-looking Baneshwar Temple in the centre of the river and watch the sunset over the water. One of my favourite retreats in India, a place with heart and soul.

Baghvan Jungle Lodge

Pench National Park (south-west of Kanha)
www.tajsafaris.com

A stylish, eco-friendly safari lodge from the Taj Group, this property lies at the southern part of the state, one of central India's lesser-known reserves. The most direct access is from Nagpur, about two hours by road, and it's worth staying a few days before venturing to another part of the state. I like it for its size and laidback ambience – an intimate property with only twelve bungalow suites, each with its own covered rooftop platform, set amongst the undulating forest landscape near the river. This is a great place for birdwatching, taking an elephant safari, and the game drives in the jungle searching for wildlife can be quite adventurous. The food is fitting for its surroundings with an emphasis on light healthy flavours for breakfast and lunch (I am a fan of their stuffed rotis, especially the cauliflower (*gobi*) roti), while dinner can be a feast of the regional specialities of Madhya Pradesh – the vegetable dishes play a starring role, and don't miss the nourishing spicy lentil soup.

The Lalit Temple View Hotel

Opposite Circuit House, Khajuraho
www.thelalit.com

This boutique hotel makes an ideal base for visiting the ancient temples of Khajuraho;

its rooms overlook the lush gardens. I usually liaise with the chef and arrange a menu to avoid the monotony of the buffet table, so whether you're having lunch or dinner in the Panna restaurant, ask them to prepare the Murgh Matka (their signature chicken dish, cooked in a clay pot in a curd gravy with aromatic spices) and *Baingan ka Bhata* (eggplant roasted on the wood grill, then mashed with garam masala and green chilli), served with *thadula*, the local *puri* bread, made with ground yellow lentils and spices.

Mahua Kothi

Bandhavgarh National Park
www.tajsafaris.com

This deluxe safari camp (above) is cradled in the picturesque Vindhya and Satpura mountain ranges and the renowned tiger reserve of Bandharvgarh National Park, one of India's most beautiful natural sanctuaries. The dramatic landscape features tropical forests and woodlands, intermingled with steep, rocky hills, flat grasslands and ancient fort ruins with an enormous statue of Lord Vishnu. This park boasts one of the highest tiger densities in India, who cohabit along with the sloth bear, leopard, grey langurs, jackal and hundreds of species of birds. There are twelve private guest pavilions designed to look like the local houses. Head out on safari every morning and late afternoon with an expert naturalist guide. The food at this camp is a standout – dinner around the long wooden communal table is a roll call of shared plates from *makhmali kofta*, potato and cheese dumplings in a rich gravy, *methi malai mutter*, green peas, spinach and fenugreek leaves cooked with ghee and cream and a vegetable biryani to name a few. You leave feeling very nourished in so many ways.

Pashan Garh
Panna National Park
www.tajsafaris.com

I drove for a couple of hours from Khajuraho to reach this little slice of paradise situated on the banks of the Ken River (with crocodiles), a place that kickstarted my curiosity about exploring this central region further. Staying in one of the twelve luxury modern stone pavilions surrounded by bushy wilderness, I felt pampered and spoilt by everything on offer at this safari lodge (above). Drinks are served in the spacious central courtyard and dinner is served either in the outdoor area near the barbeque and live kitchen where your food is cooked in front of you – an Indian version of an Aussie barbie; think

tikka, kebabs, tandoor and grilled meats – or a thali dinner indoors in the lavish dining room. This location is best for birdwatchers, as sighting of the big cats is pretty rare in these parts, but it makes a great starting point for further safari adventures.

Samode Safari Lodge
Bandavgarh National Park
www.samode.com/safarilodge

This sophisticated eco-lodge is designed around a series of ten separate pavilions, each with its own living space, bedroom, expansive bathroom (I love the outdoor shower) and a private verandah (above). The design is contemporary and melds effortlessly with its surroundings, maximising the outstanding experience you will have. Take time to visit the ancient Bandhavgarh Fort between your daily safari excursions. Fly into either Khajuraho or Jabalpur, the closest airports, then drive for a few hours from either. There is an airstrip at Umaria for private charters, if that's your gig. They mix up the menus each day – the best are the evening barbeques around the campfire in the forest, with terrific dishes like *kasundi* (mustard) prawns and *murgh tikka* (both cooked over hot coals), and the *thali* menu with lots of wonderful tastes and textures to keep you happy – especially the *bhindi kurkuri* (crispy fried okra).

Singinawa Jungle Lodge

Kahna National Park
www.singinawa.in

A safari lodge in sacred Sal forests and grasslands. Drive from either Jabalpur or Nagpur, the nearest airports, and head out on safari to see tigers and other wildlife in their natural habitat. The biscuits served with afternoon tea are shaped like a tiger's paw – too cute! – while dinner around the campfire of rustic Indian dishes is a spectacle in the golden glow of lanterns hanging from the trees. Take a bicycle ride around the local villages or learn how to cook some of the dishes you have tasted, with organic produce sourced from their nearby farm. They pride themselves on ecologically responsible tourism and you leave with a better insight into and appreciation of the art and culture of the indigenous Gond tribe – their evening dances around the campfire remind me of an Aboriginal corroboree.

1) Jahaz Mahal, Mandu 2) Holy man, Maheshwar 3) Bicycle transport, village road, near Maheshwar
4) Family bathing, Namada River, below Ahilya Fort

AGRA

City

THE EARLY-MORNING TRAIN FROM DELHI TO AGRA takes two hours and is infinitely more pleasurable than being stuck in stifling traffic on one of India's busiest highways, although the new freeway is a huge improvement, so if you have engaged a car and driver, I suggest you leave early. People flock to Agra for one reason – to stand before the Taj Mahal (opposite), a monument to love, and a magnet that draws everyone into its majestic spell. It elicits an emotional response each and every time. Visit at sunrise to catch the soft pink glow that bathes the white marble. Later in the day, a sunset visit shows a different perspective again, and to stay after the sun has gone and see the moonlight dancing on the turrets is another thing altogether. It's mesmerising – words cannot do it justice as you walk through the gates and see the vision of white marble in front of you. It is impossible not to get emotional, looking at its shimmering, majestic white beauty. This building alone defines the city, but it is also essential to spend a few hours wandering through the ramparts of the Red Fort. Eating in Agra centres around hotel restaurants, but there's also some good street food if you take the time to find it. Mughlai cooking is the speciality. ⚙

ESSENTIAL SIGHTS

The number one priority when you visit Agra is to go to the Taj Mahal (opposite top), a masterpiece of Mughal architecture. It took twenty-two years to build, tens of thousands of labourers worked on it and the marble was brought in by elephant from over 300 kilometres away – an extraordinary feat. It was built by a Mughlai emperor, the Shah Jahan, as a memorial to his wife who had died in childbirth. The perfect symmetry, the detail of every surface, the internal chamber, and the marble filigree all demonstrate the decadent excess and vision of its creator.

The other 'must see' monument is the Red Fort (above and opposite bottom), with its dusty red sandstone ramparts across the Yamuna River. A favourite spot is the white sandstone Diwan-i-Am pavilion, and the other is within the royal pavilions. Their filigreed windows look across to the Taj Mahal, offering one of the finest views.

For historical perspective, drive forty-five minutes west to Fatehpur Sikri, which was established as the original capital of the Mughal empire but was then abandoned. It's a magnificent, perfectly preserved fortified city of red sandstone, now a monument. The city was built during the reign of Emperor Akbar before a lack of water forced him to shift his empire to Agra. The buildings are a fusion of Muslim and Hindu designs and were created from the same dusty red sandstone as the Red Fort in Delhi. The abandoned buildings remain intact after many centuries, and it's quite surreal wandering around the walled city. The place has a similar feel to the Ottoman cities of Turkey and the design is a symbol of religious tolerance. It's now one of the world's most noted UNESCO heritage sites. The touts are the only pest.

In the centre of Agra, there's a bazaar right next to the main mosque. If you're looking for precious gems, Agra has a couple of terrific, reputable dealers (Kohinoor) that are worth visiting, for emeralds and rubies in particular.

Arrange a Mughal heritage walk (ask at your hotel) to experience village life, and be sure to take in the Moonlight Garden with its stunning views across the river to the Taj Mahal.

Agra is known for its pure vegetarian food traditions in deference to Lord Krishna and this is expressed in the variety of street food on offer, so venture out and try *mathura ki dubki wale aloo* (a thin spiced potato curry without onion, garlic or tomato) and *puris*.

EAT

Chimman Lal Puri Wala

Chimman Lal Chauraha (near the mosque)

For a taste of Agra's street food, come to this small hole-in-the-wall to sample their delicious *puris* – an essential snack to have at any time of the day or night.

Esphahan

The Oberoi Amarvilas, Taj East Gate Rd
Tel: 5622 231 515

The most interesting food in Agra, with a menu of Mughlai specialities, cooked with care and attention to detail. The flavours are exquisite. Available to house guests of The Oberoi hotel only – good enough reason to come and stay.

Panchhi Petha Store

Sadar Bazaar, MG Rd (opposite State Bank)

A wonderful shop with all manner of sweet, syrupy treats and *namkeen* savoury snacks packaged up ready to go. Try the local specialty – *petha* (after which the shop is named): a soft candy of white pumpkin in a dense sugar syrup, sometimes flavoured with *kewra* (pandan), as well as the caramel-like *gulab laddu* stuffed with dried fruit. I stop here to buy supplies for a road trip to Jaipur. There is also a sister shop on Bypass Road, NH2 (Guru Ka Taal) if you're heading out of town.

Peshawari

ITC Mughal Hotel, Fatehabad Rd
Tel: 0562 2331 701

Sister to the Bukhara in Delhi, the menu features kebabs, roasted meats, breads and other staples from the north-west Punjabi region. The butter-rich *makhani dal* and the flaky *parathas* are not to be missed.

Ram Babu Paratha Bhandaar

National Highway, Sikandara Rd, Belanganj

An essential authentic street food experience in Agra, with mouthwatering, flaky flatbreads, many varieties of stuffed parathas – my favourite is the *methi muttar*: fenugreek leaves and green peas. Open all day from around 9 or 10 a.m. until about 10 or 11 p.m.

SLEEP

Amarvilas

Taj East Gate End, Taj Nagri Scheme
www.amravilas.com

This much-in-demand Oberoi hotel (opposite) is the definitive place to stay if you want to be up close and personal with the monument to love. It is built within the

grounds and every room has a private balcony from which to admire the view. The Taj Mahal is so close, you feel you can reach out and touch it, and the elaborate gardens reflect the opulent Mughal legacy. The pool pavilion beckons in the afternoon, encouraging lizard lounging. Don't miss a sumptuous dinner feast at Esphahan, and at breakfast, it's impossible to go past a plate of hot flaky parathas smothered with the house-made pineapple and watermelon jam, with a *masala dosa* to follow.

The Gateway Hotel

Fatehabad Rd, Taj Ganj
www.thegatewayhotels.com

A former Taj property, this is a good base for exploring what's on offer in the city, with good rates in the off-peak season. The expansive garden and pool are wonderful for relaxing, and the staff are charming. You can see the Taj Mahal in the distance from a few of the better rooms on the upper floors.

ITC Mughal

Fatehabad Rd, Taj Ganj
www.itcwelcomegroup.in

This was my home base on my first visit to Agra and has been renovated recently with contemporary splendour in mind. It sprawls over acres of luxurious gardens, and while the rooms may not have views, this luxury hotel is a fitting tribute to the great Mughal architects, with excellent representation of Mughal architecture, full of modern-day opulence. Situated within a few kilometres of the Taj Mahal, it is home to Peshawari, one of my favourite restaurants in Agra.

LUCKNOW

City

THE CAPITAL OF UTTAR PRADESH IN NORTH INDIA, this culturally rich city was once the centre of the Mughal kingdom, and was intended to be the last bastion of courtly Islamic culture. Now, the modern city co-exists with the crumbling relics left behind by the *Nawabs* (noblemen) of Awadh, creating a strangely surreal feeling as you drive through the city. Many of its once-grand buildings now stand dilapidated, casualties of the brutal atrocities by the British colonisers when they besieged the city in the mid-nineteenth century, but you can still sense its past grandeur. The rich complexity and refinement of Mughal cuisine was born here, and anyone interested in the art, history and culture of India absolutely must visit.

The *Nawabs* who ruled Lucknow were a Muslim dynasty of rulers who enjoyed the good things in life – extravagant architecture (both Islamic and British), exquisite, delicate *chikan* embroidery and liberally spiced cuisine. Their influence lingers in the food: cream, raisins, cashews, saffron, rosewater and almonds are all used to enhance depth of flavour. The art of royal cooking, with fine ingredients and culinary expertise, truly orginated with the Lucknow *Nawabs*. The royal chefs – *bawarchis* – were given elevated status, food was raised to an art form under royal patronage and a qualification from Lucknow was a ticket to success for a chef, as they became the most popular and sought-after in the land. Given complete freedom to experiment and create, they invented new styles of cooking, testing new recipes with newfound ingredients and flavours. They developed the *dum* style of cooking – long cooking in a sealed pot over a slow fire to enhance the delicate aromas of each magical blend of spices, and preserve the flavour of each dish.

Also, as in the rest of India, family heritage recipes have been passed down through the generations; the home cooking of Lucknow is incomparable. An invitation to dinner is guaranteed to mean a feast of immense proportions; Lucknowis are known for their large hearts, generosity and, like most Indians, a love of good food. They like nothing better than to share dishes such as *khichda* (spiced beef and lentils), *rasawal* (a sweet rice dish), *uzbeki* (meat and rice cooked together, like a pilaf), *zarda* (a sweet rice dish with milk, spices, dried fruit and nuts), *kaali gajar ka halwa* (a sweet made with carrots), *ande ka halwa* (an egg dessert) and *khatti machchli* (mackerel in tomato and tamarind sauce). The list of Lucknow specialities is endless, so when you eat out, make sure you try their *korma*s (mild, creamy curries), *zarda*s (sweet rice dishes), *sheermal* (saffron-flavoured flatbread), *warqi parathas* (flaky flatbreads), *kofte* (meatballs), *shami kebabs* (soft meat patties with chickpeas and eggs), *boti kebabs* (made from marinated lamb), kakori kebabs (made from the most tender cut of lamb), *ghutwa kebabs* (made with minced meat), *hariyali kebabs* (made from chicken marinated in herbs), *patili-ke kebabs* (cooked in a copper pot), *nukti kebabs* (diced lamb marinated in green papaya and roasted spices, then cooked with mustard oil and green chilli) and a million other uniquely Lucknow food experiences. ❁

ESSENTIAL SIGHTS

The most spectacular edifice is the **Bara Imambara** (below) on the banks of the Gomti River, in the old city: a labyrinth of chambers, rooms and terraces. The view from the roof terrace is definitely worth the effort of getting there.

Wander the streets around the **Janpath market**, stopping to taste street food such as spiced chickpeas in take-away bowls made from dried neem leaves – ingenious and ecologically friendly. The market is also home to the *vark wallahs*, makers of edible gold and silver leaf. The metal sheets are beaten into a super-fine foil and used to embellish many Indian desserts and *paan* (a mixture of areca nut and betel leaf, chewed for its narcotic effect).

Visit the *Chikan* shops, where the signature white-stitched embroidery for which the city is prized is sold.

Taste the delicious mutton *biryani* at **Idris** when you wander through the Chowk, the historic city centre.

If you are there during the monsoon, make sure you taste the **mangoes** from Malihabad, considered among the best in the world. They are ripe only during the monsoon season.

EAT

Arora's Achar Shop

Aminabad market

This is the place to try *mirchi ka achar*: chilli with navratan (mango) chutney.

Aryan Restaurant

90 Mahatma Gandhi Marg, opposite Raj Bhawan
Tel: 522 223 8000

Best for lunch. Ignore the rest of the menu at this modest local haunt (a mix of Chinese and pizza that appeals to the locals) and opt for the Indian vegetable dishes with their fresh flavours and textures – the vegetable koftas, *paneer nawabi* (a creamy curry made with cheese and cashew nuts), *aloo dum hyderabadi* (potatoes cooked in a red curry gravy) and the mushroom *masala* all make it worth visiting.

Chote Nawab

Sagar Hotel
14a Jopling Road, Gohale Marg, opposite Butler Palace
Tel: 522 220 6601

Some of the best food in Lucknow, with a solid local following. Its name means

'Little King'. I had lunch here one day and the eggplant curry, chicken kebabs and *roomali roti* (handkerchief bread) are not to be missed. There are some delicious Persian-style dishes on the menu too, so be brave and give it all a go.

Oudhyana

Vipin Khand, Gomti Nagar
Vivanta by Taj Residency Hotel
Tel: 522 239 3939

Classic Awadhi cooking of the Mughals, with elaborate biryanis and kebabs in a grand dining room. This is the place to have a dinner feast in grand fine dining style.

Rahim ki Nihari Kulcha

Akbari Gate, Chowk Bazaar

The must-try dish is *nihari,* a gently spiced mutton stew; the meat and marrow are slow-cooked overnight until meltingly tender and served with rich, flaky kulcha bread (cooked in the tandoor) for breakfast. Extremely popular with local Muslims, especially during Ramazan for the breaking of the fast in the evenings. A hidden gem well worth discovering, it has long had the locals raving – it's all about the spicing.

Shukla Chaat House

Shah Najaf Rd, Janpath Market, Hazratganj

One of the oldest chaat shops in Lucknow, this place serves up melt-in-the-mouth spicy, tangy and sweet *chaat* snacks. Try the *dahi bhalla*, split black gram dumplings stirred through tangy yoghurt sauce and a sweet mint chutney; *aloo tiki*, fried potato patties; and don't miss the *papri chaat,* crunchy flat *puri* disks with potato, chilli, tamarind and yoghurt.

Sri Lassi Corner

Golewaza entrance at Chowk Bazaar

Stop here for a glass of really, really good *lassi*, thick with fresh cream.

Tunday Kebabs

Naaz Cinema Rd, off Aminabad
main Chowk (in the centre of town,
near Akbari Gate)

Considered to be Lucknow's best kebab shop, this is one of the city's landmarks, situated in Aminabad Bazaar. There's history here – the *Tunda ke Kebab* is Lucknow's highly regarded speciality. The uniqueness of this kebab is the masala that seasons and flavours the meat, a zealously guarded secret prepared by the women in the family and passed down through the generations. Also try the *kakori* and the *gilawat* – silken *shami* kebabs, literally meaning 'melt in the mouth'. It's more of a meat paste, seasoned with herbs and garlic and spread on to hot naan bread. This is a quintessential Lucknow experience.

SLEEP

Vivanta by Taj Residency

Gomti Nagar
www.tajhotels.com

This is by far the best option when visiting Lucknow; hotels are few on the ground, given that most travellers leave this city off their agenda. The outer walls still bear the bullet marks from India's bid for freedom in the mid-nineteenth century; it's a city steeped in history. The staff here are charming, the swimming pool is set in lovely gardens at the rear of the hotel and the location makes you feel as if you're in a private oasis away from the frenetic bustle of the city. Be sure to have dinner in-house at Oudhyana during your stay. The menu is a feast of Mughlai royal cooking.

SHOP

Ritz Sweets

17/3 Sapru Marg, Sapru Marg
(near Horticulture Directorate),
Hazratganj
Tel: 522 220 1384

Buy a small box of *motichur ladoos*: melt-in-the-mouth sweets made with pure desi ghee. There are also other branches in Gomti Nagar and Mahanagar.

VARANASI

City

OFTEN REFERRED TO AS BENARES OR KASHI, THE CITY of Light, the ancient city of Varanasi is one of the oldest continuously inhabited living cities in the world. The culture of Varanasi is closely associated with the River Ganges and the river's religious significance. Mark Twain's comments about Varanasi are fitting: 'Benares is older than history, older than tradition, older even than legend and looks twice as old as all of them put together.' Hindus believe that anyone who dies in Varanasi will attain salvation and freedom from the cycle of birth and re-birth, so it is considered to be Hinduism's most sacred place. It is considered essential for every Hindu to make a pilgrimage to Varanasi at least once, and the city is an equally important pilgrimage site for Buddhists and Jains. It's home to some 4 million people, and 20 000 pilgrims come every day to pay their respects to the sacred waters of the Ganga – the river of heaven. The city seems to be enveloped in its own divine aura throughout the year, but one of the best times to visit is during Diwali, the famous festival of lights in October.

The city's holy status means that anywhere near the river, the food is Satvik: no onion, garlic, meat or fish. Ginger, chilli and asafoetida form the primary flavourings. Rice, *roti*, and *puri* are the basic everyday foods. At breakfast, expect to be served fried *kachori* (vegetable pastries) with *sabzi* (cooked vegetables) or *choorha matter*, made with flattened rice and green peas. A typical Banarasi *thali* (lunch or dinner) consists of rice, vegetable curries, *dal* and *sabji*. Snacks are an integral part of the Varanasi food landscape, and the locals love to snack – *kachori*, *samosa* (a fried pastry stuffed with potatoes and peas) and *pakora* (vegetables coated with a spicy chickpea batter and deep-fried) are the most popular. *Chaat* snacks are made by mixing various crispy snack bits together to create a unique dish. *Aloo chat* and *pani puri* are some famous *chaat* dishes of Varanasi. Alcohol is not an option in this holy city, so the locals offer *panna* (raw / green mango juice) and *lassi* (made with yoghurt) – both are great thirst quenchers. ✵

ESSENTIAL SIGHTS

At sunset, board a small boat to witness the traditional *Aarti* **(prayer) ceremony** and rituals performed by the priest and pilgrims, with thousands of lamps sailing along the *ghats* (steps leading down to the river). This is a very touching and spiritual experience.

Arrive at one of the main *ghats* on the river to watch the sunrise and observe the daily ritual of people cleansing themselves in the river, offering prayers to their god – a magical sight.

Visit a **weaving community** and buy some Varanasi silks to take home for presents.

Walk through **Kachori Gali** near Vishwanath Temple in the old city and taste a few delicious fried snacks and milk-based (*khoya*) sweets.

Visit the **early morning milk market** – milk is a vital ingredient in the 'pure' Satvik Hindu diet.

Take a day trip to **Sarnath** (opposite; 10 kilometres from Varanasi), one of the most important pilgrimage sites for Buddhists – where Lord Buddha gave his first sermon under the Bodhi tree. Wander around the temple ruins and the massive **Dhamekh** *stupa* in the village.

EAT

Kashi Chat Bhandar

D 37/49 Godowlia
Tel: 0542 241 2116

This open-fronted street cafe offers some of the best *chaat* snacks in Varanasi. It's open 3–10 p.m. daily, so make it an early evening pit stop on your way down to the river to see the *Aarti* rituals (a ritual to remove darkness). The Golgappa, Aloo Tikka and Tomato Chat were my favourites. The place is bustling with locals – always a good sign.

Keshari Ruchikar Vyanjan

Dasaswamedh Ghat Rd
(near the intersection to Mandanpura Rd)

Owned by the Keshari brothers, this is another place to taste various *chaat* snacks – you can take them away or eat in the air-conditioned room upstairs, but being on the street amongst all the lively action is what this city is all about. Try the *jhal muri*, spicy puffed rice with *channa bhaja*, or any of their fried puri snacks.

Lakshmi Chaiwallah

In the bazaar quarter of the old town, near the Shree Vishwanath Temple (ask your guide or locals for directions), this small shop can be difficult to find in the maze of narrow alleys in the busy chowk. This is where you head for the most sublime chai and butter toast. The toast with *malai* (the cream that collects on top of milk as it turns to yoghurt) is even more decadent. This is the only chai stall to serve tea in porcelain cups. A treasured find. I buy a pot of their masala chai spice mix to take home each time I visit.

Raman Niwas

Raja Sir Motichand Rd, Mahmoor Ganj – opposite All India Radio Station
Tel: 0542 236 0421

An old palatial *haveli* (noble house) of the Raman family serving authentic Satvik vegetarian cuisine (no onion or garlic), so think pure, clean flavours and simple cooking. They usually serve *thandai*, a refreshing drink made of a cashew, rose petal and spice paste stirred into cold milk. Sometimes a few *bhang* (cannabis) leaves are added. The heritage house is also home to visiting artists in residence, with artwork shown in their Kitri Gallery.

Sarnath Highway Inn

Gautam Buddha Rajpath Rd,
Ashapur Crossing, Sarnath
Tel: 945 426 2836

Lunch at this modest cafe is a good choice
if you are spending the day sightseeing in
Sarnath. The functional a la carte menu
is set price (500 rupees for non-vegetarian
or 400 for vegetarian) and will give you
a variety of dishes such as *paneer butter
masala*, *aloo dum Benasari*, chilli fish, *jeera*
(cumin) rice, *raita* and *moong halwa*.

Vaatika Cafe

Asi Ghat
(next to Kashi Annapurna bookshop)
Tel: 983 809 4111

Their tandoor oven makes the most divine
Indian breads (naan and roti) and their
wood-fired oven makes decent pizzas
(all vegetarian). Apple pie is baked freshly
every morning and they do a good espresso
coffee. Seating is on an outdoor terrace
overlooking Asi Ghat and the river. Service
is friendly and efficient. A great option
when you need a break from Indian food.

Varuna Restaurant

Taj Gateway Hotel,
Nadesar Palace Grounds, Cantonment
Tel: 0542 250 3001

The city's grandest dining option, with
a menu of Vananasi and northern Indian
classics. Must-haves are the *makai ki seekh*
(corn kebabs), aubergine cooked on the tawa,
baigan ka bhatha (smoked eggplant with
tomato and chilli), *murg sirka pyaz* (chicken
roasted in the tandoor then simmered in a
spicy tomato onion gravy) and the *dal dhuaan*
(green dal cooked in a clay pot with spices).
Right next door to Nadesar Palace, thirty
minutes from the river.

SLEEP

Ganges View

Asi Ghat
Tel: 0542 231 3218
www.hotelgangesview.com

This river-facing hotel, the ancestral
home of owner Shashank, is considered
the cultural hub of the city. It has a prime
location at Asi Ghat (near the Benares
University). Style is modest but inviting.
Request a room that looks directly over
the river – breakfast on the terrace is a
perfect way to start the day. Food is home-
style, and pure vegetarian traditions are
practised. The houseboys are terrific and
helpful. This is a real gem.

Nadesar Palace

Nadesar Palace Grounds, Cantonment
Tel: 0542 2503 001 | www.tajhotels.com

Situated by the Varuna River, a tributary
of the Ganges, a half-hour drive from
the river in off-peak traffic, this exclusive
property is the former summer palace of
the Maharaja, set in 28 acres of beautifully
landscaped gardens. Live the pampered life
and feel virtuous having the delicious Satvik
thali for dinner one night, then an indulgent
non-vegetarian feast the next. The *khatti
mithi kaddu* (pumpkin and fenugreek curry)
and *Nihari Gosht* (slow-braised spiced lamb)
are memorable. The kitchen team produce
consistently excellent cuisine from the royal
kitchen of Kashi Naresh. The suites are
sumptuous and expansive, though it's
best to avoid the Laos Room as it's close
to the service area, where the noisy
breakfast set-up starts early. The Bhutan
Room is lovely and the Nehru Suite is
rather decadent.

Suryauday Haveli

Shivala Ghat www.amritrara.co.in

Commanding a riverfront location,
this *haveli*, formerly owned by the
royal family of Nepal, has been restored
to its former life as a riverfront retreat,
perfectly positioned to either take
a boat ride up the river or wander the
narrow alleys that lead to the Kashi
Vishwanath Temple in the centre of the
old city. The loyal team always welcomes
you warmly, encouraging a return visit.
Rooms are comfortable, and are plainly
furnished, in keeping with its three-star
category. Free wi-fi is available, which is
an unusual bonus. Ask to have dinner on
the roof terrace. Their menu is strictly
Satvik ('pure' vegetarian).

SHOP

Annapurna Sweets

J-12, 16-A Ramkatora
Tel: 0542 220 0151

Take-away sweet shop – various
barfi, *ladoo* and milk sweet specialities
to choose from.

Raswanti Sweets

Nandan Sahu Lane
Tel: 0542 240 5967

There are many sweet shops in Varanasi;
this one is considered one of the best by
many locals. Their *barfi* and *ladoo* selection
is worth exploring.

Shree Rajbandhu

Kachori Gali, Old Town
(near Vishwanath Temple)

One of the best shops for *khoya* (cream-
based) sweets such as *rabri* (a thick custard)
and *mallaiyo*, milk foam sweetened with
jaggery (palm sugar).

Varanasi Weavers

Flat 3, Maa Janki Apartment
Sant Raghuvanagar Colony, Sigra
Tel: 0542 222 3075
Gitendra mobile: 88743 08218

Hindu weavers keeping the weaving
traditions alive – Varanasi silk saris are
considered the best in India. Bring cash.

AMRITSAR, THE PUNJAB

City

THE PUNJAB IS THE RICHEST STATE OF INDIA, WITH the most fertile farming land, and its home to the proud Punjabi Sikhs and the revered Golden Temple – the most visited place in India after the Taj Mahal. Guru Ka Langar is the enormous communal kitchen in the temple, run by an equally enormous team of volunteers who produce food for a staggering 100 000 people per day, and many more during festival days; everyone who visits is welcome to sit on the floor in the dining room and be given a plate of rice, vegetable dal and chapatti. The region has an egalitarian quality, as well as a deep spirituality, and there's an openness and sense of welcome for everyone, regardless of religion, class or caste. Sharing and hospitality are integral to the character of the Punjabi people.

The bounty of the land is apparent in its food culture – lashings of butter and cream are a recurrent feature of many dishes. For instance, the trademark *ma ki dal* (*urad* (black) dal cooked with tomato and cream and enriched with butter) is wickedly good. This is the home of the tandoor oven, whose popularity spread as Punjabis relocated across India and the world. There is an addictive quality to the food; it's impossible to pass up another buttery stuffed *kulcha*, *bhatura* or syrupy *jalebi*. Wear flexible clothing. ✿

ESSENTIAL SIGHTS

Your first stop should be the Golden Temple, the most famous *Gurduwara* (Sikh temple) in India and its extraordinary communal kitchen. An important aspect of the Sikh belief system is the idea of equality (*langar*): every human should be treated equally, without prejudice to class, caste, religion, social status or gender. The emphasis is on sharing everything with the community and the kitchen work is done by volunteers, to feed the masses of people who visit the temple each day.

Visit the old bazaars: the city's most atmospheric shopping district is the maze of small bazaars around the Golden Temple. Each street has different items, from bangles to wooden utensils, dried fruits and *pappad*s.

Pappad workshops – head to Pappadam Galli in Pappad Warian Bazaar and turn left down the lane at the spice market when you leave the temple. You will see shops at street level – walk up one of the narrow staircases between the shops to the open roofs where pappads are made, rolled and dried on bamboo racks in the sun.

Arrange a private village excursion to get a real sense of the traditions and routine of rural life in the Punjab. Walk through a local village to experience the warmth of the Punjabi villagers and have lunch prepared in a village house.

Head out to Wagah Border Gate where the guards on both sides (Indian and Pakistani) perform the Beating Retreat ceremony every day at sunset (above). It's a true spectacle. The drive from the city centre takes about 50 minutes.

Explore the old city behind the Seven Gates and discover small *dhabas*, most without names. This is where you will find the local foodies – the street food is the best, cooked freshly every hour. Punjabi street food is not as spicy as Mumbai's, nor as sweet as Delhi's, and is seasoned mainly with cumin and coriander.

Explore the Basant Avenue area in the new town with its *kulcha* and *lassi* shops. Try a few different *kulcha breads*, a Punjabi speciality, with various stuffings, rich with ghee and baked in the tandoor.

Try the local *chachh*, a thin *lassi* made with buttermilk. It's an acquired taste, flavoured as it is with black salt and cumin seeds – but is a great aid to digestion, and a good antidote to the rich food.

1) Sikh at Golden Temple
2) Bhangra folk dancers
3) Dining hall at the temple
4) Dish washing area, *guru ka langar* (temple kitchen
5) Making *dal* in the temple *langar* (kitchen)

EAT

Bharawan da Dhaba

Circular Rd, Town Hall
Tel: 0183 253 2575

This family-owned business is usually my first pit stop when I come to visit Amritsar. It has a great vibe. Even though it's always packed with locals, the wait is never long for a table. Order the *bhatura* (puffed wheat bread) with *chole* (chickpea *dal*), *paneer burjie* (perhaps my favourite *paneer* dish in India), *ajwain paratha*, *palak paneer* and *jeera aloo*. All the dishes come with a wonderful tangy lemon pickle. Don't pass on their delicious yoghurt *lassi* either. Simple and sensational – and the locals will be as curious about you as you are about them.

Bombay Chat

Laneway at side of Queens Road flyover
(along from wooden furniture shops)

I was introduced to this tiny shopfront by a local foodie who showed me many of her favourite haunts – shops that specialise in just one thing. Blink and you'll miss it; get a local to take you. This place serves the best *bhel puri* in town. Make sure you also try a glass of *kaanji*, the tangy, refreshing tamarind water that is used to season the *puri* snacks.

Chand

Hall Bazaar (close to Amar Talkies Theatre)

Known for its aromatic chicken curries. The korma with *rice pulao* makes a great lunch.

Crystal Restaurant

Crystal Chowk
Tel: 183 222 5555

A classic family hangout, this air-conditioned restaurant (a blessing when it's hot) is upstairs from the more informal streetside cafe. It's well patronised by locals, so I follow their lead and order the tandoori platter to start – lots of different meats, fish and *paneer* cooked in the *tandoor* and served with *podina* (mint chutney). Then order several dishes to share – it helps to go with friends. I recommend the sensational *murgh peshwari* (chicken cooked in a spicy tomato and garlic gravy), *mutton rogan josh* (Kashmiri mutton curry flavoured with red Kashmiri chilli and tomato), *fish tawa* frontier (fish fillet rubbed with fragrant spices and fried on a flat tawa pan), *dal makhani*, *jeera* (cumin) rice and a few different breads such as onion *kulcha*, butter *naan* and *missi roti*. This place is filled with the Punjabi spirit, where it's all about feasting and having a good time.

Gurdas Ram Jalebi Wale

Mewari Stretch, Hall Bazaar

This jalebi shop is directly opposite Chat Bhandar and has the best *jalebis* (made with semolina, not flour), *mathhi*, a popular evening snack (like savoury *papri* disks seasoned with black pepper), wonderful *besan ka ladoo* – balls of ground chickpea flour mixed with sugar and a little ghee and *patisa*, rather wicked little biscuits made with flour, besan, pistachios and almonds bound together with sugar and ghee. Look for the queues; it's not hard to miss with its corner location, a five-minute walk from the temple.

Haveli

Grand Trunk (GT) Rd, Jandalhar-Phagwara Highway, Jandalhar
Tel: 01824 501011
www.haveliheritage.net

An essential stop if you are driving to or from Amritsar, about 45 minutes out of town. They have also just opened a branch in Amritsar, on the outskirts of the city. It's modelled on a traditional *dhaba* (a truck driver's roadside canteen); the owners have successfully recreated the look on a larger, more modern scale. It has obviously worked, as there's a constant stream of enthusiastic locals. A mandatory stop for

Gian Chand Lassi Wale

Katra Sher Singh (opposite Regent Cinema)

An institution for this city, which has been specialising in lassi since the 1930s. The buttermilk lassi with a thick layer of *malai* (cream) floating on top is pure heaven and the *bedhi lassi* made with *koya* (evaporated milk), jaggery and yoghurt with a generous dollop of *malai* on top is utterly decadent. The locals have these to finish off breakfast. *Malai* is held in the highest esteem by Punjabis – where a dish elsewhere may be decorated with silver leaf, here this precious layer of creamy curd is used.

Giani Tea Stall

Queens Rd

Join the queue of locals who hang at the front of this hole-in-the-wall place on busy Queens Road early in the morning to get their breakfast fix of flaky hot *kachori* (a stuffed, fried pastry) and a glass of chai.

all travellers, it serves fantastic food with authentic flavours – spotlessly clean, efficient, friendly service. Be sure to try *chole bhatura* (chickpea curry with flatbread), green chilli *parathas, malai* (butter) *kulcha* (flatbread) and a very impressive *papri chaat* (crisp fried dough wafers with potato, chickpea and chilli).

Kanha

Lawrence Rd
(opposite Mandir Bijli Pehalwan)
Tel: 221 1518

It's a sweet shop and take-away at the front, so walk down the side lane and watch as they fry *puris* in large *kadhais* (dome-shaped vessels, like woks), then go in to the air-conditioned dining room for breakfast or lunch. *Puris, chole* and other local staples are on the menu.

Kesar de Dhaba

Chowk Passian, East Mohan Nagar, Old City
Tel: 255 2103

The original and oldest *dhaba* in Amritsar – it opened in the early twentieth century. It's hidden down a small passage in a labyrinth of narrow lanes in the old town. You have to walk there as it's inaccessible by car. The dining room is very rudimentary and looks as if it hasn't been touched since it opened. The food is vegetarian, hearty and basic and can feel overly rich (with lashings of butter and cream), so keep it simple with *parathas* and a bowl of rich *makhni dal* – a Punjabi speciality made with *urad* – black lentils and finished with the ubiquitous cream and butter. They also do brisk takeaway business from the front window. A popular local.

Kulcha Land

District Shopping Centre, Ranjit Ave
(opposite MK hotel)
Tel: 505 0552

Samarjit Singh is perhaps one of the best *kulcha wallahs* in town. Come for breakfast – the cooked-to-order flatbreads are to die for and one is never enough! *Kulcha* is a crisp flaky *roti*, stuffed, usually with potato, cooked in the tandoori and seasoned with ghee. Order the *masala* (spicy) *kulcha* and

the *paneer* (cheese) *kulcha* – served with *chloe* (chickpeas) and fresh mint chutney. They also serve a great chai.

Rajasthani Chat Bhandar

Chowk Katra Ahluwalia, Hall Bazaar

An easy-to-find corner location at one end of the Mewari Stretch, this is a good pit stop for a few *golguppa* and various *chaat* snacks – upstairs you will find Rangla Dhaba, serving reliable regional dishes, and across the road is the *jalebi wale*, so this is a great corner to hang out, try lots of different snacks and get those tastebuds firing.

Sharma's

Circular Rd

Stop by for the best authentic chai in town, and the owner also serves freshly baked buns slathered with butter, sandwiching crumbled samosa – a local delicacy.

Surjit Food Plaza

3–4 G F, Nehru Shopping Complex, Lawrence Rd
Tel: 0183 329 4334

A menu of north Indian favourites – tandoori chicken and grilled meats – mutton *tikka*, fried chicken, butter chicken and *malai tikka*. This is a good place to try the local specialty – Amritsi fish, where chunks of *singhara* (a local river fish) are dipped in a chickpea batter that is seasoned with *ajwain* and red chilli then fried in hot oil till crisp. The flavours are authentic, the canteen-style dining room is pleasingly functional, and the owner is very friendly and only too willing to help with menu suggestions if you have trouble deciding.

SLEEP

Hyatt Amritsar

Next door to Alpha One City Centre, GT Rd
Tel: 0183 287 1234
www.amritsar.hyatthotels.hyatt.com

This is currently the best option in the city if your preference is for a modern international brand hotel with a contemporary Indian design aesthetic. Situated on the Grand Trunk Road (the main thoroughfare of Northern India), it's a 15-minute drive to the Golden Temple and old town centre, and makes a perfectly acceptable choice. There is a good indoor swimming pool, great for a refreshing afternoon swim after spending a few hours exploring the streets, especially if it's hot. I like the corner rooms on the higher floors as they have more space and good views across the city.

Ranjit's Svaasa

Heritage Spa Haveli
47A The Mall
Tel: 0183 256 6618 | www.svaasa.com

Colonial-style bungalow set in a lovely established garden off the street. This modest 250-year-old family-owned and managed eco-retreat is in a quiet part of the city. Opt for one of the suites as they offer a more generous space – Rattan Chand is my favourite, looking out over the garden. (Many of the other rooms are too dark and small.) This is a typical heritage hotel, so don't expect all the bells and whistles of a smart hotel. The best time to stay is during the cooler months. It's big on personality and offers a warm welcome, helpful service, great insider knowledge of how to make the most of your city stay and terrific home-style food.

A wonderful lunch prepared by inhouse chef Vincent can be arranged on their rooftop terrace when it's not too hot, with a menu of grilled kebabs, *masala bhindi* (okra), *paneer* in a tomato and nigella gravy, *petha sarso bheej* (sweet and sour pumpkin), potatoes stuffed with dried fruits and paneer in a rich spicy sauce, and *dahi wala methi*, chicken cooked in a mild yoghurt gravy with fenugreek leaves, using organic produce from their kitchen garden. For dinner, ask Gayatri (Ahbimanyu's wife) to make *falooda and kulfa* – slippery rice noodles in sweet milk scented with green cardamom and served with a scoop of local Punjabi ice cream, made with reduced milk – it's heaven.

It's essential to make time for charming managers Abhimanyu and Deepak to escort you on a village excursion about 20 kilometres out of town, where you'll gain a real insight into Punjabi rural life. Kick off in the morning after breakfast, be welcomed into a local village by a colourful Bhangra dance performance, walk around the village, visit a local school and engage with the kids, ride through the fields on a tractor trolley to check out the crops – wheat, rice, mustard and corn are the staples – then have a home-cooked lunch in one of the village houses before heading back to indulge in an Ayurvedic treatment in the Svaasa spa.

SHOP

Harjundir Singh Papad Warian
Near the Golden Temple

One of Amritsar's famous *papad warians* –
go on to the rooftop to see the *papad*s being
rolled and dried on bamboo mats before
they are packed for sale.

D. Mahajan Store
New Ghanta Ghar Market
Shop 189, opposite Shani Mandir,
near Golden Temple
Tel: 0183 505 2000

*Papad*s, dried fruits, spices and nuts,
packed ready to take home for a few
Punjabi taste memories.

Munim di Hatti
Opposite Bijli Pehlwan Mandir, Lawrence Rd
Tel: 0183 222 2430

One of the city's favourite shops for the
best *desi ghee* sweets in town. Try the
various *barfi* and *ladoo* flavours.

Ram Lubhaya and Sons
Lawrence Road

Street vendor set up under a tree just
down from Munim di Hatti (same side)
and diagonally opposite Kanha. Famous
for special *amm papar* – mango leather
and mango jam.

GUJARAT

State

THE WESTERNMOST STATE OF INDIA, GUJARAT IS home to many treasures and enormous diversity. It's a state with a wealth of history, art and culture that has remained one of India's best kept tourism secrets, from the desert plains in the west (Rann of Kutch and Bhuj) to the fertile plains in the east, to the vast tidal shoreline facing the Arabian Sea. Now that tourism in the state is starting to flourish, the infrastructure has improved. You will find distinctively ornate Jain temples and forts, ancient palaces and marine parks, romantic desert landscapes, wildlife and a dazzling array of textiles, from the double *ikat* weaving of Patan to the glittering embroidery of Sankheda and Kutch.

Gujarat is the birthplace of Mahatma Gandhi, and his *ashram* in Ahmedabad has been sensitively preserved in his honour. Many people come to pay homage and meditate. Ahmedabad, the business and cultural capital of the state, is one of the fastest growing cities in the country, with some of the best roads and highest literacy rates. Gujarat is a dry state where no alcohol is served (out of respect to Ghandi), so be conscious of this when you visit. The powerful influence of its largely vegetarian population dictates that the food is predominantly vegetarian, except in the Muslim quarters, whose cafes and restaurants (such as Bhatiyar Gali in Ahmedabad) are popular with everyone, including Hindus who do not cook meat at home but like to eat it. India is never short of a paradox! As Ahmedabad continues to develop into a larger metropolis, the food on offer is changing to meet the demands and obsessions of its world-savvy citizens. Gujaratis love their sugar; the food has a distinctive sweet and sour flavour with salty and spicy characteristics and many dishes may taste sweeter than you would find in other parts of the country. This is also the milk capital of India and it is widely used in cooking. You will usually find an array of fruit chutneys on the table to use as condiments. There's a staggering diversity of flavours and textures to explore; a visit to Gujarat is a festival of eating. ❁

ESSENTIAL SIGHTS

Spend an hour or so at the faithfully maintained Mill Owners Building, home to the postmodern architecture of Le Corbusier (above) – call the office and ask for an appointment to get a personalised tour of the building and the exhibition of Le Corbusier's works in India. It stands in contrast to everything else in the city.

Join a group tour of the Calico Museum of Textiles (organised through the museum) – considered the very best textile museum in India, this place is world renowned, with a distinguished and comprehensive collection of textiles and artefacts. www.calicomuseum.com

Explore the amazing street food – from the vendors on C.G. Road at Municipal Market to Manak Chowk and Bhatiyar Galli in the old city (the Muslim quarter, distinguished by its butcheries and meat restaurants – try the chicken heart or liver kebabs from Ganni Bhai's cart), and around the Law Gardens on Netaji Road. The streets come even more alive at night, when it seems each district has a plethora of street food vendors and everyone is outdoors being social, so it's worth considering a night walk to take in some of the lively action.

Take an early morning visit to Sabarmati Ashram, where Gandhi lived for twelve years during the early years of the struggle for Independence, until he began the Salt March in 1930. It is a wonderful, peaceful museum on the riverfront, with an excellent display of photos and personal letters – many pilgrims come to meditate in its calm environs.

Step back in time and visit the eleventh-century Dada Hari ni Vav Stepwell in Asarwa and compare it to the stepwell in Adalaj, about a thirty-minute drive from the city centre, and also Rani ki Vav, the Queen's Stepwell in Patan (above). All three subterranean temples are architecturally magnificent and not to be missed; they are the oldest and largest in India: elaborate, maze-like structures that descend seven or so storeys and feature ornate stone carvings of Hindu religious scenes.

Time your visit to coincide with one of the many festivals scattered across the year, as this is a great place to experience them. Navrati, for nine nights in late September and early October, is like Mardi Gras, with singing, dancing, eating and more eating.

Check out the Hutheesingh Jain temple, with its ornate, elaborate carvings in the old town, built in the late nineteenth century by a wealthy Jain trader.

Find the Grilled 'n More food truck parked on SG Highway in the Bodakdev district of Ahmedabad and order a juicy chicken burger: meat straight from the hot grill, sandwiched in a bun with salad and chutney. One is called Hot Chick and another is Mother Clucker – love the cheeky humour. If you have difficulty finding it, call Sethu on 098 2507 4419 and he will give you directions.

Take a day trip out of town to explore the smaller towns of Patan for the impossibly intricate double ikat weaving at Patola House, a showroom and museum for this extraordinary craft that opened in late 2014. It is possible to arrange a typical Jain thali lunch during your visit to the museum. Some of the charm has not transferred from the intimacy of sharing the family table in their house to the canteen-style basement in the museum, but it does allow them to cater for the crowds.

Start your morning heritage walk in Ahmedabad at the ornate Swaminarayan Temple before heading into the Pols (residential sections) and havelis of the old city, stopping off for some excellent *masala chai* at one of the street vendors along the way.

Visit the eleventh-century Sun Temple at Modhera (above), a two-hour drive from Ahmedabad, where the natural elements and the Vedic gods are revered; it's breathtaking.

Wander the dusty streets of Sidhpur, past camels pulling drays and the intricate wooden *havelis* of the Bhori Muslim community, unlike anything else you will see in India. Bhoras are trading communities and the men wear distinctive white caps and the women wear colourful burqas. If you plan ahead, you may be invited into one for lunch with a family, making the visit even more meaningful. I stopped for lunch with the Bhaimomin family, who served a refreshingly light chicken consommé to start then chicken pieces simmered in a white gravy made with ground almonds, cashews, cumin and milk, vegetables braised with red masala and a mutton biryani. It is nigh-on impossible to find Bhora food cooked outside the home, so this makes for a special experience.

Another culturally important city is **Vadodara** (Baroda), home to art and music schools and many of the leading contemporary artists of India. A two-hour drive south-east from Ahmedabad through agricultural tracts, it's possible to do this as a day trip if you head off early. Come and explore the beautiful *havelis* and bazaars as well as the **Maharaja's palace**, and stop for lunch at **Raju Omelet Centre**. Its wall menu is a list of egg dishes that you choose to have cooked in butter or oil – go for either the *masala* half fry or the *crush bhurji* wrap.

Visit **Rajkot**, the town where Gandhi went to school, and taste the freshest milk sweets from the local dairies, or have a vegetarian Jain lunch at the **Hotel Imperial Palace.**

Come during monsoon season to witness the many festivities that celebrate the rains. Dishes are created with the weather in mind – taste *rajgrani puri, methi na phulvada sheero, batata kachoris, jalebis* and *fafda*, delicious local specialities.

If textiles are your thing, visit **Calico Craft Centre** near the Gandhi Ashram in Ahmedabad, well stocked with woven cloth, block prints and all manner of fabrics from all over Gujarat. www.calicocraft.com

Spend a couple of days at the tented lion safari camp at **Sasan Gir National Park** in the south to see the fascinating wildlife. This is the only place on earth where you will see the Asiatic lion. You can either fly from Mumbai to Dui Islands, then take a two-hour drive, or it's a seven-hour drive from Ahmedabad.

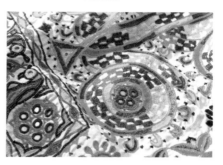

Head west to Bhuj, the gateway to the **Great Rann of Kutch**, an inhospitable desert saltpan near the Arabian Sea, home to semi-nomadic tribes and weaving communities. Their dazzling clothes and jewellery are extremely ornate and colourful against the barren landscape. Their desert cuisine is also unique – *rotla* is a dense flatbread made with millet and served with hot ghee for added moisture. Water is scarce, so milk plays a vital role; *chaas* (buttermilk) is used to quench thirst and is usually flavoured with green chilli and chopped coriander. *Khidchi*, a porridge-like staple made with rice and lentils, is served with a tangy, sharp chilli and mint chutney. *Ringda* (eggplant) is a common vegetable, used in many vegetable preparations such as *ondhiyu*, where chopped vegetables are spiced and mixed into a chickpea batter and fried to make crisp dumplings. They have their own Kutchi version of a favourite Indian snack, *pao*, where spicy potatoes are sandwiched into a soft white bun with a lick of intense chilli oil chutney. You will find this at popular street carts in and around Bhuj if you fancy a quick local snack.

1) Chickpea and potato mix, street cart, Netaji Road, Ahmedabad
2) Camel on Sidhpur street
3) Gandhi's room, Sabarmati Ashram, Ahmedabad
4) Lime soda vendor, Ahmedabad

AHMEDABAD: EAT

Agashiye

House of MG, opposite Sidi Saiyad Mosque,
Lal Darwaja
Tel: 079 2550 6946

Celebrate the art of the Gujarati thali
at this family-owned heritage hotel's
fine dining restaurant on the seductive,
expansive rooftop terrace, with a seasonal
and perfectly balanced menu that changes
daily. You choose either the standard or
the deluxe thali – both offer a good variety
of dishes, but it depends entirely on your
appetite. Standouts were the *lilva kachori*
(fried lentil balls with tamarind sauce),
smoked *brinjal* (eggplant) and the *kadhi*,
a yoghurt gravy (made with very fresh
yoghurt so it isn't sour) thickened with
chickpea flour and flavoured with cumin,
ginger, mustard seed and a dash of sugar,
served in a small bowl. It was impossible
to stop eating. The flatbreads are cooked
to order – *fulka roti* (*chapatti*) and the more
dense *bhakhari*, made with millet and whole
wheat, and they will serve you as many
as you desire. A Gujarati *thali* is about the
balance of flavours – sweet, salty and sour,
and they will offer a bowl of fresh jaggery
if you wish to add a dash of sweetness to
anything. This is a typically Gujarati habit,
as they prefer their food sweeter than in
other parts of India. The salted *chhas*
(buttermilk drink) was a perfect digestive.

Anand Dal Wada

Ashram Road, Usmanpura
(next to Gujarat Vityapith College)

Anand and his son Suresh run this street
cart that does a roaring trade, dishing out
plates of crisp *dal wada* (fried lentil balls),

sold by the 100-gram weight for a mere
20 rupees. Sprinkled with *amchur* (dried
mango powder) and served with slices
of raw red onion, fried green chillies and
half a lime to squeeze over, it makes an
ideal snack any time of the day. The place
is always packed with students and workers,
who were very curious whenever I joined
the throng.

Atithi

1st floor, Mohini, Judges Bungalow Rd
(near Shraddha petrol pump), Bokakdev
Tel: 2685 8806

A terrific place for a vegetarian thali and
packed with locals – always a good sign;
not a tourist in sight. I was introduced
to this place by Gautam, an expert on
Gujarati cuisine who insisted I try as
many different *thali* places as my stomach
would allow. The *thali* plate has a wide
assortment of dishes, more than any
other place I visited, and for a mere
250 rupees, you eat until you burst.
The dishes change daily so you can go
a couple of times a week and not have
the same thing. It is ingenious just how
versatile people are with vegetables and
legumes. The place is like a big, bustling
family restaurant and waiters come by
often to fill up your dishes and offer
more bread.

Famous Samosa House

Baba Baarulla Chawl, Shahibaug
Delhi Gate Road, near Rani Gupmati Mosque

Stop off here for some of the best bite-size
non-veg (mutton) samosas and meatballs
in town.

Farki

Delhi Gate (opposite BG Towers),
Shahibaug Rd
Tel: 6523 3255

This is the place to go for good *lassi*,
milkshakes and *kulfi* ice-cream. They
come in various flavours – choose from
the colourful menu boards on the wall.
If you don't want yours sweetened, opt for
the *lassi namkeen* – plain yoghurt with salt;
otherwise the local favourite is *rajwada*,
a thick *lassi* with dried fruit. Don't miss
the milk *halwa* cake (pictured).

Gopi Dining Hall

Ashram Rd (opposite Town Hall), Ellis Bridge
Tel: 2657 6388

A local haunt for office workers, with classic
Gujarati vegetarian *thalis* on the menu that
will include a selection of pickles, breads,
a *faarsan* fried snack, *dal, kadhi* (a thick
gravy made with chickpea flour and served
with fritters), *undhiya* (mixed vegetables
cooked in a clay pot with buttermilk,
a regional speciality), a seasonal vegetable
dish and rice.

KK Tea

Near the I.I.M. (India Institute of
Management), near AMA, Vastrapur

The city's most famous tea vendor. Go
during the day – he is shut in the evenings –
to taste what is considered the best chai
in town. Demand is huge and the shop
is always busy pleasing the crowds who
swarm here non-stop. Try the *masala* bun
too – it's a soft bun (bread roll) cut in half
and fried in butter with his own blend of
garam masala (like a spicy toast): delicious.

Lucky Tea Restaurant

Baba Baarulla Chawl, Shahibaug (diagonally
opposite House of MG)
Sidi Sayyed Jali intersection

Highly regarded for their excellent *chai*
made with the pure rich milk of Gujarat,
this is a simple cafe that keeps busy
throughout the day and evening. I also
tried their *maska* bun – a soft (almost
cake-like) bread roll spread with white
(*desi*) butter and pineapple jam. Look for
the *maska* bun menu on the wall.

Maharaja Samosa
Stadium Rd, Usmanpura

My guide Gautam brought me here to sample the best vegetarian samosas, and these small, perfectly formed parcels with delicate pastry and spicy potato filling certainly lived up to their reputation.

Mummy Nukitchu
Relief Rd, near Calico Dome

This street vendor sets up every morning in the same place and works throughout the day serving *kitchu*, a local staple made with rice flour, green chilli and ginger paste, cumin and salt. It cooks in a large pot to a thick porridge consistency and is served in small disposable bowls with chilli powder, black salt and ghee sprinkled on top. You can ask for extra spicy, as I did – he just adds more chilli powder. It's typical comfort food and is perfect during the cooler months.

SEWA Café (Self Employed Women's Association)
4th floor (above the Levbi Store)
CG Rd, near Municipal Market

The menu focuses on simple, healthy food, and I like supporting this place, as the money goes to a most worthwhile cause.

Shree Govind Farsan House
Swami Nayaran Temple Rd

A street vendor on the left-hand side of the road as you walk towards the Swaminarayan temple. The signage is in Hindi, so you need a local with you, or just look for the busiest cart; it's the one under the large tree. There are always locals milling about, munching on snacks and food non-stop. The counters are piled high with plates of *papadi*, all manner of fried tidbits and *fafda* – wafers made with a chickpea dough, rolled by hand into a flat strip then deep-fried in oil, served with slices of raw green papaya, green chilli and a thin *dal* gravy – the quintessential city breakfast.

His *jalebi* are truly wonderful and complete the experience after you have tasted *fafda*. A mix of sweet and savoury is considered essential in early-morning food.

Swati Snacks
Sera, Law Garden, Panchavati Rd, Ellisbridge
Tel: 2640 5900

A Gujarati benchmark with all the well-known vegetarian favourites on the menu, from snacks to more substantial dishes. Locals flock to this place for lunch and dinner every day, with its inviting casual atmosphere and friendly service.

For starters, try *pani puri* (puris in spicy pepper water) or *dahi sev puri* (with yoghurt) and the *chola methi dhokla* (made with chopped methi leaves and flour, steamed and drizzled with tempered mustard seeds and shredded coconut) are light as a feather; the best I have tasted anywhere. Other highlights from the menu are *paper dosa* with coconut chutney, *sambhar* and any one of their *roti* breads. Whatever you do, make sure you order the *panki chatri*: savoury chickpea pancake flavoured with turmeric, spread like a paste on to banana leaves and steamed, served with mint chutney and green chillies – they are sublime. There is also a branch in Bombay (in Taredo) which has a cult following, but I reckon the food is superior at its home base.

Vishalla

Sarkhej Narol Highway (opposite Vasna Tol Naka), Vasna
Tel: 2660 2422

It's worth the effort to visit this environmental centre for heritage art and architecture on the southern outskirts of the city. Privately owned, it's laid out as a village with an open-air restaurant. You sit on mats on the floor around low tables in the traditional manner – it's not high on comfort, but think rustic charm. The food is wonderful and authentically spicy, not toned down for the tourist market, as this place caters mostly to a local clientele. The dinner *thali* is a vegetarian feast served on disposable leaf mats, and much of the organic produce comes from their farm garden, focusing on indigenous ingredients and traditional preparations – this food has heart and soul. The *khichdi*, a lentil and rice preparation, is a perennial favourite with tiny *moong* sprouts. Leave room for the delicious *jalebi* (you can have as many as you like, or dare) and make sure to try a fresh date coated with *masala* sugar on your way out. Open for dinner only, it's worth coming a little earlier to spend time wandering through the Veechar Museum, with its stunning collection of traditional Indian household utensils and vessels from the past thousand years, beautifully displayed – best to check ahead of time that it will be open. There are also folk singers, dancers and puppet shows you can sit and watch in the garden before or after dinner if you wish – it's a veritable cultural package.

SLEEP

House of MG (The House of Mangaldas Girdhardas)

Opposite Sidi Saiyad Jali (mosque),
Lal Darwaja, Ahmedabad
www.houseofmg.com

A former private mansion that has been converted into a family-owned boutique heritage hotel, this place (above) is in high demand for a quintessential Ahmedabad experience. Ideally situated in the heart of the old town, it captures the spirit of the city, so be prepared for a constant cacophony. The grand deluxe rooms are generously proportioned; avoid the rooms at the front (numbers 4 and 19 particularly) as the traffic is incessant and noisy. You just have to love a place whose breakfast menu offers 'a healthful gratification', with an array of egg dishes, *dosa*s, *uppam*s and *upma* (steamed vegetables seasoned with tempered spices and green chilli. They also do a decent *bataka pauha*, a Gujarati version of the much loved *poha* – pressed rice flakes cooked with potato and spices. With choices like this, who needs toast?

SHOP

Gwalia Sweets and Kandoi Sweets

www.gwalia
www.kandoi

Gujarat is the largest producer of milk in India and sweets are invariably made from *mawa*, a sweet dough made with fermented milk and flour. Both these sweet stores are established chains of shops that have spread across the city and the state, and have a huge following with the local clientele. I visited both to sample some of the Gujarati specialities – *monthal*, sweet with jaggery; the creamy soft *sonpapadi*; *ghughira*, cardamom and coconut-stuffed dumplings; *ghari*, rich with ghee and spices; and *sutarfeni*, a fine semolina-looking mix made with pure milk, cream, sugar and wheat flour, flavoured with saffron and almonds or pistachios – truly melt in the mouth. Visiting during Holi (March) or Diwali (late October) festival time means the variety of sweets on offer is amazing, when sweets are consumed at a rate of knots. Ask your guide or at your hotel for the closest branch to where you are staying. Gujarat prides itself on its sweet treats and it would be remiss not to indulge while you are here.

Induben Khakharawala

C.G. Rd (near Girish Cold Drinks),
Navrangpura
Tel: (m) 0989 898 5560 – Ashish

The definitive farsan (snack) shop in
the city, this is a treasure trove of edible
delights, like a mini-supermarket with
everything from dried *pappad*s to *khakra*
(I am in love with their *methi khakra*s),
namkeen, spiced nuts, *dosa*s, *puri* puffs,
biscuits, pickles, chutneys and more. Buy
something to take home as a taste memory.

Patel's Ice Cream

Stadium Rd (opposite Sports Club),
Navrangpura
Tel: 6521 7124

You can buy by the scoop and eat at one
of their tables; it's packed during summer
evenings, or you can buy by the kilo and
take your treasure away. Flavours include
the ever-popular *chikoo* (sapote), *kesar pista*
(saffron pistachio), strawberry and roasted
badam (almond). Try the fresh mango when
it's in season (April / May).

BHUJ: SLEEP

Hotel Prince Residency

College Rd (opposite Toran Raan Resort),
Mirzapar Highway
www.residency.hotelprinceonline.com

When you're on the tourist trail, this
modest, recently renovated hotel is the
best option in this small, out-of-the-way
town in the Kutch region. The kitchen
prepares decent and simple Gujarati food,
served *thali* style.

RAJASTHAN

State

TO TRAVEL THROUGH THE DESERT STATE OF RAJASTHAN in West India is to discover a region overflowing with an embarrassment of riches. It is perhaps the most dazzling state of all, the 'land of the kings', ablaze with colour everywhere you look – from saris and turbans to forts and palaces to spices and food. It's total visual overload. Descendants of the mighty Rajput warriors, the Rajasthanis are striking and proud. The people are tolerant, respecting each other's religious beliefs. The men wear their distinctive moustaches and turbans with great pride. Rajasthanis emit a radiance and lust for life that underpins their innate strength and energy. They are devoted to their deities through music, dance and places of worship; religious festivals dot the calendar. It is one of the poorest states in India and most of the population live in rural villages, eking out a living from the land.

Rajasthani food has been influenced by the warfaring lifestyle of its inhabitants and the availability of local ingredients. Because water is scarce, milk, buttermilk and curd are liberally used to add moisture to food. Dried lentils, indigenous *sangri* desert beans, millet grain, corn and other cereals replace leafy greens, and local spices include mustard seeds, turmeric, fenugreek and coriander. The pungent leaves of the fenugreek plant (*methi*) are used extensively and are wonderful when mixed with fenugreek seeds, spinach or mustard greens and tomato. Because of their adverse conditions, Rajasthani cooking is imaginative and creative, making the most of what's at hand – so grains and pulses, red chillies, onion and garlic form the basis of their repertoire. ✿

ESSENTIAL SIGHTS

Palaces and forts are scattered across the state. There are a host of rock fortifications and important historical sites close by as we weave our way across the landscape. The **Jaisalmer Fort**, the sixteenth-century **Amber Fort** near Jaipur, and the enormous, imposing **Mehrangarh Fort** in Jodhpur, which defines that city's skyline, are just a few of the best examples. Other fortified palaces that have been neglected over time are now privately owned and operating as boutique hotels. They offer a unique experience, a mesmerising insight into what it would have been like to live as a member of the nobility.

Kumbhalgarh Fort, built in the fifteenth century, is the second longest wall fortification in the world after the Great Wall of China and is a UNESCO world heritage site.

The **Jain temple** at Ranakpur (above), with its hundreds of ornately carved marble columns, is a must-see.

Taste the perfectly textured *gatte ke saag* – besan (chickpea flour) dumplings poached in a spicy curd gravy, a Rajasthani speciality.

The golden city of **Jaisalmer** (above) – this dramatic desert city is one of the oldest kingdoms in Rajasthan and is centred on the historic twelfth-century fort with buildings that reflect red in the bright sun and pale golden in the soft morning and evening light. Several hundred families continue to reside within its ramparts, making it one of the very rare living forts in India. Inside are palaces, *havelis*, a beautifully carved Jain temple, and craft work by local artisans.

Take a **camel ride** over the sand dunes, through the desert.

Visit a **rural farm** and see how crops are grown and harvested.

Explore **village life** – the Jain villages, the tribal Bishnoi or Rabari villages and the gypsy villages all have unique ways of living.

1–2) Kumbhalgarh Fort 3) Leopard at Jawai 4) Village house in Rajasthan 5) Patwa Haveli

SLEEP & EAT

Amanbagh

Near Alwar, a two-hour drive east
from Jaipur
www.amanresorts.com
amanbagh@amanresorts.com

A modern palace modelled on a Rajasthani
haveli that blends seamlessly into its
environment (above). Enter a walled
compound of refined, contemporary
elegance that pays homage to its remote
surroundings while drawing on its Mughal
history. They offer wonderful cultural
opportunities during your stay, such as visits
to local ancient ruins and village walks.
The food is sensational, with much of the
produce sourced from its organic kitchen
garden; chef Bharghav (call him BG) is
only too pleased to show you around.
I usually stick with one of his lighter dishes
for lunch, such as the *gutti vankaya koora*
(gunpowder-stuffed eggplant with tamarind
and dried chillies) or the *bhindi masala*
(spiced, stir-fried okra), and for dinner,
either a vegetarian thali or something
cooked in the tandoor such as *lagan ki boti*
(lamb marinated with yoghurt and onions
and seasoned with ground mace). Whatever
you do, make sure you try the crisp okra
and pomegranate salad, dusted with *chaat
masala*, just one of the house specialities.

Aman-i-Kas Wilderness Camp

Near Sawai Madhopur
www.amanresorts.com
aman-i-khas@amanresorts.com

A high-end wilderness camp that set
the bar in Rajasthan, and has since been
followed by other discerning properties.
It's a three-hour drive south of Jaipur,
or a twenty-minute drive from Sawai
Madhopur station. Trains depart from
Nizamuddin station in Delhi and you are
accompanied by an Aman butler for the
five-hour journey. The property looks out
to the curvaceous Aravalli Hills at the edge
of Ranthambore National Park, and staying
in one of the ten luxury tented pavilions
is the most pampered way to experience
a wildlife safari. March and April are good
times for tiger sightings. During your stay,
be sure to visit Surwal Lake, Khandar Fort,
Ranthambore Fort (on the opposite side of
park), and the nearby, completely preserved
Moghul forts and rural villages. Sit around
the divine campfire pit (below) at night
and feast on *maas ke sooley* (lamb chops
marinated in yoghurt and spices, cooked in
the tandoor oven), *paneer hare mirch* (fresh
cheese and green chilli in a rich onion and
cashew gravy) and *dal palak* (yellow lentils
cooked with garlic and spinach). The menu
changes each night and epitomises the best
of camp-style cooking.

Bijay Niwas Palace

Bijay Nagar (south of Ajmer)
www.bijayniwaspalace.com

Roughly halfway between Jaipur and
Udaipur, about twenty minutes off
National Highway NH79, this boutique
heritage hotel is a great place to stop for
a day to break up your road trip, or if you're
pushed for time, it makes a great lunch
stop. Expect warm, friendly service, home-
style food and honest flavours – lunch *al
fresco* in the garden is the way to go.

Chhatra Sagar

Nimaj, District Pali
www.chhatrasagar.com

A pleasant ninety-minute drive south-east
of Jodhpur, along the NH112 highway that
connects to Jaipur, passing through small
towns and villages. Chhatra Sagar (above)
is an idyllic tented campsite, owned and
managed by the Singh family, brothers
Harsh and Nandi and their wives Shrinidri
and Vasundhara, who collectively make it
a memorable experience. Situated near the
village of Nimaj and closed during summer,
it takes three weeks to build each year. The
season starts in October and finishes at the
end of March. It's a blissful hideaway with
uninterrupted views of the bird sanctuary,
overlooking a vast reservoir lake to the

Aravalli mountains – an oasis of calm
and tranquility. The fifteen tents are set
up along the top of a large dam wall,
a catchment for the monsoon rains; full of
water at the start of the season (if the rains
have been sufficient) and empty by March.
This contributes to the water supply for
the property and the surrounding villages
and farms, with bore water as a back-up.

It's the cooking by Shrinidri and
Vasundhara that makes it an essential
pilgrimage. Both are exceptional cooks,
passionate about their regional food and
eager to share their culinary heritage.
They cook in a time-honoured tradition,
yet with a modern sensibility with produce
sourced from their camp's garden.
Vegetables and pulses feature heavily,
textures are fresh and crisp, flavours are
light, some of my favourite dishes are
tamarind eggplant, pomegranate *raita*,
til aloo (sesame potatoes) and *khada masala
maans* (goat curry) served with white dal
(split *urad dal* cooked with onion, garlic
and yoghurt) and the best tomato chutney
imaginable. Pre-dinner drinks are served
around a blazing fire (if it's cool enough)
built in an enormous cast-iron pit that
allows the flames to leap a few metres
into the air. Dinner is a leisurely feast
under the stars.

Jawai Leopard Camp

Bisalpur (near Perwa village), District Pali
www.sujanluxury.com

Tented luxury beyond compare – lavish
yet contemporary in design, every detail is
just perfect. The bed was one of the most
comfortable I have ever slept on. This is
a place to feel totally pampered. There are
only ten tents, making the camp private
and exclusive, and each tented pavilion has
a private outdoor deck looking out to the
bush (above). The service is unobtrusive –
things happen magically when your back
is turned. If you want to keep it really
private, you can arrange to have breakfast
in the bush, a picnic lunch by the lake or
a candlelit dinner in one of the granite
outcrops. The organic kitchen garden
provides the salad greens, herbs and some
vegetables, the *surmai* fish comes from the
lake, and other produce is sourced locally.
The food is healthy and delicious: usually
salads and fish for lunch and a typical
Rajasthani *thali* for dinner, often seated
around the campfire. There is an obvious
and strong commitment to community
and eco-friendly tourism; the ethos is to
tread lightly and leave no footprint. And
then there's the reason you are here: elusive
yet ever-present leopards roam the craggy
granite hills amid breathtaking wilderness.
There is plenty of wildlife to observe –

birds, marsh crocodiles and flamingos. You
will also spot the nomadic Rabari herdsmen
with their distinctive red turbans; take the
chance to stroll along with one of them and
his herd of goats, or take a brisk two-hour
walk to the lake and back, or grab one of
the mountain bikes and cycle through the
bush to explore the beauty of the camp's
environs. This is the place that demands
that you just be. Take it all in. The camp
is a comfortable three-hour drive from
either Jodhpur or Udaipur. Just note that it
is closed during the hot summer months,
from May to September.

Manvar Resort and Desert Camp

Khiyansaria Village, Milestone 110
(midway between Jodphur and Jaisalmer)
www.manvar.com

The perfect pit stop for a lunch break
when driving to Jaisalmer – a welcome
desert oasis. Timeless charm and country
hospitality is what characterises this place,
where lunch at a courtyard table under the
tree is served from silver handi pots and
may include sisodia paneer – local paneer
cheese cooked with curd and tomato in
the style of the local Sisodia tribe, and
jangali maans, lamb cooked in a spicy,
creamy gravy. Dessert is gajar ka halwa –
carrot halwa, a Rajasthani staple.

Mihir Garh

Khandi Village, Rohet, District Pali
www.mihirgarh.com

The luxurious purpose-built fort (above
right; its name means fort of the sun) and
glamorous sister property to Rohet Garh

(see page 120), with nine beautifully
appointed, spacious suites (a few with
private plunge pools), this is the ideal
place to just relax and be, with spectacular,
expansive views of the Thar desert. It's
a short fifteen-minute drive further on from
Rohet, and has a wonderfully relaxed yet
exclusive ambience, like staying in a private
mansion or chateau. The food is prepared
to the same exacting standard as at Rohet
Garh. Aside from giving in to the gentle
pace of life, you can take a jeep safari
through the nearby tribal villages, check
out the wildlife, indulge in the magical
experience of a royal picnic under a typical
Rajasthani open-sided tent, usually set up
under a large tree near the small lake. You
can also arrange a private candlelit dinner
in the sand dunes. For the more energetic,
they offer horse-riding safaris, boasting the
best stable of Marwari horses in India. This
is run from their nearby tented campsite,
Wilderness Camp, within sight of the fort
with eight pavilion tents.

Ranvas

Ahhichatragarh Fort, Gandhi Chowk, Nagaur
www.jodhanaheritage.com

Ranvas, 'The Abode of Queens', was
established as a pleasure palace in the mid-
eighteenth century. The hotel is within the
ramparts of the fort, and is beautifully

restored, complete with a swimming pool – essential in this part of the world. There are ten *havelis* (houses) within the fort and each has a suite and two bedrooms looking on to a private courtyard. Gaj Singhji II, the current Maharaja of Jodphur and the Mawar region of Rajasthan, is very active in the region's cultural life and hosts the World Sufi Spirit Festival every February (in Jodphur and at Nagaur), where well-known singers and musicians converge from all over the country to perform in various parts of the fort. It's a magical experience, with candles lit in recessed walls of the pavilions – like fairyland. If you want to avoid crowds and have a more leisurely stay, plan to visit at a different time.

Rawla Narlai

Narlai, near Ranakpur
Tel: 2934 260443 | www.narlai.com

For the ultimate authentic Rajasthani experience, this charming place (above) is a hidden gem; it's a little off the beaten track but well worth the effort. The small town of Narlai looks towards the undulating hills in what seems like a forgotten corner, tucked out of the way. What a discovery. They focus on the total experience. The food is sublime, perfect for its backdrop, and the service is friendly and attentive. Make sure to arrange

sundowners on the shores of Ghora Dhara Lake and a candlelit dinner in the nearby stepwell, and take a sunrise walk up Elephant Rock to the temple. A wonderful heritage hotel awaits, filled with personality and understated country style and charm. This delightful seventeenth-century retreat is the former hunting lodge of the Maharaja of Jodphur. You are greeted by a shower of falling rose petals as you arrive through the gates into the compound, the stone walls draped with bougainvillea, and suddenly the outside world disappears and you enter a magical wonderland. There's a generously sized swimming pool in another private courtyard hidden beyond one of the stone walls. Everything on offer at Rawla Narlai is considered and unhurried, perfectly executed and done with a sense of ease, in keeping with its environment. Breakfast was a perfectly ripe papaya and a *paratha* stuffed with potato and herbs, served with yoghurt and mango pickle and a pot of tea. Lunch stays light, with a few vegetable pakoras and *moong dal vadas* (lentil fritters), both served with mint chutney. The house chef, Avinash, is keen, generous and helpful. He cooks with great pride in his region, and his distinctive desert food has left a lasting impression on me: *ker sangri*, Rajastani desert beans, dry-fried in a spicy curd with mustard oil, served with *gatta* curry made with lentil dumplings, *rabori* and *laal maas*.

Rohet Garh

Rohet, District Pali
www.rohetgarh.com

A 45-minute drive south-west of Jodhpur, Rohet is a small village where the Singh family ancestoral home has been converted into an idyllic heritage hotel that has expanded over the years since my first visit.

Siddharth and Rashmi make gracious hosts, personally overseeing the different activities offered and greeting the guests each day, either over a sundowner drink on the manicured lawns, or at dinner. It's the ideal base for horse riding, jeep safaris and visiting the local Bishnoi tribal communities. The purpose-built kitchen hosts cooking class workshops featuring the heritage family recipes of Thakurani Sahiba Jayendra Kumari (Sid's mother), overseen by his wife Rashmi and head chef Kadar Khan, who has been with the family since they opened Rohet Garh in the mid-nineties.

I have enduring memories of several dishes: tender, melt-in-the-mouth *lal maas* (the signature Rajasthani lamb dish), buttery *laccha paratha*, *zafrani phirni* (saffron rice flour dumpling served with a granular-textured soft custard in a martini glass), a modern take on traditional flavours. Rashmi and the kitchen use the recipes inherited from her mother-in-law Jayendra, who oversaw all culinary productions when I visited in 2000 and has since passed away. She had written two small cookbooks: *Rohet Garh Cuisine* and *Quick and Easy Rajastani* – family heirlooms that are a legacy to the house cooks and guests, recipes that have been faithfully preserved – the passing down of family traditions.

Two of my favourite dishes are Mama's Chicken – chicken cooked with yoghurt, spices, and sweet and sour tomatoes. A dinner feast may include a thali of sweet and sour tomatoes, a yoghurt eggplant number, potato *aloo rassa*, spicy chicken and chutney. *Churma* is the house favourite for dessert, a sweet traditionally made with *dal batti*: whole wheat dough that is sun dried and crumbled, then cooked with sugar, ghee and almonds, pressed into small cakes and dressed with edible silver leaf.

It's rich and dense, and a small piece is more than enough.

When you are driving away from Rohet, stop off for one last snack at **Parlad Chand Mangilal Patjapat**, on the edge of the village on the main road to Jodhpur – there are always locals hanging round having snacks and a gossip. Their *mirchi wada* (fried stuffed chillies) is the best I have tasted, the chillies more fiery than elsewhere, and they are famous for their *kachori*s (fried flaky pastries stuffed with *moong dal*); many Jodhpur families send their drivers here to collect some for them.

Roopam Resort
Ranakpur, District Pali
Tel: 02934 285321

About two kilometres along the road from the Jain temple, this modest roadhouse comes highly recommended by Abhay, my local driver in Rajasthan, and it's where we stop for a tea break when driving through the area. Don't be misled by its name; it's a roadside cafe and serves everything from breakfast staples to *biryani*. I keep it simple and order their spicy vegetable *pakoras*, a plate of butter *chapatti* and *masala chai*. The food is honest, simple and freshly prepared.

Samode Palace

Samode
www.samode.com

A majestic palace (above), ninety minutes' drive north-west of Jaipur. Spacious rooms with expansive views, ideal for a quiet retreat away from the city when you prefer just to stay put and marvel at the countryside. Arrange a dinner at their nearby Samode Bagh (about twenty minutes from the palace) during your stay, where the chefs prepare typical Rajasthani dishes cooked over hot coals in a lovely garden setting. The kitchen makes a terrific *dahi baigan* (eggplant in yoghurt sauce).

The Serai Luxury Camp

Bherwa, Chandan, Jaisalmer
www.sujanluxury.com

A pleasant four-hour drive west of Jodhpur on a good road across the flat, stony Thar Desert, close to the Pakistan border and

forty-five minutes' drive from the medieval fort city of Jaisalmer, this is remote desert living at its best. The luxury tented campsite is set on an expansive private estate amongst the indigenous desert scrub, and offers a stylish and sophisticated camping experience. Its magical location gives a sense of solitude and calm, and it's an ideal base for exploring the desert and this far-flung city. Each of the twenty-two tent pavilions are spacious and comfortable, and the Royal Pavilion comes with a private plunge pool in a walled garden. The large swimming pool has been designed to mirror the traditional architecture of a stepwell and is the perfect place to relax after a day exploring or for an early-morning swim. I have treasured memories of sunset drinks on the sand dunes, so arrange with the front desk for a desert safari in the late afternoon that takes you out to the dunes by jeep, where you can then roam around on a camel before sunset drinks are served. The food is deliciously authentic and rustic, reflecting the flavours of the Rajputana. The Rajasthani *thali* suits its surrounds and vegetable dishes are a highlight, made with produce sourced from their expansive kitchen garden and indigenous produce such as *sangri* desert beans, wild mushrooms cooked in a creamy yoghurt gravy, ripe tomatoes stewed with spices, tiny eggplant braised in a *masala*

gravy and a yellow *dal* cooked with Indian spinach leaves. I loved the delicacy of the *murgh sharrmili* kebab – chicken chunks bathed in beetroot juice and cooked till meltingly tender in the tandoor oven and the *sailana murgh* – chicken confit in ghee with garlic and red chilli. Lunch and dinner can be taken in a different spot each time. Their sustainable conservation ethos, established by the forward-thinking Sujan group that also own Jawai and Sher Bagh, is commendable. The camp is closed from April to the end of September, when the temperatures soar to scorching heat.

Shahpura Bagh

Shahpura, Bilwara district
www.shahpurabagh.com

A four-hour drive south of Jaipur, this magnificent family property (above), set in a 40-acre wooded estate with wonderful lakeside views, offers a sense of timelessness. It is owned and managed by the Singh family, who are fabulous hosts, and it is one of my favourite Rajasthani home stays. Once the summer residence of the Rajadhiraj of Shahpura, the house has been beautifully restored and furnished with a wonderful mix of antique and contemporary pieces. As there are only seven suites and two rooms, guests are

welcomed and treated as family. There are two residences: Nahar Nivas (where family also live) has one suite and two rooms, and Umaid Nivas has six suites – this building is the pick. To get there, you drive from either Jaipur or Udaipur – it's about halfway between each. The surrounding wetlands are terrific for bird watching and fishing. With sustainability in mind, the houses are solar powered, and a farm and village visit in an open-air jeep is essential to experience the daily rituals of rural life, where agriculture is the mainstay. Jump in the jeep and drive out to Nahar Sagar farm, part of the family estate, where they grow wheat, mustard and lentils. Visit the nearby Ram Dwara temple complex, then head out to Dhikola Fort for sunset drinks with expansive views of the countryside.

A superb hostess, Maia personifies the modern Indian woman with strong allegiances to traditional values as she oversees the Shahpura household. A bevy of aunties help supervise the kitchens, where delicious home-cooked Rajasthani cuisine is produced from the local gardens and cooked on open wood and charcoal fire stoves or in terracotta pots. Sundowners are served in the garden by the pool each evening, and a gin and tonic is poured to welcome you on arrival.

Sher Bagh

Sawai Madhopur district (about three hours' drive southeast of Jaipur), near entrance to Ranthambore National Park
www.sujanluxury.com

An alternative to Aman-i-Khas (its neighbouring property), for a tented campsite close to the private wilderness of the world-renowned, historical Ranthambhore Tiger Reserve. The welcome is warm and genuine; the compact tents are lavishly decorated in a cosy heritage style (conjuring up images of a Royal Raj lifestyle) – my favourite is The Burra Sahib Suite (tent number 10) with a more expansive living space and a private swimming pool and walled garden. Part of the Relais & Chateaux portfolio, its ambience casts its magic spell, whether you are heading out for a tiger and wildlife safari with expert trackers, having sunset drinks around the campfire being cosseted by attentive service, or enjoying delicious home-style cooking in the dining tent.

Like other tented camps, it is closed during the summer months. Pinch yourself and revel in every minute of your stay.

LUXURY TRAIN TRAVEL

More recently, luxury trains have started to offer a travel experience in Rajasthan, and they've become very popular. Both these train journeys are fitted out with suites and dining cars, having recreated the grand style of the palaces and the romantic glamour of decadent train travel, travelling from Delhi to Agra, Jaipur and Udaipur. The trains travel at night while guests are sleeping and stop during the day for some on-foot exploration and sight seeing at each stop of their journey.

Maharaja's Express
www.maharajas-express.com

Royal Rajasthan on Wheels
www.royalrajasthanonwheels.co.in

JAIPUR

City

THE PINK CITY OF JAIPUR IS KNOWN AS THE GATEWAY to Rajasthan and is the largest and busiest of Rajasthan's fortified imperial cities, and an essential stop if you're planning to explore the magnificent nearby Amber Fort (left), with its lakeside garden in the summer pavilion planted like a Mughal carpet. The city gets its colour from locally mined rock, reflecting the colour of the desert. The museums of the City Palace display the opulence of palace life and are definitely worth a look to appreciate the richness of its culture. The Johri bazaar, shops and markets here make a shopping trip mandatory, and it is nigh-on impossible to leave empty-handed. The vegetable vendors, whether on the sides of the streets, in vendor carts or small shops, display their colourful and diverse produce invitingly, everything sparkling fresh and clean. The shops have a narrow frontage and the owners sit out front on well-worn *charpoys* (traditional woven beds) inviting every passer-by in to browse. Wherever you look, business is brisk. For an authentic taste of Jaipur and Rajasthani food, venture into one of the busy *dhabas* (roadside cafes), often set up under makeshift canopies or overhanging trees – places that rely on fast turnover and more often than not, where the best food can be found, as they are where the locals eat. Food is served from large *handis* (conical pots) and breads are cooked to order at a furious pace. It's an experience not to be missed.

The late Maharani of Jaipur, Rajmata Gayatri Devi, championed the royal cuisine of Jaipur, writing a cookbook that's full of family heirloom recipes from the royal palace kitchens, with recipes centred round the extravagant entertaining of her royal household. The restaurant at Rambagh Palace carries on the traditions of the Khansamas, the royal cooks of the Rajasthani palaces, and offers a culinary tour of the kingdom with its menu. ✿

ESSENTIAL SIGHTS

The Jaipur Literary Festival, held in the third week of January each year at Diggi Palace, is a must for keen readers and writers; there's always an exciting line-up of noted authors from India and abroad, considered by many to be the best literary festival in the world.

Wander past Hawa Mahal (Wind Palace), the pink stone façade that has come to symbolise the city (avoid the snake charmers with their trained cobras on the opposite side of the street at all costs, they are a rip-off).

Spend time at Jantar Mantar (above), the astronomical observatory, with its massive sundials built by Maharajah Jai Singh.

Visit City Palace (opposite) – a museum of the city's heritage and royal family.

Drive out to Amber (about forty minutes) and spend a morning wandering through the ramparts of the spectacular Amber Fort, a former Rajput palace (above), and its Mughal gardens, then stop off at the nearby Anokhi Museum to see the wonderful displays of handcrafted textiles and block printed fabrics.

Explore Johri Bazaar and food market; there are many tempting things to buy.

Princess Diya Kumari of the Jaipur royal family has established an NGO (Princess Diya Kumari Foundation – PDKF) focused on the education and empowerment of women and girls in Jaipur, with headquarters at the historic Badal Mahal (Cloud Palace), located within the City Palace complex. A private visit can be arranged with prior notice.

EAT

1135 AD

Amber Fort, Jaipur
Tel: 0141 253 1048

One of the most stunning locations in Jaipur, this recently opened restaurant is tucked away inside the Jaleb Chowk's main gateway at the Amber Fort. Feel like indulgent royalty as you dine in this sumptuous room with gilded mirrored tiles; the food is every bit as good as the setting. Order the Rajasthani *thali* – a feast for the senses.

Anokhi Cafe

2F, KK Square, C11 Prithviraj Road, C Scheme (near M.I. Rd)
Tel: 400 7245 | www.anokhicafe.com

A chic cafe that is open every day, with a menu featuring simple, flavoursome dishes using organic produce from their farm near Amber. It's ideal for when you need a break from Indian food; order a sandwich, a salad or one of the delicious vegetarian dishes and leave space for a cake to have with tea or coffee. It's a quiet retreat, even though it's in a shopping complex. Anokhi is known for its beautifully crafted hand-printed fabrics

and textiles. A socially aware brand that combines age-old traditions and conservation with sensitive development.

Aryan Niwas

Sansar Chandra Rd (Behind Amber Tower) near Post Office, off M. I. Road
Tel: 237 2456

This modest hotel is a favourite with locals in the know, whether for families or those travelling solo. A quiet oasis in the centre of the city with a walled garden space and free wi-fi, it's modest, clean, simple, cared for and great value. We come for the food – home-style cooking that is nourishing and authentic. It reminds me of an old-fashioned tuck shop. The dining room serves some of the best vegetarian food in Jaipur, and they also make the best *masala chai*. Lunch starts at 12.30.

Lassiwala

312 Tiwari Building, M.I. Rd
(opposite Niros Restaurant)
Tel: 237 8692

The original and the best – ignore the neighbours that have moved in to open up copycat versions. The lassi is served, with a thin layer of pure cream on top, in disposable clay beakers, available in two sizes. The flavour is sublime.

Nanda Lal Aloo Tikka

Outside 147 Johari Bazaar, Jaipur

A street cart offering very delicious potato snacks – a great place to stop for an early-evening snack after shopping in the bazaar. The fried potato balls in masala gravy are wickedly good and easily become addictive.

Niros

M.I. Rd (near Panch Batti)
Tel: 237 4493

A local institution and a city landmark, although more popular with tourists than with locals these days. A fun place for lunch – try the *malai tikka* (chicken kebabs cooked in a ginger, garlic and yoghurt paste), the *bhuna* chicken (cooked in a *masala*-spiced onion and tomato gravy) and the *paneer* butter masala.

Pandit Kulfi

Hawa Mahal Rd

Definitely the best *kulfi* (Indian ice cream) in Jaipur; stop off for a treat after checking out Hawa Mahal Palace just up the road.

Rawat Misthan Bhandar

Station Rd, opposite Polo Victory Cinema (near main Rail Station)
Tel: 236 8288

For the best *kachoris* in town and recommended by many locals – be sure to try the *masala* onion and potato (*pyaz ki kachori*) or the sweet *kachori*, sticky and gently spiced. The counter displays a huge array of sweets – try the Rajasthani speciality *ghewar* with cream and saffron on top, or the threadlike *fini* or wholewheat *rabri*.

Samosawala

A street cart at the city gate on the Amber Road, just beyond the old city. Make this a pit stop when you head out to visit Amber Fort, arrive early when the pastries are freshly made, there are usually people queued up to get their fix.

Sharma Dhaba

Jaipur-Chomu Rd – about thirty minutes from city centre on a main arterial road

A favourite with the locals, this roadside cafe under a canopy of trees serves home-style vego food, and the menu is also available in English.

Surya Mahal

Rajvilas, Goner Rd, Jaipur (about thirty minutes' drive out of town)
www.oberoihotels.com

The setting is dramatic and dinner on the courtyard terrace is a must, with beautifully cooked food from their lavish menu that features regional dishes of India. The chefs offer cooking classes to resident guests; this is where I first learnt the art of cooking in a tandoor, and their meats and breads cooked in the tandoor are second to none. If you choose to stay here, make it worthwhile and request a luxury tent; they are spacious and well appointed with a lovely ambience.

Suvarna Mahal

Rambagh Palace, Jaipur
Tel: 221 1919

Live like a *maharajah* or *maharani* – get your butler to dress you up in traditional clothing and dine in this grand palatial dining room. The menu is a showcase of regional specialities of the royal cuisines of Awardhi (Raj), Punjab, Hyderabad and Lucknow (Moghul). The service is attentive and helpful and the wine list offers plenty of choice. This is the city's ultimate fine dining experience, so expect some pomp and ceremony. I usually arrange for a set menu, which might include the most delicious *dahi ke* kebabs (curd dumplings), *khara seena* (chicken marinated in aromatic spices

and cooked over hot coals), *awadhi gilawat* (spicy lamb kebabs) and *warqi paratha*, a *Hyderabadi tathi* kebab, *dum ki gosht biryani* (lamb and rice), *murgh tikka* butter *masala* (butter chicken) and a silky rich *dal suvarna mahal*, their signature dal preparation.

SLEEP

Dera Mandawa Haveli

Sansar Chandra Rd (outside Chandpole Gate)
www.deramandawa.com

A lovingly renovated *haveli* with seven suites, overseen by the owner Durga Singh, a proud, aristocratic Rajput and generous host who brings his culture and country vibrantly alive with a wonderful sense of humour and storytelling. Durga is a renaissance man whose interests are as diverse as philosophy, religion, contemporary politics, farming, tribal culture, music, poetry and food – conversation is always lively. It's a treat to stay at this intimate boutique property, where every effort is made to make you feel like part of the family; hospitality is second nature. For dinner when I visited, the house cook prepared a wonderful Rajasthani barbecue out in the garden: *gaj ka sula* (lamb kebabs) were marinated in yoghurt and spices and threaded on to long steel skewers, then cooked over hot glowing coals, accompanied by *sooka aloo* (*masala* potatoes), *baingan bharta* (eggplants smoked over coals and mashed with chilli and onion), and a lovely fresh vegetable and *paneer* (fresh cheese) salad.

Rajmahal Palace
www.sujanluxury.com

Jaipur has a new benchmark for a luxury urban retreat. Check in and live it up like a royal prince or princess in the oldest private palace in Jaipur (former residence of Maharaja Sawai Man Singh II), faithfully restored and transformed into an ornate oasis of calm in this fast-growing urban metropolis (above). Experience the flamboyant palatial grandeur of a bygone era; the decor is seriously over the top (channel your inner Versace). Colours, fabrics, textures and fittings jump out

at you from every direction. Doing a few laps in the Art Deco swimming pool is pure decadence on a hot afternoon, and splashing out on a grand dinner in their restaurant completes the fantasy. I opt for the *thali* menu, which changes daily (rather than the a la carte menu of Western dishes) and may include classic preparations like *murgh khada masala* (chicken cooked with aromatic whole spices and ghee), *aloo methi* (potatoes and fenugreek leaves), *matar pattaghobi* (green peas tossed with shredded cabbage) and *safed maans* (mutton marinated in curd and spices and slow cooked). Every mouthful is delicious with the flavour and spirit of good home cooking. You'll depart Jaipur with a sense of euphoria.

Rambagh Palace
Bhawani Singh Road, Jaipur
www.tajhotels.com

The ultimate palace hotel (above) for indulgent pampering with polished, considered service, and definitely one of the most opulent places to stay in central Jaipur – a sanctuary that ticks all the boxes. The suites and rooms are sumptuous (request one that looks on to the garden), and lunch or a well-deserved gin and tonic on the Verandah Terrace, overlooking the perfectly manicured gardens, is not to be missed.

Samode Haveli

Gangapole, Jaipur
www.samode.com

A charming and sensitively restored heritage *haveli* with an ideal central location in the old city near Jorawarsingh Gate, moderately priced with well-appointed rooms. Poolside drinks in the garden courtyard are a good way to kick off the evening before heading out to dinner. Service can be lacking and the food is so-so – don't let it detract from your stay, just make wise decisions about where to eat. There is lots of choice in this city when it comes to good food, so don't squander a moment.

SHOP

The Gem Palace

MI Rd, Jaipur
Tel: 237 4175

The ultimate Indian jewellery shop and one of the best-known shops in Jaipur, where you can choose from an endless array of dazzling gemstones and finely crafted jewels. If you are serious about your jewels, make an appointment for a private viewing in the upstairs room with brothers Munnu or Sanjay.

Laxmi Misthan Bhandar (LMB)

100 Johari Bazaar, Jaipur
Tel: 256 5844

In the main street surrounded by market shops, this place has been operating for more than 300 years and in some ways, it looks it – worn with age and more often than not, the service can be on the surly side. The menu offers typical Rajasthani staples and next door is the sweet shop, a good place to buy take-away sweets.

JODHPUR

City

THE MEDIEVAL CITY OF JODHPUR IS DEFINED BY THE colour indigo, and is at its most beguiling just before sunset. It is positioned at the edge of the Thar Desert that stretches west to Jaisalmer and beyond. Another of Rajasthan's imperial cities, Jodhpur is dominated by the powerful and imposing presence of the Mehrangarh Fort, with the sprawl of indigo-hued houses around its base. It's a clear reminder that they knew how to build on a grand scale hundreds of years ago. It gets scorchingly hot during summer, and water is a precious resource, piped down from the Himalayas along the Indira Gandhi Canal, a massive pipeline that brings life to so many farming communities and the city. The bazaar and streets around the Clock Tower at the edge of the old town are home to produce markets and shops that sell everything from lentils, flour, rice and spices to furniture, clothing, hardware and jewellery. The street vendors churn out a never-ending supply of specialty snacks such as *mirchi wada* – a hollowed-out long green chilli stuffed with a spiced lentil mix, dipped in a chickpea batter and deep-fried. There are also *samosas*, *parathas* and the Jodhpuri speciality *mawa kachori* – small, deep-fried balls of dough made with flour and milk and sweetened with cardamom. ❁

ESSENTIAL SIGHTS

Go for a wander to explore the old town, the narrow laneways around the bazaar, the *haveli*s and so on.

Visit **Clock Tower Market** – check out the street vendors and taste the *mirchi wada* and chilli *pakora*s from any one of the street vendors. Make sure you taste *mawa kachori*, Jodhpur's gift to India's expansive culinary repertoire. A fried *poori* stuffed with *khoya* (milk), nuts and sometimes rose petals, and coated with edible silver leaf, it is sinfully good – total sugar overload and hard to stop at one.

Have a sunset drink on the outdoor terrace at **Umaid Bhawan Palace** and take in its opulent extravagance and manicured lawns. Available to hotel guests only, so book a room.

Jodhpur is considered the centre for the best Rajasthani **handicrafts and antiques**, so head to one of the factory outlets dotted around the main roads of the city, where it's like entering Aladdin's Cave and difficult to leave empty-handed.

Spend a day wandering through the imposing **Mehrangarh Fort** (above and opposite top), one of India's most magnificent forts, packed with history and legend. It has commanding views across the city.

Taste the local **Mathania chillies**, used widely in Mawari and Rajasthani cooking: rich deep red in colour with a fiery flavour, they are legendary in India.

Jodhpur is the home of polo (the game of the royals) and it's possible to watch a game at the **Equestrian Institute**. www.jodphurpolo.com

EAT

Bhati Tea Stall
Bhati Choraya (Circle)

Join the flock of locals and drivers who stop by this modest but famous tea stall (above) on a busy corner for a glass of *masala chai*. There are queues from early morning throughout the day. They will bring your order to your car, so you don't even need to get out – now that's service.

Chokhelao Mahal
Mehrangarh Fort, Jodhpur
Tel: 255 5389

A terrace restaurant in the gardens of the fort, it's one of my favourite places to sit for lunch after spending the morning there. The menu showcases regional favourites: vegetable dishes, *dal*, lamb curry and rice *pulaos*. If you go for dinner, you will be entertained by a performance by Rajasthani dancers.

Janta Sweet Home

3 Nai Sarak (Clock Tower Rd near Choraya Rasta (main circle))
Tel: 263 6666

A fast food shop that specialises in *namkeens*, *samosas*, *kachoris* and sweets. Do try the *mirchi wada*. Also, make sure to taste *malai ghevar*, a fine sugar pastry case filled with reduced cream and nuts – a typical Jodhpur sweet and a house specialty during the monsoon season.

Hanwant Mahal

Umaid Hills, Circuit House Rd
Tel: 0291 2510 803

Part of the Maharaja's royal estate, with great views across to Umaid Bhawan Palace on the opposite hill, managed by the same group as 1135AD at Amber Fort in Jaipur. Expect a flourish of service and a menu of classic Rajasthani dishes.

Karni Bhawan

Jodphur
Tel: 941 4126 2900

Mrs Singh will welcome you into her bungalow guesthouse with delicious flavours from the royal cuisine of the House of the Sodawas, local Rajput warriors. Ask to sit in the Dhani, an open-air hut in the garden, and enjoy a homely Rajasthani experience with food served from large brass pots on the buffet table by engaging staff.

Shri Mishrilal Hotel Lassi shop

Right by the clock tower at the entrance on the right side as you enter facing the bazaar, this modest shop (above) has been here since 1927. I have tasted *lassi* all over India and this place rocks; one of the best you will find anywhere. The *lassi* are flavoured with cardamom; be indulgent and go for the one with extra cream, it's utterly delicious. They also serve fried snacks and sweets but it's the lassi menu that has everyone coming back for more.

SLEEP

Devi Bhawan

1 Defence Lab Rd, Ratanada Circle
www.devibhawan.com

An authentic homestay, this intimate
hideaway in a lush garden setting offers
great value. This budget-priced *haveli* is
packed with Rajput charm and hospitality –
a classic heritage hotel where the rooms are
comfortable if somewhat spartan. I suggest
you opt for the deluxe rooms, as they are
more spacious and have private balconies.

Raas

Tunvarji ka Jhalra, Makrana Mohalla
www.raasjodhpur.com

One of the more stylish contemporary
urban properties to open in Rajasthan,
this boutique hotel (developed from an
old *haveli*) is an oasis of calm in the most
stunning location, packed with glamorous,
understated style in the heart of the old
walled city (above). You are transported in
by the hotel's auto-rickshaw, as the lanes
are too narrow for cars. It's a great way to

arrive. Each of the luxury rooms have
unparalleled views of the fort. **Darikhana**
is their fine dining restaurant, with a menu
featuring regional specialties – *dahi kebabs*
(sesame-coated yoghurt dumplings) are
exemplary, as is their *laal mas* (Rajasthan's
signature dish of lamb, slow braised with
spices) and *gulab jamun ki sauji* (chena
dumplings cooked with yoghurt and
fenugreek). Don't miss the *malai ghewar*
for dessert, a creamy concoction with
a crunchy sugar topping – utterly divine.
The more casual **Baradari**, in the courtyard
by the pool, where they serve breakfast
and lunch, features a casual menu of
Asian and Western dishes using organic
vegetables. Favourites include the Raas
garden salad with refreshing crunchy
textures and clean flavours and a simple
pasta with roasted tomatoes. Both dining
areas have spectacular views of the fort.

Umaid Bhawan

www.tajhotels.com

One of the grandest and largest palaces in
Rajasthan, an impressive sandstone building
that defines Jodhpur, sitting high on a hill
like a grand wedding cake looking over
the city (above). It's a fifteen-minute drive
from the old city. The royal suites are mindboggling in their extravagance and chic Art
Deco style. One of its wings remains the

private residence of the Maharaja of Jodhpur, and the rest has been converted into a luxury hotel, capturing a finely tuned sense of space, proportion and opulence. Its restaurant **Rishala** is fine dining formal and you have to be a guest to eat there. Be sure to reserve one of the tables on the terrace overlooking the spectacular gardens, even if just for a leisurely sunset drink. Private dining can be arranged in the garden – perfectly in keeping with palace living.

SHOP

M.G. Spices

Shop 206A, Sadar Market (vegetable market), Clock Tower Bazaar
Tel: 093 5291 3349

There are a few spice shops next to each other along this stretch, all with similar names (M.M., M.B. etc – each mimicking the original M.V.) Each place vies for the title of spice master of the city. This particular shop sells excellent flavoured green teas, a great *masala chai* mix and quality Kashmiri saffron.

M.V. Spices

Shop 209B, Sadar Market (vegetable market), Clock Tower
Tel: 291 510 9347

While he was alive, Mohanlal Verhomal was long considered the authentic spice master of the city, a man I visited in 2000 on my first trip to Jodhpur, and took home a stack of aromatic spices to cook with. It's like a pilgrimage to return each time I visit the city. The shop is now run by Mohanlal's wife, who maintains the same high-quality product and attentive service.

UDAIPUR

City

UDAIPUR, IN THE SOUTH OF RAJASTHAN, IS THE WHITE city of the state. Its palace buildings of locally quarried white marble are reflected in its beautiful lakes, which adorn the city despite its being in the driest state in India – not to be missed is the romantic, iconic Lake Palace. The Maharana Arvind Singh Mewar and his family live at the Fateh Prakesh Palace next to the City Palace complex, and his HRH Group owns and manages several hotel properties in Udaipur and the Mewar region of Rajasthan. Udaipur is surrounded by the undulating Aravalli Hills and is at its most magical when the sun goes down – the golden glow is reflected across the waters of the lakes, leaving a lasting impression of serene beauty and calm. The hills turn a verdant green after the first rains of the season, one of my favourite times to visit.

ESSENTIAL SIGHTS

Take a sunset or sunrise boat ride on **Lake Pichola** and admire the **Lake Palace** from different angles.

Visit **Jagmandir Island Palace** in the centre of Lake Pichola (above), once the pleasure palace for the royal family, and have a drink in the courtyard.

Explore the **City Palace**, the largest palace complex in Rajasthan (above), now a museum of royal opulence.

Drive up to **Bansdara Hill** and walk through the ruins of **Monsoon Palace** overlooking the city.

Explore the local handicraft bazaar along **City Palace Road** and the narrow lanes that lead around to Lal Ghat, the oldest bazaar in the city.

Walk through the old city on the eastern side of the lake to **Lal Ghat** (above).

Venture beyond Picola to the other two lakes: **Fateh Sagar**, a favourite haunt with young lovers, and **Sukhayra Circle**, popular with families and kids. Both lakes have fast food vendors, paddle boats, and camel and horse rides.

Visit the Shiva temple at **Eklingji** – the temple of the royal Mewar family, about twenty kilometres from Udaipur and close to Devigarh Palace – and stop at one of the street vendors across the road from the temple entrance to sample the addictive local speciality, *mirchi wada*: long green chillies stuffed with masala potato and deep fried in chickpea batter, like a pakora.

EAT

Ambrai

Amet Haveli, Brahmpol Rd, Chandpole
(Lake Pichola Hotel, opposite Lal Ghat)
Tel: 4243 1085

Lake-facing garden restaurant with tables
set under large trees on the terrace and
a wonderful view of the city across to
City Palace and Lake Palace. The menu is
typically extensive; it's best to choose the
Indian dishes. This place offers some of the
better Indian food in Udaipur – authentic
flavours and Rajasthani favourites. The *lal
maas* (a Rajasthani mutton curry where the
meat is cooked in red chillies, spices and
curd) is second to none, the kebabs are
cooked perfectly with the right degree
of spice, and the breads are moreish.

Neel Kamal Restaurant

Tel: 294 242 8800
Lake Palace Hotel
Lake Pichola

The fine dining restaurant at the Lake
Palace hotel is for house guests only, and
it's worth booking a room just to eat here.
Feast on the Rajasthani specialities on the
menu: choose a few appetisers to start –
the tandoori quail is perfectly spiced and

meltingly tender, and the crisp okra
sticks dusted with ground spices are
divine. The kitchen also makes a sublime
lal maas and wonderful breads and pickles.
A candlelit dinner on a private terrace
can be arranged with prior notice and
is a wonderful way to experience the
extravagance of palace life.

Paantya Restaurant

Shiv Niwas Palace, Udaipur
Tel: 294 252 8016 | www.eternalmewar.in

The last time I visited, the fine dining
restaurant of this palace hotel offered
flavoursome Indian food, but as with
anywhere, the quality depends on the
resident chef. Bypass the Western dishes
on the menu and go for authentic local
food. The wine list offers good choices.
My best tip, though, is to pre-arrange
a private table on the rooftop terrace for
dinner and gaze out over the city and lake
as the stars twinkle above, or if you're
fortunate enough to be there at the right
time (February or March, depending on the
year), watch the fireworks that mark the
Maha Shivaratri, a festival for Lord Shiva's
birthday. I distinctly remember a few of the
kitchen's crafted desserts: a signature *gulab
jamun* cheesecake that could easily become
a modern Indian classic; *lapsi*, made with
broken wheat, rosewater and shredded
coconut, presented in a brandy-snap wafer;
an indecently rich *churma laddoo*, rolled in
small balls and coated with silver leaf, and
little silver cups filled with *makai ka
jhanjaria*, another milk-based dessert.

Paliwal Kachori

Jagdish Temple

Introduced to me by my driver Abhay,
who lives in Udaipur and has a knack for

discovering the best places for street food and snacks. The owner Sutho is well known and the most highly regarded *kachori* maker in Udaipur, favoured by locals. He serves up the best, non-greasy onion *masala kachoris* with mint chutney imaginable.

Palki Khana

City Palace, Udaipur
Tel: 294 252 8016; 294 252 8017

The cafe inside the main gate of the City Palace Museum. Grab an outside table overlooking the courtyard – an ideal spot for a refreshing cool drink after visiting the palace. I can recommend a *badam* (almond milk), *aam ka panna* (green mango juice) or a *nimbu pani* (fresh lime soda). There are a couple of excellent shops right next door; my favourite is **Aashka**, upstairs on the right, for contemporary design pieces (jewellery, clothes, homewares).

Sunset Terrace

City Palace, Udaipur
Tel: 294 252 8016

An ideal outdoor location, where you can sit and gaze out across the lake. Great for a simple lunch of curry and rice, a sunset cocktail, or a glass of champagne with a few plates of Indian snacks. Service is attentive.

Udai Kothi

Hanuman Gate Rd, opposite Lal Ghat,
Lake Pichola
Tel: 243 2810

Grab an alcove on this rooftop terrace by the pool facing the lake. Seating is on floor cushions to make the most of this wonderful location. The menu is small; go for the vegetarian Indian dishes and soak up the view. The kitchen cooks with organic produce grown on their nearby farm at Udaibarg. Try the *Mewari kheer*, a sweet rice pudding, for dessert.

Vintage Car Museum Canteen

Garden Hotel, opposite Sajjan Niwas garden, Gulab Bagh Rd
Tel: 241 8881

Down the hill from the City Palace and part of the HRH Hotels empire, this is a definite must for lunch. Nothing glamorous, it's a canteen in the building by the front gate to the museum, with good food for just a few dollars. Order the authentic Rajasthani vegetarian *thali* and be sure to try their *chaj*, a local yoghurt drink similar to lassi made with yoghurt and milk (no cream) that's tangy and refreshing. View the collection of royal twentieth-century cars housed in the former Mewar State Motor Garage before or after lunch.

SLEEP

Amet Haveli

Brahmpol Rd, Chandpole (Lake Pichola Hotel opposite Lal Ghat)
www.amethaveliudaipur.com

A cute little gem with a prime location on the lake, looking across to Lal Ghat and City Palace. More modestly priced than its glam neighbours, this is a reliable budget hotel. For a few extra dollars, it's worth opting for a suite. This hotel is also home to Ambrai Restaurant (see page 148).

Bujera Fort

Bujera Village, Via-Nai
www.bujerafort.com

A new addition to the local market, this luxury compound is available for exclusive use only (that is, only your party will be staying there) and can sleep up to fourteen – a brand-new, purpose-built fort house that is both traditional and contemporary in its design, with a focus on yoga, holistic wellness, organic food and rejuvenation. A labour of love for its English owner Richard Hanlon, who has been an Udaipur resident for several years, it is a thirty-minute drive from Lake Pichola and the centre of town in a lovely rural setting.

Devi Garh by Lebua

Delwara, near Eklingji
www.deviresorts.com

A fabulously decadent hilltop fort restored with contemporary style and great attention to detail near the village of Delwara, a forty-minute drive from the centre of Udaipur (above). You'll have to pinch yourself as you are sprinkled with fragrant red rose petals when you arrive and walk through the enormous elephant gate. The service is attentive and pampering and the food menu is broad, but I would recommend trying their Rajasthani *thali*, a great balance of flavours and textures – the *malai palak* (corn and spinach) is a knockout. Sunset drinks on the terrace with *chaat* snacks set the tone for a perfect evening. My favourite breakfast is an Energiser Smoothie (ask them to make it for you) and *poori bhaji*, a fried puffed wheat bread with *masala* potatoes, especially after an early-morning yoga session, village walk or bike ride.

Fateh Prakesh Palace

City Palace, Lake Pichola
www.eternalmewar.com

Part of the HRH group, owned and operated by the Maharana's family, this small palace hotel has two wings that give a sense of being part of the rich Mewar traditions (opposite). Opt for a premier suite in the Dovecoat wing for expansive rooms, recently renovated, with fabulous views across the lake. Pop downstairs and spend some time in the Crystal Gallery, a spectacle of royal wealth that transports you to its rich and authentic heritage.

Lake Palace

Lake Pichola, Udaipur
www.tajhotels.com

Rajasthan's most iconic hotel, floating romantically in the middle of Lake Pichola (above), is a lovely place to stay. You are

ferried across the water by boat and showered with rose petals on arrival. The rooms and suites have water views and are luxuriously appointed. There is a large internal garden courtyard and a swimming pool on the terrace. I can highly recommend booking an exclusive dinner on the Mewar rooftop terrace as it's such a romantic setting: candlelit white marble, rose petals, glistening water, magical views and sumptuous food.

SHOP

Ganesh Handicraft Emporium

City Palace Rd, Udaipur
Tel: 252 3647

This labyrinthine, blue-painted shop is hidden down a covered walkway and sells quality handicrafts: textiles, clothing, homewares, furniture and woodwork. Ask Manoj, the affable owner, to show you around his Aladdin's Cave.

Mandi Markets

Mochiwada Rd, Nada Khada
(inside Delhi Gate)

Fabulous sprawling food bazaar with huge array of fresh produce and spices.

Om Handicrafts

45 New Fatehpura Rd
Tel: 29 4256 0250

Renowned for its beautiful detailed miniature paintings, a specialty of local artists. The owner Dinesh Sharma will engage you with his enthusiasm and knowledge.

CALCUTTA (KOLKATA)

City

INDIA'S CULTURAL CAPITAL, WITH ITS FADED COLONIAL charm, has a beguiling magic to its crumbling beauty – it's a city that leaves nobody indifferent. It's intriguing, chaotic and congested beyond compare; it has immeasurable possibilities yet to be explored. It has begun to evolve commercially, after being stifled by bureaucracy and a political hegemony for the past few decades. Its palpable sense of decay is saddening; when you chat with locals who've seen some of the world, there's a real desire for Calcutta to rediscover and celebrate its rich arts heritage – music, dance, visual art and literature. This city is dynamic, diverse, fascinating, historical, scenic, colonial and dramatic. Today, teeming, bustling Calcutta (its Indianised name Kolkata is rarely used in everyday speech) is a veritable microcosm of India, in an intensely concentrated form.

Bengali food has a well-deserved reputation for its subtlety, elegance and richness. Kolkata is at the epicentre of Bengal's distinctive cuisine, and travellers and those who have settled on its shores have left an indelible mark, from the Chinese, Tibetan, Burmese, Arab to European. Bengalis are staunchly non-vegetarian; fish and meat are central to their repertoire, and even Bengali Brahmins eat fish. Fish curry is inseparable from the Bengali temperament, as are sweets. *Sandesh* (a sweet, moist fudge made with fresh paneer) is perhaps the most renowned; it is the Bengali word for 'message' and is especially highly regarded, eagerly consumed by the city's pleasure-loving hedonists. *Mishti Doi* is another essential culinary experience, one that every Bengali is brought up on and very much revered. Milk is reduced and mixed with caramelised jaggery (Indian sugar), then mixed with curd and set in small earthenware cups or vessels: rich and luscious. Calcutta's close ties to its Burmese heritage prevails in dishes like *kawswe*, a coconut curry noodle soup that epitomises comfort and nourishment. And in the days of colonial rule, the British initiated the tradition of *tiffin* – little snacks to nibble on, which have become an essential component of Indian culinary culture. At the same time, the British memsahibs taught and encouraged their house cooks to make cakes and breads, which have become integral to Calcutta's sweets and desserts.

Spicing is more subdued, even delicate in Bengali food; lightness of hand is the key and great stress is placed on how spices are ground and how much water is used to make a paste. The finesse of the paste is paramount. *Panch Poran* is a Bengali five-spice mix in which the whole spices are fried in hot oil; the flavours define the Bengali kitchen. The food is richly flavoured and elegantly textured. The ritual of eating plays such an integral role in Bengali life that it is considered that 'Bengalis live to eat'. Dishes are served one at a time and eaten in sequence, with rice. There is a deliberate adherence to the six primary tastes – bitter, salty, pungent, sour, sweet and astringent – hence the order and the tasting of each dish separately, to appreciate the distinct flavours. This marks an obvious difference between Bengalis and the rest of India. Finish with a small bowl of *ragri*, the Bengali equivalent of *kheer*, or creamed rice. ⊛

ESSENTIAL SIGHTS

Take an early-morning walk through the Maidan and colonial quarter near **Dalhousie Square** – past the **Writer's Building**, **Town Hall**, **High Court** and **Governor's House** – architectural treasures of the city.

Calcutta is renowned for its street food everywhere across the city, so it's possible to pick up a snack wherever you are – I usually head to **Camac Street** for breakfast street food, where vendors dish up eggs and butter toast, *idli* and *vada* with coconut chutney, rice and *paratha*, *lucchi* and *dal* or *kakori*, then drop into **Russel Street Dhaba** (just off Park St) for a plate of delicious samosas (called *shingoda* in Bengali) or *bhelpuri* at **Sarat Bose Rd**.

To immerse yourself in the city's history, check out the **National Library**, **The Indian Museum**, **Asiatic Society** and **Victoria Memorial** for some wonderful insights.

Visit the **Kalighat Temple**.

Walk through **Mechua Fruit Market**, the largest in Asia – two kilometres north of Dalhousie Square – open daily from 10 a.m. to 5 p.m.

Visit **Mother Theresa's home** (above) at the Missionaries of Charity. Her spartan dwelling symbolises her life's work, dedicated to helping the poor and underprivileged of the city.

Visit the **Marble Palace** in north Calcutta – just up from the food market – and also the nearby **Potters Market**.

Join the locals and play golf at the **Tollygunge Club**.

Take a private **cruise up the river** and get a great view of the ghats along the river – the unseen side of the city – a relaxing way to experience this frenetic city.

Join the throng of locals and walk through **Decras Lane**, near Curzon Park in the central Esplanade district, and stop at the food vendors to try *kachori*, fried pastries stuffed with green peas, tray coffee and inexpensive street food.

Food is always on the minds of Bengalis, so suggestions for what to eat come thick and fast. Indulge in a **traditional Bengali breakfast** – *lucchi cholar dal*, puffed *puri* bread and lentil stew made with yellow (*channa*) lentils and flavoured with cumin, ginger and tiny chunks of fresh coconut.

Try *shorshei ilish* – the famed Hilsa fish prepared in a variety of ways, a favourite staple during the monsoon months.

Mix it with the well-heeled locals and spend an afternoon at the Calcutta Races at **Royal Calcutta Turf Club** at the Maidan near **Victoria Memorial** (below).

EAT

6 Ballygunge

6 Ballygunge Place, South Kolkata
Tel: 2460 3922

Authentic flavours and an extensive menu of regional Bengali specialities. Always full of locals – a good sign. Try the *beguni*, Bengali pakoras made with eggplant (*brinjal*) and fried in mustard oil, *khichuri* (lentils and rice), fish head *dal* (a Bengali signature dish) or the *bhekti* fish, marinated and fried in turmeric, chilli and lime, then simmered in a spicy coconut-milk sauce. For dessert, try *khejur gud pithe*, small rice dumplings sweetened with dates and jaggery.

Aheli

Peerless Inn Hotel
12 J.L. Nehru Rd, Chowringhee
(central Kolkata)
Tel: 4400 3900

A Bengali specialty restaurant and a favourite with locals; go there for the typical Bengali fish dishes or try their *kosha mangsho* (mutton), while vegetarians can have *chhanar dalna* (fresh cottage cheese) or *shukto*, vegetables stewed with *bori* – *urad dal* lentils that have been ground, formed

into small balls and sold dried, which then soften when added to sauces or gravies.

Arsalan

Ripon St – at Free School Crossing, opposite Mocamba Restaurant
Tel: 2281 3921

This is a casual no-frills diner serving some of the best Muslim food in the city. I go for their wonderful kebabs (chicken and lamb) and mutton biryani prepared by the chefs who left the once-popular Nizam's in New Market when it changed hands a few years ago. There is also a takeaway shop at Park Circus.

Bhojohori Manna

23A Priyanath Mullick Rd
(and other branches across the city)
Tel: 2454 5922

Serving authentic local food, this is a lunchtime favourite with office workers. The jumbo prawns in spicy gravy (*jumbo chingri malaikari*) are sensational, as is the *bhekti rongpuri* – fish fried with mustard, ginger and garlic paste and the *chhanar dalna* (cottage-cheese curry) and *shukto*, a vegetable staple of Bengali cuisine, is a perennial favourite.

Blue Poppy

Sikkim House, 4/1 Middleton St
(off Camac St), Elgin
Tel: 973 503 6117

Steamed *momo* dumplings are a Sikkimese staple and a popular snack in Bengal (as they are in Bhutan), and this is a good place to taste them. Served with a spicy hot chilli sauce, they are very similar to Chinese dumplings, stuffed with vegetable or pork or chicken.

Buzz

Taj Gateway Hotel, 1930 Rajdanga Main Rd, EM Bypass
Tel: 6666 0000

I come here for the authentic flavours of Bangladeshi food. If you want the same, ignore the buffet or regular menu and request a few dishes from chef Asish Joy's repertoire. He has done extensive research into the food traditions of neighbouring Bangladesh (former East Bengal), and stand-outs include *doi begun* – small disks of eggplant deep-fried, hollowed out and filled with a yoghurt curd spiced with green chilli and ginger; *laal saag* – red spinach cooked with red lentils and onion, earthy and balanced; and *sorshe chingri bhapa* – prawns marinated in mustard and steamed in banana leaves. *Patisapta*, rice-flour pancakes stuffed with a sweet, rich coconut cream and rolled, is a dessert not to be missed.

Calcutta Club

Lower Circular Rd
www.calcuttaclub.in

You need to know a member to get into this private social club (as you do for its rival, the Bengal Club). The white building is grand in the colonial style and can't be missed as you drive along the main road. I was taken there for lunch by my friend Arun, and it was a step back in time to the days of yesteryear's polite gentlemen's clubs – an experience I would not have missed for the world. The food is basic, reminiscent of colonial times, so take it in the spirit that it is served and order a gin and tonic to get started. Our lunch was fried fish with a couple of simple vegetable dishes and the obligatory *dal* and rice. Perfectly acceptable and a little glimpse of part of the city's social fabric.

Flury's

18 Park St (at Middleton Row)

Whether it's stuffed omelettes or a chicken croissant for breakfast, an array of sandwiches or gaudy cakes and pastries, the place looks and feels like an endearing time warp, and is a perennial favourite with locals. It's a tradition for first-time visitors to include this place on their list.

Hot Kati Roll

1B Park St (next to Asiatic Society)
Tel: 2217 7308

This roadside stall, renowned for its kebab rolls, makes the very best *kathi kebab* rolls: succulent meat cubes wrapped in egg-coated *paratha*s (the chicken and egg are my favourite) and garnished with onions, green chilli and yoghurt – it's the best fast food snack imaginable.

Indian Coffee House

15 Bankim Chatterjee St (off College St)

Opposite Calcutta University and Presidency College, in an area crammed with bookshops, this literary meeting place and city landmark is crowded every day and night with students and intellectuals. You come here for the lively atmosphere, to sit and watch the vibrant local life. It's cheap and cheerful, and it's worth having either the onion pakoras or the vegetable *singaras* (Bengali samosas) with chilli sauce from the 'caterings' section of the menu. Absolutely classic – just don't expect a food epiphany!

Jhaal Farezi

42 Circus Ave, Park Circus
Tel: 6502 0202

Spread across different spaces with quirky contemporary decor in a renovated old Kolkata wooden house, the cafe is on the ground floor, or you can head upstairs for a more expansive menu: a mix of Indian and western dishes. I can recommend the *gandharaj kasundi fish tikka* (fish kebabs with mustard) and the chicken *shahtoosh* (cooked with pistachio and cream), both cooked in the clay tandoor; *begun basonti* (fried eggplant in a creamy mustard yoghurt sauce), and the *bhatti ka prawns* (chargrilled in the tandoor with *bhatti ka masala* (chicken cooked with yoghurt and spices)). The roof terrace is open during the cooler months when it's bearable to sit outside – the perfect place to sit, order a drink and munch on snacks like *samosa*, *golguppa* (*pani puri*), *vada pao* (potato fritter in white bun), *jhal muri* (like *bhel puri*) and *aloo dum* (potatoes slow-cooked in tomato gravy).

Kewpie's Kitchen

2 Elgin Lane (off Heysham Rd)
Tel: 2475 9880
www.kewpieskitchen.com

Rakhi Dasgupta opened this restaurant in her renovated house in 1998. Her mother wrote the definitive *Calcutta Cookbook*, and Rakhi is spreading her mother's gospel through her own cooking and classes at Kewpie's. The restaurant features typical Bengali specialities, and it's best to let the staff create a menu for you – engage with them, but make sure to try the *panch phoran* (Bengali five-spice) prawns, Kewpie's tomato chutney, their *kasundi* (a mustard condiment), *shorshe chingri* (mustard prawns) and the spiced poppyseed chicken if they are on the menu.

Mitra Cafe

Shri Aurobinda Sarani Crossing, Jatindra Mohan Ave, Sovabazar, North Kolkata

With more than a hundred years of operating under its belt, this no-frills canteen is famous for fried food, such as prawn cutlets (known as *chingri cutlets*), brain chops, fish fry and chicken *kabiraji* (chicken cutlet marinated in green chilli, garlic and ginger then crumbed and fried). If you come with an appetite, the chicken roast is pretty good too.

Oh! Calcutta

4th floor, Forum Mall, 10/3 Elgin Road
Tel: 2283 7161

Classic fine dining with a menu showcasing the best of traditional Bengali dishes – they have branches in Mumbai and Delhi, but the food at its home base is the best as far as I am concerned. Try the *bhekti maacher paturi*, fish steamed in banana leaf with

mustard sauce; *chingri malai curry*, prawn curry with coconut; the railway mutton curry and the *hilsa* (fish) if it's in season, a Bengali specialty that comes steamed, smoked or fried. I like it with poppyseeds, green chilli and yoghurt, and the fillets fried in mustard oil make a great snack.

Prema Vilas

63/1 Rash Behari Ave (opposite Lake Market), Desapriya Park
Tel: 2463 1961

One of my favourite places for a breakfast of south Indian food – their *idlis* and *vadas*, made with the finest rice flour, milk and curd are ethereally light, and the coconut chutney is to die for – try the *sada dosa* with *dal* and chutney.

Sonargaon

Taj Bengal Hotel, Alipore
Tel: 2223 3939

Authentic Bengali flavours, refined and perfectly executed. I suggest you ask chef Sujan to prepare a special Bengali *thali* for dinner – small dishes on an elegant silver plate that include mutton *kakori* kebabs or their signature chicken kebabs flavoured with star anise and cooked in the *tandoor*, *bhakti*, a local fish braised whole in a coconut mustard sauce or with red chillies and onions; and *kosha mangsho*, spiced, slow-braised lamb with buttery rich *dal sonargaon*. Their breads are among the best I have tasted.

Suruchi

89 Elliot Rd, Central Kolkata
Tel: 2229 1763

Run by the All Bengal Women's Union, this modest place is fine for a humble

home-cooked Bengali lunch that consists of a simple salad, pulses, rice, vegetables, fries and fish or mutton. The minimum spend is a mere 40 rupees (about 80 cents).

SLEEP

The Glenburn Penthouse

Kanak Towers, 7A Russell St
(off Chowringhee Rd)
Maidan Central East
www.glenburnteaestate.com

The first luxury boutique property in Kolkata and new sister property to Glenburn Tea Estate in Darjeeling, with uninterrupted views across to Victoria Memorial, the Maidan and the historic quarter, this is chic city living at its very best. In this intimate haven with roof gardens, the nine suites are furnished with discerning taste and contemporary sensibility. Owner Husna-Tara Prakash is the ultimate host and offers a unique collection of private, bespoke excursions in Calcutta, with her crack team of city experts who share the soul of their city and their insider knowledge with you to bring the city to life, with cultural walking tours, a discovery of food, architecture, art, history, literature and temples, authentic Bengali home-style cooking in a private house, private river cruises and a picnic at the Botanical Gardens.

Taj Bengal

34B Belvedere Rd, Alipore
www.tajhotels.com

Opposite the Calcutta Zoo and National Library and fifteen minutes from the city centre (in light traffic), this hotel offers outstanding service and ambience – the best in the city. For extra pampering, request one of the larger rooms or suites on the club floors. The little clay pots of baked yoghurt and *mishti doi* (sweet yoghurt) are an absolute essential at breakfast. The hotel is home to the fine dining **Sonargaon Restaurant**, which specialises in Bengali cuisine and Chinoiserie, with the best Chinese food in the city, strongly supported by the local community. The sizzling lamb with Sichuan pepper and chillies and the crispy eggplant in chilli plum sauce are two of my go-to dishes when I dine here.

SHOP

Dolly's The Tea Shop
Ground floor, Dakshinapan Shopping Centre
Gariahat Rd South, Dhakuria
Tel: 2423 6445

A tea shop and cafe, where you can order a pot before you buy from their vast selection. They also do a mean toasted sandwich and have a display of cakes baked in-house. Warm, friendly service.

Ganguram
46C Chowringhee Rd, near Victoria Memorial

Another noteworthy sweet shop when you are on the sugar trail – try their *sandesh*, *rasgoola* and *mishti doi*.

K.C. Das
11A+B Sidhu Kanor Dahar
(off Chowringhee Rd)
Tel: 2248 5920

Legendary sweet shop with the best *rasgoola* in the city.

Mithai
48B Syed Amir Ali Ave, Beckbagan
(near Park Circus)

This is one of the best shops for *mishti doi* and a wide variety of *sandesh*. I am also a fan of *paatishapta*, a sweet rice pancake stuffed with shredded coconut, cashews and condensed milk, rolled up to resemble a small spring roll. Totally yummy.

Nauhom's Jewish Bakery
F20, New Market (near Lindsay St)

Legendary breads, cakes and pastries from this city favourite, smack bang in the middle of New Market.

SHE (Self Help Enterprise)
Mallika's Kantha Collection
4/1 Alipore Park Rd, Alipore
Tel: 2479 9002 | www.sheindia.org

Small showroom of beautifully embroidered textiles in the private house of Shamlu Dudeja. Her enterprise has helped to keep alive the Kantha tradition of textile stitching, a centuries-old technique from rural Bengal. Self-Help Enterprise (SHE), which she established, provides training programs and employment opportunities for village women. Call beforehand to make an appointment.

Subodh Brothers
Sambhu Chatterjee St, College St Market area
Tel: 2241 4662

A tea shop for connoisseurs, recommended to me by Ranobir Sen, one of India's expert tea tasters, whom I met at Glenburn Tea Estate. Come to taste, get some expert advice and purchase premium grade teas from various Darjeeling estates.

HYDERABAD

City

HYDERABAD IS A MELTING POT OF MUSLIM AND HINDU cultures and has a legacy of both Persian and Islamic influences due to the long rule of the Nizams, who made the city famous. This legacy pervades all aspects of Hyderabadi culture, from the way the language is spoken, the appreciation for the arts, architectural styles (such as in the Charminar minarets, opposite) and the renowned Hyderabadi hospitality. It is a city of contrasts, where the ancient Orient and the modern world collide. The city has three distinct areas: Hyderabad (the city of the Nizams); Secunderabad on the north side of the river, the administrative centre for the British during their reign – a legacy that can still be seen in its colonial architecture; and the modern city of Cyberabad (or Cyber City) in the Jubilee Hills and Banjara Hills districts. And just to confuse you, Telangana became the twenty-ninth state of India in 2014, consisting of ten north-western districts of Andhra Pradesh, with Hyderabad as its capital. The city of Hyderabad will continue to serve as the joint capital for Andhra Pradesh and Telengana until 2024.

This city is home to some of the hottest chillies in India (outside of Assam and Nagaland), with the hottest considered to be the *gingur* (also called the bomb chilli or the bum stinger). The *gingur* chilli is used to make the fiery, tangy fish curry called *chapu pulusu*. Small amounts of the curry are mixed into steamed rice to temper the heat. Typical Andhra (Hindu) cooking is deliciously spicy and hot, while Hyderabadi cuisine, the food of the Muslim Nizams, is richer and less spiced, heavily influenced by the royal culture. Its most famous preparation, *kacchi biryani* (lamb in a yoghurt marinade and rice layered in a wide pan and cooked over a slow fire), has come to define the city. Restaurant menus show the three cuisines that define this city – fiery Andhra (Hindu), Hyderabadi Muslim food and Indo-Chinese, a testament to the city's history over the past four centuries. ⚙

ESSENTIAL SIGHTS

Explore **Golconda Fort** (above), about forty minutes from town, one of the most spectacular fortress complexes in India – look for the whispering walls.

Visit **Qutab Shahi tombs** (above), the world's largest royal necropolis, with extraordinary Indo-Saracen architecture.

Walk across to the **Laad Bazaar** to experience the action-packed local bazaars for bangles, *ittars* (essential oils), Soorma (kohl), Mehendi (henna) and spices.

Spend a morning at **Chowmohalla Palace** (above), the beautiful palace where the Nizam kings lived and ruled from. This should be followed by a visit to The **Nizam's Museum**, which houses the world's largest wardrobe, amongst other fascinating artifacts. Find a local caterer who can provide a picnic lunch on the lawns.

Climb the **Charminar** (above) and see the **Mecca Masjid** from the top floor.

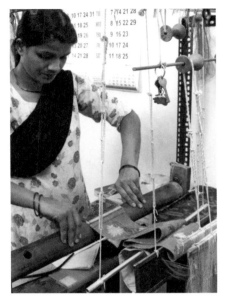

If you're feeling philanthropic, visit Suraiya's – home to traditional weavers and crafts established by Mrs Hassan. It is a training centre for the revival of traditional weaving and crafts, and its main objective is to empower underprivileged women. Mrs Hassan has also established the Safrani Memorial School on the same grounds for the children of the workers. 1–86 Darga Hussain Shah Wali, Raidurg Tel: 3258 8542

Visit one of the many Irani (Persian-style) cafes across town for tea, coffee and snacks.

Arrange an architectural tour of the city's finest buildings with an expert guide.

Take a drive around Hussain Sagar, the large artificial lake in the centre of the city, with its massive Buddha statue in the centre.

If you are an adventurous foodie, engage my friend, colleague and renowned local food expert Jonty Rajagopalan (above) for a personalised tour or join one of her small group adventures. Jonty gave up her successful career as an international marketing guru and founded her travel company Detours India (www.detoursindia. com; email: jonty@detoursindia.com) to introduce visitors to her native city's bounty with customised guided adventures. To spend time with Jonty exploring the city's diverse food cultures is one of life's great joys; her enthusiasm is infectious and her knowledge is extraordinary. She has the inside scoop on where to find the best and most interesting food places in the city and the state, and looks at food in the context of the city's history and culture. For instance, her Biryani Detour winds its way through the city's many biryani hubs and explores this Hyderabadi staple in all its variations.

EAT

Adaa

Falaknuma Palace Hotel
Engine Bowli
Tel: 6629 8585

The menu reflects the abundance of royal
Nizam life. The tasting menu prepared by
chef Arun and his team may include classics
such as feather-light *dahi ke kebabs*, melt-in-
the-mouth *kakori* kebabs, *lassoni hara pyaz
tikka* (chicken cooked in a clay oven with
garlic, cream and green onions), *pathar ke
gosht* (meltingly tender slices of baby goat
cooked on a hot granite stone), *tarmezi
khorma* (chicken cooked in a yoghurt gravy
perfumed with sandalwood and mace),
and the *Hyderabadi kacchi biryani* (tender
mutton cooked with aromatic masala
spices, yoghurt and basmati rice) is the
best you will taste anywhere. This is
a feast for the senses – pure decadence.

Agra Sweets

21-2-112, Charkaman, Hyderabad, Andhra
Pradesh 500002, India
Tel: 40 2457 8787

Just around the corner from Govind's,
this place serves the best *lassi* (yoghurt and
cream drinks) in town and their savoury
and sweet snacks are worth trying too.

Chutney's

Road 36, Jubilee Hills
Tel: 040 6662 8484

Vegetarian South Indian Andhra food –
part of a chain; there are five scattered
across the city. Reliable, and the menu also
lists some Chinese dishes (as do most
restaurants in Hyderabad). Lively and
popular, it's a great place to try the local
Andhra cuisine, which includes such dishes
as the spicy Guntur *idlis*: steamed rice cakes
topped with a red pepper-heavy powder.

Firdaus

Taj Krishna Hotel
Road Number 1, Banjara Hills
Tel: 6629 3306

Inside one of the city's original business
hotels; don't be put off by the lacklustre
(hotel formula beige) room; the food here
is renowned in the city and came
recommended by one of my local guides
the first time I visited. Walk through the
lobby out to the garden and down the
stairs and explore the menu that reflects
old (or royal) Hyderabad. The passion of
the kitchen is expressed in its food. Try any
one of their signature aristocratic dishes –
from *nalli gosht* to *dum ka murgh* (chicken
cooked 'dum' style in a pot) or *haleem*
(lamb and wheat porridge), if meat is your
thing; otherwise their *paneer khatta pyaaz*
or *guthi vankay* (small round eggplants
stuffed with spiced peanuts and tomato).
Don't miss the *phulki* (delicate, paper-thin
wheat roti bread). For dessert, order the
kubani ka meetha (rich bread pudding).

Four Seasons

9-4-77/3/D/4/5/6, Yousuf Tekri Complex,
Prof C.R. Rd (opposite R.T.A. office), Tolly
Chowki (near Golconda)
Tel: 2356 3320

A typical local serving good Muslim food.
I go for the *lassoni* kebab (chicken chunks
marinated in cumin, yoghurt and cream
then grilled on skewers), *katha ka gosht*
and *akari gosht* (pickled lamb).

Govind's Dosa

Mutti Ka Shaed, near Charminar,
around the corner from Agra Lassi shop
(Charkaman 2)

One of the city's favourite street vendors,
he starts in the early morning and packs
up when the *dosa* batter runs out, usually
by 12.30 p.m. – best to go for breakfast and
indulge in a sublime butter dosa, and make

sure you also try his *idlis* (steamed lentil
cakes), *tava idli* (snack made with leftover
idli pieces – fried in oil with spices and
tomato) with chilli and the best *vadas*
(fried lentil dumplings) imaginable. When
he packs up, **Anil's Chaat** steps in with his
cart in the same spot and works through
the afternoon, selling all sorts of fried *chaat*
snacks. The crossover is a great time to
be there – you get the best of both worlds.

Hotel Shadab

Shop 21, 140 High Court Rd –
right near Charminar
Tel: 2456 1648

The menu features typical Mughlai food
and the ambience is a blast from the past.
The place is bustling, constantly packed
to the rafters with locals. It's spread across
two levels and upstairs is air-conditioned.
Food comes out in a flurry – don't over-
order as it's quite hearty and filling, and
portions are generous. Stick with a *kheema
pulao* (minced lamb cooked with basmati
rice) and a couple of vegetable side dishes
to share among a few of you and if you're
hungry, also try the *haleem* (whole wheat
and lamb slow-cooked over hot coals with
onions and spices in a covered pot until
it becomes smooth), a deliciously rich
Hyderabadi speciality.

Sahib Sindh Sultan

5th floor, City Centre Mall, Road Number 1,
Banjara Hills

First you have to get past the train decor
setting – the Indians love a theme! More
fine dining than casual with prices to match,
the consistency and standard of food makes
it a favourite. Ignore the paltry buffet and
opt for the a la carte menu. Order the *dahi
ki kebab, murgh makhani* and the *paneer malai
kofta*, and the chilli *achar* with some bread
is heavenly – lots of choice and some okay
vegetarian options.

Southern Mirchi

Plot 76, Road 3, Nagarjuna Hills, Panjagutta
Tel: 2335 3737

The Andhra food is authentic and spicy –
start with *rasam*, a light, refreshing, peppery
broth, or other appetisers such as spicy

pepper chicken, *murgh malai* kebabs, mutton
seekh kebabs, roast chicken or chilli-fried
quail, served with mango pickle, yellow chilli
powder, black chilli powder, curry leaves and
dried red chilli, which you mix with liquid
ghee to use as a condiment – utterly
addictive. Try the Chicken 65 (made with
the famous spice blend of the same name)
or the vegetarian version, Gobi 65 (made
with cauliflower). Team some Gongura
mutton curry with *jonna* or *jowar* rotis or
that other Andhra ethnic favourite, *ragi
sankati*, steamed millet dumplings. I also love
their fried chicken *pulao*. Finish with a traditional dessert like *sorakaya halwa*. To find it,
turn left into the lane, just past Chutney's at
Mahindrah Motors; it's on your right.

Southern Spice

8-2-350/3/2, Road Number 3, Banjara Hills
Tel: 40 2335 3802

Some of the best and most authentic
Andhra cooking in the city – don't miss
their fiery *Anellwan Meriyal Kodi* (pepper
chicken), the *royualu igurur* (prawns braised
in a gently spiced tomato coconut gravy) –
perfect accompaniments to either the
Kheema Pulao, a minced lamb *biryani*, or the
vegetarian *thali*. Also try chilli-fried quails
and Chicken 65, curd rice, *appam* with
coconut milk, *kodi pulusu* – a rich, aromatic
Andhra chicken curry, and prawns cooked
with onions and a spicy masala gravy.

SLEEP

Falaknuma Palace

Engine Bowli, Falaknuma,
Hyderabad
Tel: 40 2438 8888 | www.tajhotels.com

A breathtaking royal palace (right) perched on a hill with 360-degree city views, made entirely of marble, this is the former home of the Seventh Nizam of Hyderabad (the world's richest man at the time of India's independence), restored to its former glory after an extensive and expensive renovation. Nothing can prepare you for the extravagance and opulence of this extraordinary property, which takes luxury to a whole new level. Splurge and stay in one of the lavish royal suites, featuring discreet personal service and attention to detail. An early-morning walk in the palace gardens and high tea in the Jade Room are a must. The table in the Dining Hall seats 101 guests, each with a personal butler; a private dinner here is an extravagant affair. A more intimate option is a sumptuous banquet at Adaa, the restaurant that features royal Hyderabadi cuisine, or you can arrange a private, exclusive dinner in the bejewelled Durbar Hall, full of decadent promise.

Park Hyatt

Jubilee Hills
www.hyderabad.park.hyatt.com

Opened in late 2012, this ultra-contemporary hotel in the business district of Cyberabad is plush Western luxe in its design, though it makes no reference to the city's history. This is the future vision of the new city and a good base if you are here for business. Book one of the corner suites with drop-dead views and fabulous bathrooms, and enjoy making an entrance through its dramatic foyer. The menu is written for its clientele and features classic international fare.

SHOP

Karachi Bakery

Mozzamjahi Market, Nizam Shahi Road, Abids
Tel: 2473 2785

The best place to come and buy all sorts of traditional biscuits, cakes, pastries and sweet treats. There are a couple of other locations across the city, including one in Banjara Hills.

Pradama's

Sweets, Hots and Pickles
House 70, L.I.C. Colony
(opposite Indira Park Main gate)
Behind Park View Apartments
Tel: 2761 3276
Mob: 099 0887 9512

One of my favourite food shops selling traditional Telangana spices and *masala* pastes – supplied to the local market and shipped overseas to those who are homesick for its flavours.

BENGALURU (BANGALORE)

City

THE CAPITAL AND LARGEST CITY OF KARNATAKA AND the country's major IT hub – India's answer to Silicon Valley – Bengaluru has morphed effortlessly from Garden City into City of the Future – a modern metropolis known for its landscaped gardens and temperate climate as much as for its gleaming corporate office towers, planned real estate and modern entertainment and leisure facilities. This is contemporary India. Old and new face off on either side of the river, like a fractured personality.

One of my favourite parts of the old city is around Russell Market, one of the finest produce markets in India. The quality and range of the beautifully displayed vegetables and fruit, all lovingly polished and arranged in perfect pyramids, has great visual appeal. There are glossy purple eggplants, small red tomatoes, dark purple–red onions, huge mounds of pomegranates, new-season mangoes, chillies from yellow to various shades of green and red, gongura (a bitter-tasting green leaf, similar to sorrel, that is used for making a pickle), massive stacks of betel leaves and fragrant curry leaves, and bunches of mint and coriander. A nearby street is lined with Muslim food stalls, where you can get kebabs and biryanis to go. It's sensory overload as its best.

ESSENTIAL SIGHTS

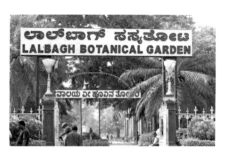

Lalbagh Botanical Gardens hold a significant place in the city, and an early-morning walk around the central lake in the cool air is a wonderful way to start the day. As you leave, stop for a breakfast snack just outside the gate at the **Mavalli Tiffin Room.** It's like stepping back in time; the room has that old-world colonial charm and it is one place that has not been affected by the rapid modern change that has taken hold of the city. This is a quintessential Bengaluru experience.

Explore **Russell Market** in the Shivajinagar district – it is well planned with wide corridors and the most inspiring arrangements of fruits and vegetables. This place epitomises the old-world charm of yesteryear Bangalore – early morning is best.

Take an early-morning visit to the **Flower Market**, which supplies 70 per cent of India's cut flowers.

Market Road area (just along from Russell Market) is home to a string of food vendors and street stalls – kebabs and all types of edible snacks; definitely worth exploring.

Check out some of the city's historical buildings, which are fine examples of British colonial architecture: **Bangalore Palace**, **Mayo Hall** and **The State Legislature Building**.

Bangalore Fort, a fort palace built for the founder of the city in the sixteenth century, gives an insight into the early days of Bangalore and will provide you with some perspective on the city.

EAT

Fanoos Roomali

17 Hosur Rd, Richmond Town
Tel: 6536 2712

Kebabs, roti rolls and handkerchief bread (*roomali*) are the order of the day. This place pulsates with frenetic energy. Explore neighbouring Johnson Market while you're here and discover the wonderful Muslim food shops – breads, biryanis and more – a food haven of the city.

Halli Mane Rural Restaurant

14, 3rd Cross, Sampige Rd, Mallesvaram
Tel: 4127 9754

A bustling place (the name means Village House and the restaurant resembles a mud brick house) and one of the city's favourites; some of the best local vegetarian food is served from this frenetic open kitchen. Order the *chow chow bhath* – a speciality of Karnataka that brings two classic semolina preparations together – one spicy, one sweet – (*khara* (*upma*) and *kesari* (saffron *halwa*) *bhath* served together), curd *vada* or lentil *vada* (dumplings) for breakfast; *ragi roi*, little balls of finger millet (a Karnataka cereal) served with sambar or a vegetable korma. Don't miss the sweets – the creamy

baasundi (sweet thickened milk flavoured with cardamom, nutmeg and dried fruit), syrupy jalebi and *holige* (coconut crepe) are my favourites.

Jamavar

The Leela Palace Hotel, 23 Old Airport Rd

For a really grown-up fine dining experience, expensive by local standards, this is one of the best in the city. The atmosphere is opulent, as you would expect of a five-star hotel property like this, and the indoor–outdoor space has a fabulous garden backdrop – a calm oasis. The menu showcases southern and northern Indian regional specialties. Be sure to insist on spicy food, as they tend to tame flavours down too much for my liking, probably to gain the approval of more insipid Western palates that don't respond to the culinary jungle drums in the same way I do. Try the *jhinga* (prawn) *masala*, lobster *neeruli* (lobster tail cooked in a sauce of coconut milk, cream and spices) *alleppey* fish curry (typical of Kerala, with coconut, turmeric and green mango), and the succulent kebabs served with an array of delicious fresh chutneys. Whatever you do, don't forget to order the *appams*, butter *naan* and *rotis*.

Karavalli

Gateway Hotel, 66 Residency Cross Rd, Ashok Nagar
Tel: 6660 4545

Set in a lush garden and considered the best fine dining restaurant in Bangalore, the menu showcases the coastal cuisine of the south west. *Kozhi malliperlan*, chicken braised in a spicy coconut milk gravy, is fragrant and the prawns with chutney are expertly spiced.

Khansama

2nd Floor, UB City Mall, Vittal Mallya Rd,
Sampangi Rama Nagar
Tel: 4111 4499

The name means 'royal Indian master
chef', and the menu reflects the imperial
era of north-west India, with rich curries,
kebabs, meats roasted in the tandoor
and other Sikh classics. In keeping with
its theme (and the Indians love a theme),
the ambience evokes a royal setting,
delivered with all the elegance you'd
expect of a fine dining establishment.
Make sure you order the lamb *raan*,
cooked on the bone to perfection.

Koshy's

39 St Marks Rd (at Church St)
Tel: 2221 3793

This family-owned all-day cafe serves
a damn fine vegetable *biryani* alongside
typical British colonial dishes such as roast
chicken or pork sausages, a favourite with
the locals, and great coffee, sourced from
Chikmagalur in Coorg, which you can
have served with toast for breakfast. Their
pastries and breads are also worth trying.

Masala Klub

Taj West End Hotel
Racecourse Rd (opposite Turf Club)
Tel: 6660 5660

There's a choice of indoor or outdoor
dining – I prefer the tables outside under
the canopy of trees. A fine dining restaurant
with prices to match, and the menu
showcases Mughlai specialities. Don't miss
the *anardana ambi paneer*, *paneer* cheese
marinated in raw sweet mango juice and
pomegranate powder, then grilled over
coals, or the *barrah kebab* – lamb chops

seasoned with onion, mace, cardamom
and nutmeg and glazed in the tandoor
oven, and their take on a fragrant
Lucknowi-style vegetable biryani is also
a must. The cardamom milk dumplings
make a deliciously spicy finale.

Mavalli Tiffin Room

14 Lalbarg Fort Rd (at front gate of the
Botanical Gardens – on the right side of
the street as you face the gate)

A favourite local canteen that is great
for breakfast and serves up endless plates
of delicious *masala dosa* (crisp lentil
pancake with masala potato curry), *idlis*
(steamed lentil cakes) and *vadas* (fried lentil
dumplings), this place has a buzzy vibe and
is constantly packed. The menu is listed on
an old blackboard on the wall; join the row
of men sipping their tea and have a *masala
dosa* and some rice *idlis* with chutney and
dal, or go for their renowned *thalis* at
lunch, then *tiffin* snacks in the afternoon.
The downstairs front room has the
best atmosphere.

Nagarjuna

44/1 Residency Rd
Tel: 2559 2233

Bustling canteen packed with families and students, with a menu that specialises in the spicy food of neighbouring Andhra Pradesh: rich *biryanis*, grilled meats and spicy curries. Make sure you sample the fiery gunpowder chutney and even spicier *kharam puri* – you will become addicted. There is also a branch in Indiranagar, at 195 Double Road.

Vidyarthi Bhavan

32 Gandhi Rd, Gandhi Bazaar, Basavanagudi

Blend in with the locals at one of the city's most legendary and popular cafes and order the *masala benne dosa*; these look like small thick pancakes and are rolled with spiced potato – crisp on the outside, soft and buttery inside, and served with coconut chutney. One of the city's defining food experiences.

Windsor Pub

7 Kodava Samaja Building
1st Main Road Vasanthnagar
Tel: 2225 8847

The best pub food in the city, the curry leaf chicken is to die for – a favourite discovery from my first visit and worth a pilgrimage alone; the spicy prawn curry is heaven and the *masala pappads* are the best snacks imaginable to have with a cold Kingfisher beer.

SLEEP

Alila Bangalore

100/6 Hal Varthur Main Road
RG Hali, Whitefield
www.alilahotels.com/bangalore

This elegant, contemporary urban resort hotel adds to the vibrant hotel scene and is situated in the centre of the business district on the eastern side of the city, out past the old airport. The rooms are spacious and big on comfort, each with a private balcony and scenic views. A good location if you're here on IT business, but a little out of the way of the main attractions. The traffic congestion in Bangalore is legendary, so bear that in mind, depending on the nature of your visit.

Taj West End Hotel

Racecourse Rd (opposite Turf Club)
www.tajhotels.com

A luxurious, grand and elegant hotel (opposite top) with an ideal central location for sightseeing in the old city – the best place to stay for some deluxe pampering. The beautiful colonial buildings are set in massive, lush established gardens opposite

SHOP

KC Das
38 Church St (corner St Marks Rd)

For definitive Bengali sweets such as
rasgullas, *sandeesh* and *mishti doi*, this place
is a landmark in the city. One of many in
a chain that stretches across India from its
home base in Calcutta.

the Polo Club and racecourse. The Blue
Bar, in an open garden pavilion, makes
an ideal spot for a late-afternoon G&T,
miles from the frenzy of central downtown.
It's home to the **Masala Klub**, featuring
contemporary Indian cuisine. Request an
outdoor table under the tamarind tree.

KARNATAKA

State

THIS STATE STRETCHES FROM THE TROPICAL WEST coast across the Western Ghats mountains to the rocky Deccan interior, meaning there are diverse regions to explore and plenty of regional differences in the food. The east of the state has a common heritage with Tamil Nadu and shares many of its food traditions, with attention and diligence paid to vegetarian dishes, and rice a constant at the table. On the west coast, Mangalore is a small city that is home to a wonderful array of seafood dishes which dominate the menus in Karnataka and all along the Konkan coast to Mumbai, while in the north, the influence of neighbouring Andhra Pradesh is evident in the liberal use of hot chillies. Everywhere you will find different versions of the same dish, depending where you are; staple dishes such as *bhaat* (rice) dishes that are tempered with a rich spice mix and coconut, or the sweet *payasam*, a dessert that is made with vermicelli, rice or semolina and cooked with milk, jaggery and nuts (cashew or pistachio). Sometimes banana, papaya, jackfruit or dried fruit is added. It has been served to me in different guises at every place I have visited in Karnataka.

In the mountains, Mysore is famous for its yoga retreats, sandalwood and incense, and compared to other cities, it's small, relaxed and uncrowded, with an old-fashioned ambience and a less hurried pace, known for its gardens and palaces, most notably the opulent Maharaja's palace, which looks like something out of a fairytale, especially at night. With a long tradition of music and dance, art and literature, the welcoming hill-station atmosphere and its hybrid personality of colonial past and techno-modern future make it an attractive place to visit for a couple of days. It's worth a visit to the atmospheric Devaraja market, a couple of blocks from the royal palace, which is packed with all manner of fresh produce. There are some interesting food stalls and pickle shops on the streets surrounding the markets. Now that there are direct flights into the city (previously you had to fly to Bangalore, then drive for three hours), it's an ideal starting point for exploring the less-travelled mountain region.

From Mysore, head south-west, driving into the mountains to the Coorg region through undulating countryside, verdant hills, fertile lands and lush vegetation, past sugar-cane plantations, bamboo forests, rice paddies and coffee plantations and the Tibetan enclave near Kushalnagar with its prayer flags fluttering in the wind. Coorg is known also by its Indian name, Kodagu. The cuisine of Coorg has evolved over the centuries, drawn from the generosity of the fertile landscape, so expect to taste tender wild greens, ferns, bamboo shoots, mushrooms, pork, wild game and birds from fields and kitchen gardens carefully tended by people who were once warriors, hunters and farmers, mostly in that order – an intriguing contrast to the rest of the state. ⚙

ESSENTIAL SIGHTS

Visit the **Mysore Palace**, an absolute must.

Wander through **Devaraja produce market** in Mysore and sample some of the street snacks on offer.

Visit **Hampi** and its amazing temples and the ruins of the old city – one of the most important religious sites in India, and off the beaten track.

Explore the **Coorg region** high in the Western Ghats mountain ranges, with its coffee and cardamom plantations.

Drive south from Goa and visit the half-moon-shaped **Om Beach** in Gokarna (a temple town) for its pristine beauty.

If yoga is your thing, spend time at the **ashtanga yoga institute** in Mysore.

EAT & SLEEP: MYSORE

Dasaprakash Hotel

Gandhi Square
Tel: 244 24444

The restaurant at this modest local hotel is vegetarian and a great place to try *idli* and *dosa*. They make a delicious stuffed *idli* (the only place I've ever seen this); the soft pancake is filled with carrot, cashews and mustard.

Green Hotel

Chittaranjan Palace
2270 Vinoba Rd, Jayalakshmipuram
Tel: 821 425 5000
www.greenhotelindia.com

A former palace built for the Mysore princesses, this tranquil oasis in the city's centre is geared more to the budget market and prides itself on its sustainable and eco-friendly practices. The best part is the fabulous garden for relaxing; the rooms are generous in size if plainly furnished, and the simple home-style food hits the comfort button.

Metropole Hotel

5 JLB Rd, CFTRI Campus
www.royalorchidhotels.com/royal-orchid-metropole-mysore

Managed by the Royal Orchid Hotel group, this is a terrific base and my preferred option when visiting Mysore. A relaxed informal dinner on the outdoor terrace is my favourite, with a menu of barbecued meats, fish and vegetables.

RRR

Shri Harsha Rd

A basic, no-frills place that's always busy with locals, serving authentic spicy Andhra food.

Vinayaka Mylari

79 Nazarbad Main Rd
Tel: 094 4869 8710

A decent no-frills vegetarian cafe – a great place for authentic Mysore *masala dosa* with coconut chutney.

EAT & SLEEP: COORG

Orange County Resort

Karadigodu Post, Siddapur
Tel: 80 4191 1000 | www.orangecounty.in

This was one of the first environmentally sustainable places to open for guests in the Coorg region. Located 90 kilometres from Mysore by the Cauvery River, the resort's cute-as-a-button (though not plush) thatched cottages (opposite top) are set among 120 hectares of spice and coffee plantations, bordered by a massive bamboo forest. The occasional elephant can be spotted if you're lucky during an afternoon walk with a guide. A good base for bird watching and trekking, the resort caters mostly to the domestic family market and also offers other outdoor activities such as boating and fishing. Like every resort in this region, there's an Ayurvedic spa centre for wellness and body treatments. I stayed here many years ago on my first visit to the Coorg region, before other resorts had opened. The kitchen prepared local specialities such as bamboo shoot curry,

a delicious egg and potato curry, and an aromatic *pandy* (pork) curry served with *akki ooty* (rice chapatis). My favourite dessert was their *semian payasa*, made with rice vermicelli cooked in subtlely spiced milk custard and garnished with pistachios, cashews and sultanas. They also make a moreish *karjikai* – Coorgi vegetable samosas to snack on with a late-afternoon drink at the bar.

Raintree

13/41 Pension Ln (behind Town Hall), Madikeri
Tel: 82 7222 0301

Located in an old house in the centre of this small town, this casual restaurant has an extensive menu, as it tries to please all tastes. Ignore the north Indian and Chinese options and cut to the chase – order from their Mangalorean coastal food and Coorgi (*Kodava*) local specialities. I love the fried bamboo shoots (sourced from the expansive bamboo forests nearby), *kandhi* (pork) curry, the *nullu puttu* noodles, the steamed rice balls are wonderful and the prawn ghee roast with chilli is not to be missed. For dessert, try their version of *payasam* – rice vermicelli cooked in cream. As you would expect in this part of the world, the coffee is good. It makes a great lunch destination when you are staying at one of the nearby resorts.

The Tamara

Kabbinakad, near Virajpet,
about 35 kilometres from Madikeri
www.thetamara.com

Surrounded by Rajiv Gandhi National Park and located within a working coffee plantation, this luxury retreat of contemporary wooden cottages is set atop high stilts resembling tree houses, each one offering an expansive vista across the forest canopy. The food is typically local, with a menu of regional specialities such as *kali mirch gosht* (tender pieces of mutton cooked in mild pepper gravy), *kadambuttu* (Coorgi-style rice dumplings with an aromatic chicken curry), and light-as-a-feather *rotis* straight from the oven.

Vivanta by Taj Madikeri

1st Monnangeri, Galibeedu
www.vivantabytaj.com/madikeri/coorg

A thirty-minute drive from Madikeri and set in a living rainforest, this luxurious eco-lodge perched high up in the forest seduces with its individual pavilions built into the hillside, with panoramic views of the Western Ghats mountain range, private plunge pools, outdoor terraces and a fireplace for when it's cool. Connect with nature and trek some of their adventure trails or go mountain biking. Take time to discover the indigenous Coorgi culture through its dance, music and food experiences that are woven into your stay. It's fun to go strawberry picking at a local farm when they are in season. Have dinner at Nellaki Restaurant, with a menu that showcases regional Coorgi cuisine. I also like the food at Dew, with its emphasis on wellness cuisine. It's great for a quick detox: fresh crunchy salads, freshly squeezed juices, light nourishing broths and simple grills. Flavour is paramount.

EAT&SLEEP: GOKARNA

SwaSwara

Om Beach, Gokarna
www.swaswara.com

A secluded yoga, meditation and Ayurvedic retreat on a lovely crescent-shaped stretch of white sandy beach, appropriately named Om. The focus is on wellness and a holistic way of life, with a few leisurely adventures thrown in. The food is clean, healthy and extremely fresh, prepared with organic produce from their kitchen gardens and fish from the coastal waters. The retreat can be reached by either flying into Mangalore or Goa then driving along the Konkan coast. They require a minimum seven-day stay, but they prefer fourteen or twenty-one days to allow you to completely unwind. My friend Mini Chandran, whom I met years ago in Kerala, is the general manager here, and her nurturing spirit is a perfect reason to give yourself over to their care. A holiday here is an escape from the daily routine – one of relaxation and rejuvenation. Some consider this the perfect place to visit during the monsoon to nourish body and soul.

KOCHI

City

KOCHI (FORMERLY COCHIN), THE OLDEST EUROPEAN settlement in India, is a lagoon of islands and peninsulas separated by the backwaters of the Arabian Sea and connected by bridges and ferries. It has a rich maritime history and it still ships Kerala's coir, rubber, seafood, spices and pepper products to foreign ports. Influenced at various times by the Arabs, the Chinese, the Dutch, the British and Portuguese, and the Jews who first emigrated from Roman-occupied Jerusalem in the 6th century BC to Cochin. It is now a charmingly curious potpourri of Jewish synagogues, Chinese fishing nets, Portuguese churches, Dutch palaces, British cricket greens and colourful Keralan architecture. The atmosphere is somewhat Mediterranean but the climate is characteristically sub-tropical with a laidback vibe. The locals live to a different, unhurried rhythm in this part of India; there's a real sense of detachment from the hustle and bustle of the modern world. ✿

ESSENTIAL SIGHTS

Take a heritage walking tour of **Fort Cochin**, visiting **St Francis Church**, where Vasco da Gama was originally buried before his remains were returned to Portugal; the Dutch Cemetery; the famous **Jew Street** and the Jewish Synagogue; and the unique cantilevered Chinese fishing nets.

The **International Pepper Exchange** near Palace Road in Jew Town – where the price of black pepper is determined and traded on the world market each day.

The most popular and sacred dance drama of Kerala, **Kathakali**, has evolved over the past 400 years. This classical dance requires lengthy and rigorous training to attain complete control of the body, and sensitivity to emotion to be able to render all its nuances through facial expressions and hand gestures. Themes centre round the two great Indian epics, the *Ramayana* and the *Mahabharata* – it is quite a spectacle.

Sample the street food along **Gujarathi Road** with its fresh produce stalls and local shops. You will see how the Gujarati women tie their saris differently, as well as getting a look at Jain temples and schools.

The **Kochi-Muziris Art biennale** in early February, centred around Aspinwall House in Fort Kochi, is a wonderful exhibition of India's contemporary art, an initiative and investment in culture that is gaining world recognition and putting the city on the map. www.kochimuzirisbiennale.org

Visit the **Mattancherry Dutch Palace** off Palace road, built by the Portuguese and now a museum of the city's history.

Visit the Goan quarter on **Ammankovil Road** (near Krishna Temple) for pappadams, sweets, pumpkin leaves and flowers.

EAT

Arca Nova @ Fort House

Fort House Hotel
2/6A Calvathy Rd, Fort Kochi
Tel: 48 4221 7103

The restaurant of this modest colonial
hotel is outdoors on a waterfront pier –
great for a lazy lunch on a balmy afternoon
and also ideal as a candlelit dinner setting.
Specialising in Keralan seafood with dishes
such as ginger garlic prawns, fish braised in
coconut cream with aromatic spices or the
spicy *meen kallechuttathu* – whole fish grilled
with green chilli and lime juice, served with
yoghurt sauce. Don't miss the coconut
pancake with honey to finish; it's dreamy.

Badettu @ Sarovaram

NH 47 Cochin Bypass Rd, Ernakulam
(airport road)
Tel: 230 5519

Terrific vegetarian *thalis*, Kerala-style,
with several spicy curries to choose from.
Act local and eat with your hands. The
breakfasts here are fab, so order a plate
of *vada* and a *masala dosa*. I usually stop
off here on my way to or from the airport,
as it's on the main road, like a highway
roadhouse. The kitchen is open so you
can watch them preparing *dosas* on the
large flat metal pans, making it look
incredibly effortless.

Dal Roti

Church Rd, Fort Kochi
Tel: 048 4221 7655

This cool canteen-style cafe serves
wonderful flaky *parathas* and *kathi* rolls,
and is a great place for lunch or a quick

snack with friendly service. Patronised
by locals and in-the-know travellers –
always a good sign.

Kashi Art Cafe

Burgar St, Fort Kochi (off Tower Rd)

A popular, stylish cafe with a Western
aesthetic, and a great place to chill and relax
over a pot of tea, an espresso or a fresh juice
(below). The menu consists of sandwiches,

salads and cakes. Local artists exhibit their work and it has a cool, buzzy yet laidback ambience and friendly staff. Their cakes are baked inhouse, and the moist chocolate cake and the banana cake are my favourites.

Malabar Junction

Malabar House, 268 Parade Rd, Fort Kochi
Tel: 221 6666

Tables are set up in the garden under the trees for dinner and the food comprises sophisticated, authentic south Indian flavours with a modern interpretation. The tiger prawns with fresh mango and coconut are light and refreshing, the *seafood ularthiyathu* has great depth of flavour and texture, with prawns and sea bral (fish) cooked with ginger, *kokum* and tapioca, and tempered with mustard seeds and curry leaves, and the Kerala-style lamb cooked in a coconut, fennel and shallot paste with *garam masala* and a black pepper gravy is utterly addictive. The ginger ice cream to finish is just perfect.

Nimmy Paul

Variamparambil
Chakalakal Rd, Ernakulam, Kochi
www.nimmypaul.com

Lunch or dinner comes with a cooking class in a private home (above right), with one bedroom for a homestay visit, making it a very special and unique experience. Nimmy is a gracious, knowledgeable and engaging host, and knows how to draw keen cooks into understanding and appreciating the nuances and myriad flavours of the Syrian Christian cooking of Kerala. She is a professional cookery instructor, opening her family home and offering food and hospitality to foreign guests. In keeping with the traditions of their families, they enjoy having guests and serving good food. She is also a food consultant to writers, chefs and magazines, and is opening a purpose-built cooking school at Manassery (near Fort Kochi) in early 2016.

Old Harbour Hotel

Tower Rd, Fort Kochi
Tel: 098 4702 9000

Crab *rasam* (crab meat in a pepper consomme broth), coastal fish curry (with tamarind and turmeric), ginger *paneer tikka*, crispy fried sardines, pumpkin *olan* (pumpkin simmered with lentils) and a fried eggplant salad with green onions and peanut dressing make an ideal casual lunch. Simple clean flavours in a heritage hotel setting.

Rice Boat

Vivanta by Taj Malabar Hotel
Willingdon Island
Tel: 664 3000

The menu features delicious south
Indian specialities such as *prawn vattichathu*
(a tangy prawn and *kokum* curry), coconut
crab soup and *meen pollichathu* (fish fillets
cooked with spices in banana leaf), served
with delicate *appam*s to soak up all those
wonderful juices. The room is styled like
a Keralan rice barge (below) and the
atmosphere comes alive when it's full
(it can be quiet at lunch). A pleasant way
to arrive if you aren't staying at the hotel
is to hire a water taxi or local boat from
Fort Kochi (during daylight hours only);
beats the laborious road traffic any day.

SLEEP

Brunton Boatyard

Near Aspine Wall, Calvetty, Fort Kochi
www.cghearth.com/bruntonboatyard

A lovely colonial building (above) with
rooms centred around an internal garden
with a prime waterfront location. The only
downside is the location, next to a noisy car
ferry terminal, so choose a room on the
opposite side of the building if you stay
here. The front rooms facing the water have
nice views and small balconies. Stay in for
dinner and try the pork curry with string
hoppers, or their signature railway mutton
curry, rich with red masala and coconut.

Eighth Bastion

Bastion St, Fort Kochi
(opposite Malabar House)
www.cghearth.com

A charming small hotel next door to
Malabar House with an attractive price
point: well-appointed, spacious, perfectly
comfortable rooms with small balconies
and lots of natural light. They provide
bicycles for guests – a terrific way to get
around the Fort area. The traffic here is
not that scary and it's easy to navigate
your way through the narrow streets.

Malabar House

268 Parade Rd, Fort Kochi
www.malabarhouse.com

Centrally located in the Fort area, this feels like a large, elegant family beach house; its relaxed ambience makes it an ideal base when visiting Kochi – full of style and charm, and the service is excellent. My favourite rooms are the larger suites with outdoor verandahs on the upper floor (above). The house restaurant Malabar Junction in the courtyard honours the flavours of Kerala and its wine bar Divine serves wines by the glass, cocktails, delicious fruit smoothies and the best espresso.

Vivanta by Taj Malabar

Willingdon Island, Kochi
www.tajhotels.com

Situated halfway between Ernakulam and Fort Kochi and surrounded by rivers, this manmade island was created as a ship-building port. The hotel is on the island's tip, looking across to Fort Kochi. Opt for a waterfront room and watch dolphins swim gracefully among the boats and ships ploughing through the water on this busy working harbour. The garden and pool provide an idyllic retreat from the bustle of port life. Fort Kochi is easily accessed by hiring a private water taxi or the Taj speedboat (during daylight hours only), as the hotel is a little out of the way – a thirty-minute drive (longer if traffic is heavy) into the historic fort area.

SHOP: KOCHI

Cinnamon

@Trinity
Ridsdale Rd (off Parade St)

Contemporary clothing, jewellery, and some homewares.

Little Queen Embroidery

Jew St, Mattancherry

Run by Kerala nuns, this place sells white-embroidered white cloth – napkins, sheets, handkerchiefs, and so on – a speciality of the region. You can bargain a little, depending on how much you buy.

Play Clan

Petercelli St, Fort Kochi (off Santa Cruz Rd)

Funky stationery, T-shirts and contemporary graphics by hipster locals.

Spice Market

Jew St

A terrific spice shop run by local women.

KERALA

State

KERALA WEAVES A PERVASIVE MAGIC; THERE IS SOMETHING so poetically romantic about this part of India, with its shimmering emerald landscape and sun-kissed coastline. It's quite unlike the rest of India, with its unique, languid charm and heady sensuality. The state is diverse, with distinct regions, and every community has its specific religious architecture, music, arts and food. The lush, verdant jungle, thick with coconut palms, banana, jackfruit and cashew trees, spice, tea and rubber plantations, along with the rice paddies, make up the cornucopia of idyllic and enchanting images and culinary preparations. The fragrance in the air is unique to Kerala, which has long traded in black pepper, cardamom, turmeric and ginger with Arab, European and Chinese merchants, renowned as the land of spices. Another important cash crop is cashews, which are commonly used in savoury and sweet preparations. Coconuts and bananas are prolific and have a strong presence in their culinary repertoire. The coconut tree is considered a gift from the gods, a tree of wealth, as every part can be turned to profit. Coconuts are used to make cream, oil and vinegar, and then there is the 'milk' from this most versatile fruit. Even the sap from the flowers is tapped into clay pots tied to the tree – the juice ferments to make a mildly alcoholic beverage called *toddy*.

It is easy to sense Kerala's prosperity: the houses are large and well maintained, everyone smiles and their melodic Malayalam language fills the air with music. The Kerala region is diverse, full of religious and philosophical enthusiasm and tolerance, with its mix of Hindu, Catholic, Syrian Christian, Jewish and Muslim cultures, all co-existing happily. The different castes and communities each reflect their own customs, traditions and food styles, with a passionate awareness that makes for an interesting and peaceful community. ❁

ESSENTIAL SIGHTS

When you drive south from Mangalore along the north Kerala coast, stop off at the historic **Bekal Fort** at Kappad Beach, where Vasco da Gama landed in the late fifteenth century.

Be sure to taste the distinctive **Moplah (Mappila) cuisine** of the Malabar Coast in and around Tellicherry (Thalassery).

Muzhapilangad Beach, a long stretch of deserted white sandy beach, is five kilometres north of Thalassery, accessed across a couple of rivers and estuaries, then down a narrow lane. Pass what could be some of the most prime real estate in the country, through virgin jungle and a beach fringed with tall, swaying coconut palms. Locals come to relax in the late afternoon and there is a leisurely ambience, with a mix of Muslim and Hindu families, and saris, kurtas and scarves floating in the breeze. The beach is so wide, they allow vehicles to enter and drive back and forth.

Thalassary (Tellicherry) was the epicentre of the spice trade for centuries and its history dates back to Phoenician and Roman times, with a more recent colonial past of French and British settlement and the centre for Moplah cuisine. The Moplahs are an ancient trading Muslim community of Arab origin and their **distinctive food** is Persian-inspired, using the local ingredients of Kerala. Black pepper from this region has long been a highly prized commodity.

Kerala is famous for its **short eats** (snacks), so whenever you see a street vendor, stop and taste, whether it's *neichoru* (ghee-fried rice served with chicken curry and a date pickle), a coconut *puri*-type bread served with fish curry, mainly eaten at breakfast, or *ari pathiri* (thin rice pancake / crepes served up with a fish or vegetable korma). *Arikkadukka* is a spicy snack only made on the Malabar coast – mussels stuffed with coconut masala, dipped in egg white and fried. *Puttu* – rice cake layered with spiced minced meat or shredded coconut and steamed in a tube, and *kannu pathiri*, folded like an envelope, are eaten for breakfast.

The **fish markets** at **Thalassary** (Tellicherry) have an abundant array of fish and seafood on display each morning. The fishing boats unload their baskets of mussels that have been collected from the small rocky islands a few hundred metres offshore; other boats have nets full of sparkling sardines, sea mullet and seer fish (similar to our wild kingfish). The best time is just after sunrise, before heading back to your bungalow for aleisurely breakfast.

Take a guided walk through the **spice plantations** around **Thekkady** and **Kumily**, where cardamom, black pepper, cloves and allspice are the main cash crops.

Periyar Reserve, one of India's largest wildlife sanctuaries, with an active conservation policy – do an early-morning walk through its nature trails with an expert guide. You may chance on some wildlife (I have spotted a sambar and mongoose) but don't expect to see tigers; they have all but disappeared from this region.

Wear your conservation hat and book a walking tour with **The Preserve Alleppey Society**, a group of dedicated locals whose aim is to raise awareness about the town and help preserve it by documenting Alleppey and its history before it disappears under concrete. The walk starts with a slide presentation about the history and unique features of the town, with one of the members of the Society acting as a guide. The walk covers the Gujarathi quarter, canalside, a view of the Jain temple, the oldest Anglican church and the main market area. The walk ends with refreshments at a local home. www.preservealleppey.com

EAT

50 Mile Diet

Spice Village, Thekkady
www.cghearth.com

Sustainable eco-tourism at its best – all
the produce is organic and sourced from
farms within a fifty-mile radius at this
outdoor garden restaurant, which follows
the 'paddock to plate' ethos. The dinner
menu might include organic curried
pumpkin soup, green peppercorn quail
kebab, *kanalil chutta muyal masala* (spiced
grilled rabbit), cardamom chicken, or the
ranger wood mutton. A brilliant initiative
to minimise their carbon footprint delivered
with enthusiasm and care. During the day,
you can experience a farm visit by booking
through the Spice Village. The tour takes
you in an open-air jeep to a breathtaking
viewpoint over the Tamil Nadu Valley, then
on to the working farm to see the pigs,
chooks and cows.

Kanal Restaurant

Niraamaya Retreat's Surya Samudra
Vizhinjam Beach, Kovalam (45 minutes' drive
south of Trivandrum airport)
www.niraamaya.in

Sit under the large thatched roof
overlooking the ocean and watch the
twinkling lights of the fishing boats out
at sea, feasting on their daily catch of
terrific barbecued seafood, grilled with
spices and other Keralan specialities, such
as the smoky *kokam*-flavoured Malabar fish
curry (make sure you try the hot mango
pickle with the curry) and *chakka* (jackfruit)
thoran. Kickstart the evening with one
of their delicious cocktails from the
garden bar.

The Lake Palace

Thekkady/Periyar Reserve
www.lakepalacethekkady.com

A former summer palace of the King
of Travancore, situated on an island in the
middle of Periyar Lake within the reserve.
It's a twenty-minute boat ride up the lake
from the jetty and it feels as if you have
been transported to some far-flung colonial
outpost, a step back in time. I come here
for lunch after spending a morning trekking
through Periyar Reserve, to sit at a table
on the verandah and luxuriate in the peaceful
ambience. There are a few guest rooms,
should you choose to opt for an overnight
stay and if you do, choose one of the two
larger suites with open verandahs. Ambience
is antique colonial. The food is a charming
reminder of yesteryear a mix of Anglicised
Indian staples such as chicken cutlets with
an Indian version of coleslaw, a lettuce and
fish salad, a simple curry with local rice, and
cinnamon apple pie.

SLEEP & EAT

Ayesha Manzil

Court Road, Thalassery (Tellicherry)
Tel: 490 234 1590
cpmoosa@rediffmail.com

Off the beaten track, Thalassery
(Tellicherry) is home to Ayesha Manzil,
a generously proportioned nineteenth-
century heritage bungalow that has
been in the Moosa family for more than
a hundred years. It is a gem that is worth
every bit of the effort of the journey. Its
owners, Faiza and Moosa, make charming
hosts and the house, perched on a hill with
views across the Arabian Sea, with the

bonus of a swimming pool in the garden, offers a lovely respite. Dinner on the terrace is fantastic. The house has a heady aroma of spice and you wake each morning to the smell of breakfast breads (*pathiri*, fried *battura* and *mutta sirka*) and heavenly ground rice and egg dumplings with sweet cardamom syrup being prepared. This is the ideal place to discover the secrets of the Muslim food of the Moplahs, traced from its early Arab descendants.

Faiza moved here from Calicut (Khozikode) when she married Moosa, and she learnt her culinary skills from her mother. She is considered one of the most exceptional home cooks in Kerala and is very proud of her Moplah traditions and heritage. Her flavours are defined yet complex and simply sing on the palate; her repertoire includes *chemmeen varattiyathu* (tamarind prawns); cabbage *thoran*, clean-tasting and refreshing in its simplicity; and fried spiced sea mullet with a salsa of

chopped tomato, red onion, ground chilli, salt and lime juice. Ladies' fingers (okra) are simmered in a lightly spiced yoghurt sauce, and drumstick *sambhar* offers a delicious savoury sour note. Make sure Faiza cooks you her mussel dumplings: mussels stuffed with rice and flavoured with coconut and cumin, revealing the dish's Arabic and Chinese heritage. They are served with 'eyelash bread', where the dough is rolled and cut into a square, with its four corners folded in to meet in the centre before being deep-fried. The bread curls and looks like an eyelash.

Her fish *biryani* is legendary and you can spend an afternoon in her kitchen learning how to prepare it; it's a real labour of love. Little wonder it is such a celebratory ceremonial dish, reserved for special occasions. When placed on the table, it is accompanied by raita, coconut chutney and the most delicious date pickle, studded with the tiniest garlic cloves. Faiza also prepares an English-style custard pudding, which she calls the Queen of Desserts, given an Indian makeover with rosewater and cardamom, and served as the finale to a sumptuous dinner. My favourite breakfast here is *mutta kakkathil* – egg roast or sacred eggs with a plate of perfectly formed *appams*. This place is food heaven.

Hill House

Kuttikanam, Idukki District
Tel: 9847 054 615
Email: ranialpy@gmail.com

On arrival at her spice plantation and ancestral house, believed to be one of the residences of the Queen of Travancore (Kerala's former name), Rani John will give you a tour of the estate and the old house. Hill House is the newer house built just up the hill by her husband John, using recycled and salvaged timber. There are only four guest rooms, and the best two are to either side of the front entrance; the house has a spacious outdoor terrace, with wonderful vistas across the valley and the picturesque tea and spice plantations of the estate. Rani's mother Mary Kallivayalil is in her late eighties, a wonderful cook and custodian of the family's Syrian Christian heritage recipes, and directs the house cooks to prepare a delicious banquet lunch, adopting the British influence on Keralan food with Indianised versions of colonial dishes such as shepherd's pie, meat cutlets, mint chutney sandwiches, carrot and cabbage salad and chicken roast. For dessert, you can expect either those English stalwarts, trifle pudding or caramel custard (like a creme caramel) served with estate-grown tea and coffee, roasted to Mary's specifications. Rani is an engaging and generous host, a local environmental activist and the driving force behind the Preserve Alleppey Society, working towards the conservation of Alleppey and the backwaters, and will conduct a personalised walking tour of the district upon request. Hill House is a one-hour drive from Thekkady, three hours from Kochi and two hours from Alleppey.

Kalari Kovilakom

www.kalarikovilakom.com

A high-end Ayurvedic retreat with treatments, yoga and meditation. The accommodation is as grand as you can get at a wellness retreat in Kerala; the service and care is immaculate. Minimum stay is two weeks, but they prefer you to stay for a month, so come prepared with the right attitude. Kalari Kovilakom was the home of Queen Valiya Thampuratti of Kollengode, who founded the palace in 1890. It is now run as an exclusive Ayurvedic retreat and people come from all over the world to seek rest and recalibrate their burnt-out bodies and spirits. The palace has been sensitively restored and has delightful gardens full of medicinal herbs and trees, including an enormous old mango tree in which turquoise kingfishers play. Guests are cosseted behind a high wall and can hear

the sounds of the outside world only distantly, save for amplified music from the temple each morning at 5.30 and the enthusiastic singing of local schoolchildren at 8. If you peer over the fence, you can see local women doing laundry in the lake, with lots of loud slapping as they beat their soapy clothes against the rocks. According to Ayurveda, the body is made up of three *doshas*: *pitta* (fire), *kapha* (water) and *vata* (air) and each guest undergoes a thorough Ayurvedic examination upon arrival. We are all born with one or two dominant *doshas* and then must work to keep them in harmony to function well, with balanced emotions and good physical health, so each person is prescribed a diet to redress the imbalances. The kitchen prepares healthy vegetarian dishes, with different food cooked for each guest depending on their *dhosa*, so the service is highly personalised and aims to balance you with medicinal

herbs and spices, chosen according to the season. Bananas play a significant role in Ayurvedic cooking, and one of the best breakfast treats is *pazha kattey*, little banana coconut cakes served with a spicy fruit chutney. Daily yoga and meditation also play a key role. There's much to connect you to your inner child – steamed apples for breakfast, childlike yoga poses, warm milk being poured over you, sitting down to play with paints and paper. The medicine, yoga, meditation and quiet surroundings with no stimulation mean you cannot help but journey inwards.

Lakes & Lagoons
Alleppey
www.lakeslagoons.com

Ketuvellams are traditional rice barges converted to luxury houseboats that come with engaging local cooks and unobtrusive service. An idyllic escape and a wonderful way to observe the languid pace of life on the waterways. I have tasted many wonderful local specialities whenever I stay on these boats, including Sabu's coconut-rich duck curry *varutha tharavukari* – duck smothered with a spicy masala paste and baked in coconut oil – was sublime, and became a memory as enduring as his *payasam*, a coconut-milk concoction with tiny threads of rice vermicelli, sultanas and cashews, scented with cardamom, like nursery food for grown-ups. For a snack with drinks before dinner (bring your own alcohol), bitter gourd is peeled and finely sliced, then deep-fried with shallot slices until crisp – a perfect accompaniment to a gin and tonic as we watched the sun setting over the tranquil waters.

Leela Kovalam

Kovalam (45-minute drive from Trivandrum airport)
www.leela.com/hotel-kovalam

Perched on a cliff overlooking the ocean, this luxury beachside resort hotel has easy access to a long stretch of sandy beach – be sure to book an ocean-facing room for the best views. Have a sundowner at the Sky Bar or indulge in their Ayurvedic health spa. At the beachside restaurant **Tides**, where the menu is more Asian-inspired than Indian, I stick with reliable dishes such as fried prawn with coriander, and ginger and black pepper crab. The ginger crab fried rice is also good. At the **Terrace**, their all-day dining casual restaurant, choose Indian dishes from their vast menu – *vendakka ulitheeyal* (okra and shallots in roasted coconut gravy) and *cheera ada* curry – spinach dumplings in spiced coconut gravy with a layered Keralan *paratha* would be my choice.

Neeleshwar Hermitage

Ozhinhavalappu, Neeleshwaram, Kasaragod District, North Kerala
www.neeleshwarhermitage.com
www.thelotuskerala.com

At the northern end of Kerala and the Malabar Coast (either a two-and-half-hour drive south of Mangalore, the closest airport, or a two-and-half-hour drive north from Tellicherry), this tropical hideaway (above) exudes tranquillity and a relaxed vibe. An enchanting beachfront property of eighteen palm thatched cottages (opt for Prema, the only one with a private plunge pool) with enclosed outdoor bathrooms and garden courtyards, this is the perfect place to kick back, unwind and make the most of the unspoilt beach setting as you succumb to the pampering from friendly staff. Looking along twenty-odd kilometres of virgin pristine beach fringed with tall, swaying coconut palms, the aesthetic is South-East Asian-style of a bygone era, set in lush tropical gardens – cool interiors with a strong commitment to sustainable and responsible tourism. The infinity swimming pool makes an ideal spot to hang out and the Priya spa offers various massages and Ayurveda treatments. My favourite is the Kalari massage, where the therapist uses her feet to massage and leaves you feeling re-energised.

The outdoor beachside dining area, **Meenakshi**, is where you head for breakfast and lunch in barefoot elegance. The food is based on sound home cooking (a mix of Western and Indian) and is delicious, wholesome and nutritious, regardless of what you order. There are two options for dinner. At **Meenakshi**, the catch of the day (black pomfret, kingfish, sea bral, red snapper, prawns, scampi, lobster etc) is brought to the kitchen straight from the fishing boats and given the local treatment. You choose whether you want it basted with a fragrant masala paste and grilled, simmered in a mild aromatic *molee* gravy, served as a Kerala fish curry (the fish chunks cooked in a spicy coconut milk sauce with ginger garlic paste, curry leaves and chilli and soured with smoked kokum); or there is meen vattchathu, a hot and sour curry with a gravy of kokum, dried chillies, vinegar and lemon. Fish dishes are served with plain boiled mixed vegetables and rice.

You will find typical home-style Keralan dishes on the concise menu across the garden at **Annapurna** in the central living area. The vegetable dishes are particularly standout. I absolutely loved their beetroot thoran, perfect with grilled masala fish; *vendakkai puli kulambu* (tiny okra cooked in coconut milk and tamarind with chopped tomato), *ulli thiyal* (a sweet and sour curry of tiny whole shallots), and the dry fried long beans with ginger, turmeric and grated coconut is a knockout. Beetroot *pachadi*, shredded beetroot with a local leaf of red spinach cooked with cumin, grated coconut and curd is perfect with *meen pollichathu* (kingfish fillet and spicy shallot masala steamed in banana leaf). Both dining areas change their menus daily, which keeps things interesting.

During your visit, I can highly recommend having an overnight stay on **Lotus**, their sumptuous traditional rice barge, purpose-built as a houseboat that sleeps four (there are two luxury rooms with private decks) and glides through the secluded back waters of Malabar along the Thejaswini River. Unlike the clogged waterways of Lake Vermabad at Alleppey, the pace here is gentle, tranquil and traffic-free. It's an unexploited paradise with a sense of complete innocence. Think beachcomber luxury. Transferred by car from Neeleshwar, a short ten-minute drive away, you step on board and immediately enter another world. Deepak, the boat chef, prepares a banquet of dishes throughout the day; his cooking is confident and perfectly balanced. The chicken pepper fry at lunch is utterly addictive; *olan* (a mix of steamed white pumpkin pieces, long beans and black-eyed beans), cooked in a mild coconut milk sauce seasoned with mustard seed, fenugreek seed and curry leaves, is a revelation of restraint, and fried *unnipallam*, mashed steamed banana mixed with grated coconut, jaggery and cardamom, shaped like a torpedo, rolled in ground rice and fried till crisp on the outside is a delicious dessert. Dinner on the roof deck under a big moon and a canopy of stars is a defining and treasured memory of Kerala. Everything about Neeleshwar Hermitage and Lotus is of unequalled elegance and has left an indelible imprint on my soul.

Niraamaya Retreat's Surya Samudra

Vizhinjam Beach, Kovalam (45 minutes' drive south of Trivandrum airport)
www.niraamaya.in

A small boutique property consisting of thirty traditional Malayali Keralan cottages with contemporary interiors, scattered through the landscaped gardens facing the

Arabian Sea (no beach access, though) in a secluded bay. The rooms are stylish, chic and private – opt for a room facing the sea. This place reminds me of Bali in the Seventies before it was overrun by mass tourism. **Cafe Samsara** is the property's casual dining space and makes a healthy salad or sandwich, ideal for a light lunch.

Philip Kutty's Farm
Pallivathukal, Vechoor
Kottayam
Tel: 4829 276 529
www.philipkuttysfarm.com

A hideaway retreat of eight separate waterfront villas, this boutique homestay is part of a productive 35-acre organic farm (above) on a small private island in the lake to the north east of Alleppey and accessed by *vallum* (canoe), offering an insight into waterside farm life, with sustainable eco-friendly practices and the most beautiful place to stay on the lake. Matriarch Aniassa Philip, known to everyone as Mummy, and her daughter-in-law Anu are the most gracious and generous hosts and cook some of the best food in Kerala. It's a privilege to sit and watch as they expertly prepare a few dishes for dinner in their well-worn *uruli* pans (wide braising pans with concave bases): a mellow chicken curry flavoured with turmeric and ginger, *meen molee* (fish

in coconut and pepper gravy) or *karimeen* (pearl spot, a small fish unique to Kerala's backwaters), delivered each day and cooked in various ways, often simply fried with turmeric and chilli. I can also recommend a *thoran* of chopped beans and carrot, quickly stir-fried with tempered mustard seed, curry leaves and a little red chilli, each spicy flavour distinct. The coconut and candied pineapple pudding is one of the best desserts imaginable, and is always my favourite when I stay there. Their home cooking is heavenly and makes the visit even more perfect. A treasured experience, this is backwater living at its best.

Purity Resort
Meppuram Rd, Aryakara Ward 5, Muhamma
www.malabarhouse.com/purity
Tel: +91 484 221 6666

In an idyllic location overlooking Lake Vembanad at its widest point, this Relais and Chateaux property oozes calm and serenity. Generously proportioned rooms with verandahs and terraces overlook the lake; there's a contemporary ambience with splashes of bold colour here and there and perfectly positioned Keralan artefacts. The lakeside infinity swimming pool is a great place to watch the sun setting over the lake as fishermen in their small wooden boats glide by with long poles for catching fish. It's a place that exudes blissful happiness and the menu naturally has a strong emphasis on local fish and seafood. Don't miss a seafood thali for lunch and their Travancore prawn curry is lush and rich with a gently spiced tomato and onion gravy. Served with appams (string hoppers), it is complete in itself. They offer cooking classes in their lakeside pavilion, so you can take a few Keralan secrets away with you to recreate at home.

Serenity

Kanam Estate, Kottayam district
www.malabarhouse.com/serenity

A private hilltop guesthouse retreat
in a rubber plantation in the Kottayam
hills, this beautifully renovated heritage
bungalow is an ideal place for a one-
night stopover en route to Periyar and
the mountains. Go mountain biking or
walking, or be brave and ride Lakshmi,
the house elephant. The food is home-
style, similar to the menu at Malabar
House in Kochi, its sister property, and
seafood is treated with respect – try the
kingfish steamed in banana leaf with
red masala paste if it's available.

Shalimar Spice Garden

Murikkady, Thekaddy
www.amritara.co.in

A perfect mountain hideaway (above),
surrounded by spice plantations and close
to Periyar Wildlife Reserve. Private
bungalow-style cottages that mimic the
traditional *tharavad* houses are set in
beautiful landscaped gardens that create an
idyllic sanctuary of calm and natural beauty
(the best cottages are numbers 214, 202, 204
and 220). The swimming pool is a welcome
treat, as it is nearly always hot enough for
an afternoon swim. Early-morning walks

with a local guide through cardamom and
pepper plantations are a must and there are
a couple of elephant farms nearby if you
fancy a ride around the paddock, just for
a thrill. The kitchen prepares traditional
family-style Keralan recipes, and I have
fond memories of their *ulathiya irachi*:
beef strips dry-fried with shredded coconut,
tomato and curry leaves (a Syrian Christian
staple), *kozhi varatha* – chicken cooked in
a roasted coconut paste, *kallappam*, rice
pancakes and *nadan adu*, a restorative
country-style mutton broth spiced with
cardamom and pepper. Coffee is from
their own plantation. Make time to visit
the spice shops in nearby Kumily, one of
the most important spice trading centres
in the mountains.

Spice Coast Cruises

Coconut Lagoon, Kottayam
Tel: 484 258 2615
spicecoastcruises@cghearth.com

Another company that that offers
a backwater experience on a converted
rice barge where you board from a different

location on the lake. With friendly staff and decent, simple home-style food, we start with a typical banana-leaf lunch when we come on board. The long green leaf has small spoonfuls of many tastes arranged around a central mound of steamed Keralan rice, whose grains are shorter and plumper than other Indian varieties. The food is eaten with your fingers, an essential Indian tradition, and gives an immediate insight into and taste for the local dishes. There's *sambar*, spooned over the rice because of its runny consistency; crisp banana chips; pumpkin simmered in coconut milk; fish fried with turmeric and chilli and served with fresh lime; a carrot *thoran*; *avial* made with drumstick vegetables cooked in turmeric water; a cabbage and carrot *pachadi*, a wicked beetroot and yoghurt relish; *meen varathathu* (seer fish fried with turmeric and ginger paste); a fish *mooli* with chilli, ginger and lime; and a few other things – all with coconut. Before we know it, Giresh, our cook, is preparing dinner, and more treats appear from the minuscule kitchen at the back of the boat. We are served delicious, tender dry-fried morsels of chicken seasoned with spices, small green chilli and curry leaves; beetroot *pachadi*, a local leaf of red spinach cooked with cumin and grated coconut; a light *dal* curry; and two different *bhindi* (okra) preparations, one

stuffed with rice and shallow-fried, the other chopped and cooked in tangy coconut milk. A prawn curry is soured with smoked *kokum*, and *kuttanad* is a typical sour fish curry.

Windermere Estate

Munnar-Bison Valley Rd,
Poathamedu, Munnar
www.windermeremunnar.com

Perched high in the tea country of the Western Ghats, this delightful country residence is in a large cardamom estate a couple of hours by road to the north of Thekkady overlooking a vast mountain wilderness. Full of colonial charm and a hint of nostalgia with its manicured lawns, it channels the days of the British Raj era. Dinner each night is a set menu where the kitchen cooks family recipes from their Syrian Christian heritage, using produce from their kitchen garden and honey from their beehives. This is honest, simple home cooking. Like all places in Kerala that are not hotels, they can't have an alcohol licence, so it's a dry stay. You can bring your own, but it has to be consumed in the privacy of your room.

CHENNAI

City

The southern gateway to India, Chennai (formerly Madras) is the capital of Tamil Nadu and one of India's faster growing cities. It is steeped in ancient Hindu culture and tradition that has remained intact through the centuries, beyond the reach of the Mughal invaders to the north and impervious to British colonial rule during the days of the East India trading company. The summer heat is brutal, so if that turns you off, avoid visiting from April through August, the monsoon season. You will experience an immediate awakening of the senses on arrival as you breathe in the intoxicating night air on the drive into town from the airport, something that is distinct and typical of the region. Today, there is a flourishing art scene and the film industry has taken a firm grip as Mollywood fever (their version of Bollywood) consumes the city, where Tamil films compete with Bollywood for huge audiences. The movie-star business is booming, and it's not uncommon for actors to become politicians in these parts; both are equally revered.

Chennai's Tamil food culture is defined by rice; this region is the rice bowl of India. Rice is served in some form at every meal and more often than not, curd (yoghurt) rice completes the meal. The various breads of the south are made with fermented rice and white lentils – *idli*, *dosa*, *uttapam*, *vada* and *appam* are integral to any meal throughout the day, served with a deliciously fresh coconut chutney and sambhar, a tangy vegetable and lentil broth that is a staple of Tamil Nadu. The state's long coastline yields a bounty of fish and seafood, and these are woven into the everyday diet along with a plethora of vegetables. ☸

ESSENTIAL SIGHTS

Visit any number of the city's **Hindu temples** (see previous page), with their grandiose architecture and towering gateways that provide a centre for religious worship and social gatherings – you will often come across a Hindu wedding, of which you instantly become a guest.

Take a walk along **Marine Drive** on the seafront promenade – fishing boats, fish hawkers etc – the best way to view the colonial architecture facing the sea in all its glory, from Fort St George to San Thome Cathedral and the Legislative Assembly in Mylapore. The **High Court**, a regal red-brick edifice, is the pick of the colonial buildings.

Do an early-morning trip to the **Koyambedu market**, one of Asia's largest wholesale markets, and meander through the vegetable, fruit and flower sections, each housed in different vast sheds.

Eat at one of the **local mess halls** (like workers' canteens) and try some authentic Tamil food – the district of Mylapore is home to many of the best in the city. Usually there is no menu, so just follow what the locals do. This can be one of the defining food experiences of a visit.

EAT

Analaxshmi

804 Anna Salai
Tel: 4214 1210

Entering this restaurant is like stepping into Aladdin's cave. It is lavish and has a cosy atmosphere, and the operators endeavour to make their South Indian vegetarian *thali* menu a cultural experience, with a variety of vegetable dishes and chutneys, rice and breads, carefully recreated from heritage recipes. Established as a culinary arts centre by Swami Saraswathi, there are branches in Coimbatore, Singapore, Kuala Lumpur and Perth. It aims to be a service to the community and is staffed by volunteers. You pay what you wish; there is no fixed cost, so it doesn't hurt to be generous.

Anjappar

JP Towers, Nungambakkam High Rd, Nungabakkam
Tel: 44 2825 6662

Just down the road from the Taj Coromandel Hotel, this is one branch of several of the same name in Chennai. The food is authentic Chettinad, hot and spicy, with a good fried rabbit dish, chicken pepper fry, a mutton meatball curry or prawns fried with spices and garlic. Honest and simple; don't expect glam surroundings, think functional – it's all about the food.

Dakshin Restaurant

ITC Park Sheraton Hotel
132 TTK Road, Ra Puram
Tel: 44 2499 4101 | www.itcwelcomegroup.in

This is my favourite restaurant in Chennai, offering the finest south Indian food. Chef Praveen Anand, a passionate food scholar, weaves culinary magic with traditional recipes from India's four southern states of the Deccan. The menu features classic dishes from Tamil Nadu, Karnataka, Andhra Pradesh and Kerala, and it is wise to follow the staff's expert advice when deciding what to eat. The flavours are distinct, considered and tantalising. I adore the lightness and purity of *nandu puttu*, freshly picked crabmeat tossed with onion, ginger and green chilli. *Tallale jhalke* are little ladyfish lightly coated with a spicy chilli and ginger blanket and deep-fried until crisp – utterly delicious with a mild, fresh mango chutney. A Karnataka-style prawn *masala*, *khara sigadi*, consists of tiny prawns simmered in a rich and spicy tomato sauce, excellent with flaky *paratha* bread. Perfect *appams* – rice batter swirled on to a small hot pan shaped like a deep wok, so the batter sets on the outside without colouring and stays steamed and soft on the inside – is a lacy sheer pancake shaped like a vase and made to order. *Urlai sadhi*, potato simmered in coconut milk with mild green chilli and flavoured with ghee, is poured on to the centre of the spongy *appam*, which serves to soak up the juices. Don't miss their signature banana and cashew nut *dosas* as a starter.

Karaikudi

84 Radhakrishnan Salai, Mylapore
Tel: 2811 6446

A typical modest dining room with a menu showcasing food of the Chettinad region in southern Tamil Nadu, with aromatic and spicy hot flavours. Try the classic black pepper chicken fry, crab *masala* and any of their vegetable dishes, especially the dry-fried potatoes with cumin and pepper.

Myali Karpagambal Mess

20 East Mada St, Mylapore
Tel: 2462 2902

A great pit stop after you've been exploring the colonial buildings around Mylapore, this all-day diner serves up some of the best local food imaginable. Everything is freshly cooked with punchy flavours. Look around, point at what you like the look of and just go with the flow – you will probably get fantastic *idli*, crisp *vada* (fried lentil dumplings) or a sensational *dosa* (crisp pancakes) served with *sambhar* (lentil vegetable stew) and chutneys. This is one place you don't want to miss.

Saravana Bhavan

228 NSK Salai, Vadapalani
Tel: 2480 2577 | www.saravanabhavan.com

There are more than twenty branches of this vegetarian tiffin restaurant in Chennai, and more further afield. It's fast, reliable, authentic and always packed with locals, pulsating with an energetic vibe. An essential breakfast experience, where your *thali* plate will be filled with light, fluffy steamed *idli*, perfectly crisp *vada* with coconut chutney, *masala dosa* or *uttapam*, a flat *roti*-style rice pancake cooked with shredded onion, chilli and carrot. There's a bowl of *sambar* – a vegetable and lentil

soup which is eaten with rice and *idli* and is one of the defining dishes of Tamil Nadu. To follow, there's a small cup of *rasam* (a pepper water that is as versatile as *sambhar*) with a *masala dosa*. A large, crisp, tissue-thin pancake made with rice and lentil batter and smeared on to a hotplate to cook quickly, so the inside remains steamy and soft. A dollop of mild potato *masala* is added then the *dosa* is deftly folded or rolled over and put on to the plate. It is served with coconut chutney, a staple throughout Tamil Nadu. All this is made with humble vegetables, lentils and rice and a good measure of spice – and it is just breakfast! Every meal is finished with *sombu* – fresh fennel seeds that have been lightly coated with crystallised sugar and act as a natural breath freshener.

Southern Spice

Taj Coromandel Hotel
39 MG Rd, Nungambakkam
Tel: 6600 2827

The room may look like a colourful Bollywood set, but the food sets the tone with authentic flavours and generous spiciness. Don't miss the *appam*s or *idli*s made to order or the tamarind lentil *rasam*, the *denji rawa fry*, deep-fried soft shell crab with semolina crust, or the melt-in-the-mouth lamb and fennel dumplings.

SLEEP

With the city's pace accelerating at a rate of knots, international brand hotels such as the Park Hyatt, Radisson and Marriott have proliferated on the city hotel scene, giving much more choice to the discerning business and leisure traveller.

The Park Pod

23/13 Khader Nawaz Khan Rd
(off Mahatma Ghandi Rd), Nungambakkam
www.theparkhotels.com

Contemporary design has arrived in Chennai; it was only a matter of time. This small boutique hotel (twenty rooms), part of the Park Hotels Group with a courtyard swimming pool, is a little oasis in a quiet, tree-lined street, offering privacy and intimacy in the chic Nungambakkam district. Make time to visit its big sister property The Park, a few blocks away, for a sunset drink or snack on its rooftop bar. The rooms are spacious and well appointed.

Taj Coromandel

37 Mahatma Ghandi Rd, Nungambakkam
Tel: 44 6600 2827 | www.tajhotels.com

A slick city hotel offering luxury in a central location, its more recent makeover has added glamour and style. This was my first ever experience in India, where I was invited as guest chef back in the mid-nineties. Service is first rate. I have also stayed several times at its sister hotel – the Art Deco **Vivanta by Taj Connemara** on Binny Road, a few kilometres away, a more heritage property (avoid the new wing if you stay there) with a great swimming pool in the garden. On the opposite side of the road is the **Taj Club House** with its rooftop restaurant Kefi, serving Mediterranean food, a welcome respite for when you need a break from Indian food.

TAMIL NADU

State

FRINGED BY THE COROMANDEL COAST ON THE BAY OF Bengal to the east and the mighty Western Ghats mountain range to the west, the southern state of Tamil Nadu has a deep connection to its Deccan and Dravidian past. The Indian south carries an aura of distinct identity, culture and mythology; it is home to Brahmin Hindus and some of India's most significant temples (such as Mamallapuram, left) dominate its towns. The Tamil way of life is steeped in tradition; the ancient culture pervades the air but remains relevant to modern lifestyles. You can't help but notice the sense of timelessness. The food is unique – spicy and wet, and reliant on fresh curd, yoghurt, buttermilk, lentils, tamarind and an extraordinary array of vegetables, many of which are farmed inland in the more temperate climate of the hills and trucked down to the coast. The harshness and lushness of its natural landscape has helped to create an original culinary repertoire, where every ingredient serves a specific purpose in the diet for health and practical reasons. I can highly recommend taking a week and driving from Tiruchirapalli (which everyone calls Trichy) with its imposing Rock Fort to Karaikkuai in the Chettinad district, staying a couple of days then heading inland to Madurai to check out Meenakshi Temple, one of the state's most important and largest temples. Grab a freshly squeezed pomegranate juice from the market area while you are there. Then head into the mountain regions beyond, to Dindigul and the Palani Hills district or further west to Coonoor and the tea estates of the Nilgiri region. Here the air becomes misty and magical, the cooler atmosphere offering respite from the searing heat of the plains in summer. ✺

ESSENTIAL SIGHTS

Follow the temple trail, a meandering pilgrimage to the temple town of Mamallapuram, dating back to the seventh century. It is the nearest temple town to Chennai, an hour's drive south of the city. Magnificent temples are carved from the surrounding rocky hills, and taking centre stage is the Shore Temple. With its dominating pyramid tower and one of the world's largest bas-reliefs carved from stone, it is one of the few shore temples that has withstood the ravages of the sea and wind.

The temple town of Kanchipuram (see page 225), 70 kilometres west of Chennai (a ninety-minute drive), one of the holiest temple towns of India and an important Hindu pilgrimage centre, is equally famous for its fine silk sari weaving.

The coastal wetlands south of Chennai are a veritable playground for birds and wildlife and can be incorporated into a visit to the temple heartland. Fly to Tirichirapalli (Trichy) in the Kaveri Delta to see the magnificence of the Rock Fort and its decorative Ganesh as well.

Allow yourself a few days to check out the distinctive Chettinad region, a cluster of 72 villages and towns stretching from the coast inland towards Madurai, established by the Chettiars, a shrewd, prosperous banking community who brought enormous wealth to the region, reflected in their palatial houses, ornate and colourful architecture, jewellery and food. One of their legacies is the cuisine they developed, which was heavily influenced by their trade connections with South-East Asia and is distinctly different to the rest of the state's.

Take a three-hour drive south of Chennai along the coast to spend a few days in the union territory of Pondicherry (Puducherry) and Auroville, a former French protectorate with distinctive architecture (including over-the-top cathedrals) and food. The city is divided into two parts: the Ville Noire, which is largely untouched by European culture, and the Ville Blanche, whose wide, French-style boulevards and whitewashed villas with timber-shuttered windows evoke a sense of another time. The lingering French-ness gives the town a distinct ambience, and the food is an intriguing hybrid of French and Tamil influences. A visit to Pondicherry is not complete without seeing the Auroville Ashram, where you can sample some delicious organic Ayurvedic food, and the Sri Auroville handmade paper factory.

EAT: KANCHIPURAM

Kanchi Kudil

53A Sangeetha Vidwan Nayanar Pillai St
Kanchipuram, Tamil Nadu
Tel: 44 2722 7680
www.indiamart.com/kanchikudil
kanchikudil@hotmail.com

A restored heritage agricultural house
and the ancestral home of Malavika and
her family, offering a glimpse into the rural
life of yesteryear. They offer a set menu for
lunch, by arrangement. The food is prepared
by Vijiya, the house cook, and the *thali*
served on banana leaf mats includes several
vegetable dishes and a chicken curry with
curd rice and pickles. The drumstick
(a readily available green vegetable) *sambar*
is absolutely delicious, as is the potato
poriyal (potato sauteed with spices, curry
leaves and shredded coconut). This is

uncomplicated, honest rural cooking
and well worth the drive from Chennai
for a day visit.

SLEEP & EAT: PONDICHERRY (PUDUCHERRY)

Auroville Bakery

Auroville Main Road, Kuilapalayam

The best place for a breakfast treat – fresh
croissants, pain au chocolate and baguettes
baked daily by the French-trained team.

Cafe des Arts

Suffren St, White Town
Tel: 99 9448 1914

A charming courtyard cafe surrounded
by drooping bougainvillea, offering a sense
of peace and tranquillity. Patronised by
a young, bohemian crowd and serving
reasonable coffee and light snacks such
as sandwiches, crepes, waffles and salads.

Le Dupleix

5 Rue de la Caserne
www.sarovarhotels.com

This intimate, elegant boutique hotel is
centrally located in the heart of the French
Quarter, a couple of blocks from the beach.
Luxuriate in one of the fourteen suites in
this former mayoral residence and have
dinner in their garden courtyard under
the large sprawling mango tree.

La Maison Rose

8 Rue Romain Rolland, White Town
Tel: 413 421 0806

Look for the pink villa that is a boutique and restaurant and head inside to the courtyard. The menu is European and may include dishes like a gently spiced prawn noodle salad with lemongrass, a decent saffron fish soup with harissa and a few classic desserts such as chocolate mousse, strawberries and cream and a baked cheesecake, for when you want to indulge in a little of its historical French flavour.

Palais de Mahe

4 Rue de Bussy
Tel: 413 234 5611
www.cghearth.com/palaisdemahe

Located in the city's French Quarter, this boutique hotel property is charm and style personified and a few minutes' walk to the seafront, and makes an ideal base for exploring the town.

Solar Kitchen

Auroville, Bommayapalayam (off Crown Rd)

The Solar Kitchen building was designed as a collective kitchen for the Auroville community and is a good choice for a rooftop lunch, also open for dinner.

The cosmopolitan menu is vegan, prepared largely from the vegetables and grains grown organically in and around Auroville. There is a choice between Western items such as pasta, fresh salads and sandwiches, or south Indian staples such as *idli* and *dosa*, *dal* and chutneys. Don't miss their nutritious fruit and vegetable juices and gelato.

Sri Aurobindo Ashram Dining Room

Francois Martin St, White Town, near Bharathi Park

This place, like many businesses in town, is run by an ashram and this determines the style of food – a vegetarian menu of simple flavours and uncomplicated cooking, best for lunch. Buy a coupon before you go.

Surguru

99 Mission St, Pondicherry (MG Rd area)
Tel: 413 430 8082

A modest, canteen-style hotel dining room, clean and spacious, serving typical south Indian vegetarian food. I can recommend their vegetable *thali* and the *masala dosa* – best at lunch.

SLEEP & EAT: KARAIKUDI

Bangala

Devakottai Rd, Senjai
www.thebangala.com

A family-run heritage hotel in a restored mansion, rich in history with elegant charm, this authentic, simply furnished house in the heart of the Chettinad region

with delicious home-style Chettinad food, overseen by its owner, Mrs Meena Meyappan, a highly regarded food historian of the region. The set menu changes daily and may include house favourites such as black pepper chicken, pepper chicken fry (a Chettinad speciality served with *vella paniyaram*); *masala brinjal*; dry-fried potatoes; or *meen kozhambu*, a tangy fish curry, all served on vintage kitchenware. The cook makes sensational *allam dosa* (soft spongy rice-flour pancakes) so don't miss those. The swimming pool in the garden is a welcome relief after a day out exploring the local villages.

Visalam

Local Fund Rd, Kannadukathan, Karaikudi
www.cghearth.com

Close to the palace in Kanadukathan village, this is a cute-as-a-button fifteen-room boutique hotel in a renovated

Chettiar mansion with lavish attention to detail. It has a swimming pool – a bonus for when it's hot – and the outstanding food created with organic produce from the hotel's gardens is the pride of the region; the menu showcases spicy Chettinad specialities. To get there you need to fly south from Chennai to Trichy and drive 80 kilometres along dusty roads (a two-hour drive), but this region is well worth the visit, rich in culinary history.

EAT&SLEEP: RAJAKKAD

Rajakkad Estate
Palani Hills district, near Dindigul
www.rajakkadestate.com

A destination in itself, this hidden gem also makes an ideal place to stop for a couple of days as you drive through the hill region from Trichy and Madurai and across the mountains west to Kerala. A comfortable two-hour drive from Madurai (the closest airport), situated at the crest of the Rajakkad Estate in the rolling green hills, a working coffee plantation, Pallam Palace is a large eighteenth-century heritage estate house with striking wooden architecture that has been lovingly converted into a delightful garden hotel with only seven en suite rooms, making it feel like an intimate family-style home stay, in the grand tradition. The whitewashed rooms are simply furnished: clean modern lines with authentic touches that pay homage to its past, each with private garden access, exuding a sense of calm and serenity. The farm on the estate provides produce for the kitchen and the house menus –

lunch is a relaxed affair with light dishes, salads, and sometimes a delicious south Indian curry, while dinner offers a set three-course menu served sequentially, in the Western manner and in keeping with palace etiquette. The coffee plantation makes for an interesting visit and there are numerous walks you can take around the estate to keep up your fitness levels after indulging in honest country cooking.

EAT&SLEEP: COONOOR

Labarrier Inn
Coonoor Club Rd
Tel: 0423 223 2561

Situated on the road above the bazaar, this modest Raj-era abode with great views and spacious rooms that open on to flower-filled balconies is a good base when travelling through the Nilgiris and tasting tea at its source. Coonoor is a tea planters' town, less hectic than nearby Ooty (the southern version of Darjeeling), and my preferred option if staying in this region – it's possible to do a day trip to Ooty.

Tranquilitea
136B Strathearn, Porters Ave, Kotagiri Rd

A colonial-style tea lounge with appropriate snacks such as walnut tea bread, little scones and almond butter cookies to accompany the vast tea menu. The list includes Nilgiri's finest tea – try the golden tips or the organic winter frost.

THE HIMALAYAS

THESE MESMERISING MOUNTAINS STRETCH ACROSS the northern borders of India from east to west, like a rooftop over the country: a totally absorbing and mesmerising experience. My first introduction to the more remote regions of the Himalayas was with the incomparable Shakti Himalaya (www.shaktihimalaya.com), a bespoke travel company which set the benchmark for life-changing and unforgettable experiences. Shakti is the manifestation of divine female energy, and the name was chosen by its creator Jamshyd Sethna, whose vision for responsible tourism and trekking in the Himalayas is without parallel. They invite guests to 'share the rejuvenating effects of remote surroundings – to provide privileged access to places far removed from the noise and clutter of the modern world, where space, peace and epic landscapes provoke the imagination and nourish the soul'. Much about Shakti is intangible. It's their intention to provide you with the space to go, discover and fill in your own story. Their purpose is to take you on an adventure – softly – and help you to create memories that last forever. This is responsible tourism with a sharp focus on ecology; sustainable conservation tied with a strong sense of community, one that has been emulated by other savvy operators, giving the curious, intrepid traveller some excellent choices for where to sleep and eat in each of the Himalayan regions. Each destination in the Himalayas is breathtakingly beautiful, from the hill stations developed during colonial times to the vast and diverse landscapes of Kangra Valley, Kumaon, Himachal Pradesh, Rishikesh, Kashmir and Ladakh, and the wild frontiers of Assam and Nagaland in the remote north-east. Apart from being visually stunning, each has its own unique and intriguing food culture. ✸

Ladakh skyline, near Chang La Pass

Eastern Himalayas

DARJEELING

A HILL STATION STEEPED IN BRITISH COLONIAL HISTORY, Darjeeling is now a crowded town spilling down from the mountain ridge, a heady blend of Tibetan Buddhist, Nepali, British and Hindu culture, evident in its food. Driving up from Bagdogra airport, near Shiliguri (the main supply town for the eastern region), stop either at Kurseong (Kurseong Tourist Lodge) or Teesta (Teesta Tea Stall), depending which route you take, for a plate or two of steamed *momos* (dumplings). This sets the tone and the greeting is always friendly and welcoming. A day visit to Darjeeling town allows time to take a walk through the busy *chowk* bazaar, with its amazing array of mountain produce, along Chowrastra to Observatory Hill before visiting the Himalayan Mountaineering Institute and the Tibetan Refugee Centre. I always head to Dr Zakir Road and stop at one of the roadside vendors to get a taste of *shya faley* – fried round bread pastry discs with either a vegetable or chicken stuffing – a favourite Tibetan snack. It's also worth spending a day exploring Kalimpong, a nearby hill station close to the Bhutanese border, to sample the local cheese, which looks like a cheddar but has a more acidic flavour – delicious with apple. Staple proteins in this part of the mountains are pork, mutton and chicken, and they weave their way into all kinds of dishes.

EAT & SLEEP: DARJEELING

Dekevas
Ground floor, Dekeling Hotel
51 Ghandi Road

A simple cafe with robust Tibetan food, so bring an appetite. Owner Sanjee is warm and engaging and only too eager to please. Her chicken *gyathuk* soup is hearty and perfectly balanced: thin wheat noodles, little chunks of chicken and vegetables in a light, flavoursome broth; just add a spoonful of the green chilli coriander relish for a kick of heat. Her *momos* (steamed dumplings) are unbeatable, especially the vegetable ones stuffed with chopped mustard leaf and *paneer*. A simple salad of sliced tomato, cucumber, onion and chilli is taken to another level with the addition of crumbled *churpi* – a local fresh cows' milk cheese, like a salted cottage cheese.

Glenary's
Nehru Road, Chowrastra Mall

This two-storey bakery and cafe serves savoury and sweet pastries and cakes downstairs, and is highly atmospheric with its air of faded glory, Art Deco touches and

an abundance of paper doilies in the teahouse. Upstairs is a more informal restaurant style, with a multi-cuisine menu (Western, Indian and Chinese). Try the soup with *momo* dumplings. The decor is quaint and full of old-world charm, if a little time-worn. Pastries and cakes can be bought to take away.

Glenburn Estate
www.glenburnestate.com

A working tea estate (above), about a ninety-minute drive from the centre of Darjeeling, which has two colonial-style bungalow houses – Burra, the original house (with four rooms) and Water Lily, with four generously proportioned en suite bedrooms (this bungalow is the pick). There are exceptional views of the Darjeeling Valley and Kanchenjunga when the clouds behave – October and November is the best time to visit. The home-cooked food makes the experience even more magical, with much of the produce coming from its kitchen garden. They serve the local Sikkimese beer, Dansberg, and the dinner menu varies each night. This may include Nepali-style pumpkin chutney, pork curry and a stunning *sisnu dal*, made with stinging nettles, or Tibetan dishes with *momos* and chilli relish, *thugpa* noodle soup and various vegetable salads. The Burmese menu has a terrific *kawswe* (chicken noodle soup) and there's also a menu designed to showcase the flavours of tea, with tea-smoked chicken and tea-leaf fritters, and a green tea panna cotta, tea jelly and chai sauce for dessert. Owner Husna-Tara Prakash is a most engaging and elegant host who makes you feel immediately at home and pampered – you may never want to leave. There's plenty to see and do during your stay, but make sure you include either a picnic lunch down by the Runjeet river at Glenburn Camp, in front of Glenburn Lodge (a log cabin), or hike down to Rung Dung river with its sandy beach, rock pools and clear mountain water. A visit to the tea factory for tuition in the art of tea and

a tasting with Parveez Hussain, the estate manager, is mandatory. It's also a great base for exploring the region further – Darjeeling, Sikkim and Kalimpong.

Penang
Laden La Road (opposite the post office)

The rustic Nepalese *thali* alone is a good enough reason to visit.

Sonam's Kitchen
Dr Zakir Hussein Road

All-day breakfast food with terrific egg dishes – try the *masala* omelette, the good-quality bacon and various sausages.

Eastern Himalayas

SIKKIM

CARVED BY GLACIERS AND RIVERS, FED BY MORE THAN one hundred rivers and hot springs, this is India's tiniest state, nestled in the eastern reaches of the Greater Himalayas. Largely unexplored Sikkim shares its borders with Bhutan, Tibet and Nepal, and is the perfect destination to experience a melting pot of Himalayan and Indian cultures, where Hindu and Buddhist religions peacefully cohabit and interact. The largely Buddhist kingdom is renowned for its abundance of culture, its indigenous clans, its rich flora and stunning landscapes. It is the looming presence of Kanchenjunga, the world's third highest mountain, that lends the region its defining magic. The narrow winding highway leads up to the capital Gangtok from Bagdogra airport and once you cross the Tista river, you have entered this magical land. The colourful markets and their array of mountain produce determines what gets cooked. There are *isqu*s (choko), fiddlehead ferns, potatoes, squash, marrow, pumpkin leaves and tender stalks for stir frying, as well as eggplants and onions. The best times to visit are either March and April or October and November – summer can get very hot and humid. Essential sights include Rumtek and Pemayangste Monasteries, Pelling with its close-up views of Kanchenjunga, and Yuksom, the oldest village in Sikkim. Taste the local Danberg beer – a clean-tasting pale ale with a hint of sweetness.

EAT&SLEEP: SIKKIM

Bamboo Resort
Rumtek
www.bambooresort.com

A more peaceful setting than in the city, this place is close to the monastery, and a thirty-minute drive from Gangtok.

Glenburn Tea Estate
P.O. Singritam, Darjeeling 734101

Makes an ideal base from which to visit and explore Sikkim for a few days.

Hidden Forest Retreat
Gangtok
www.hiddenforestretreat.org

Peaceful, private and elegant.

Shakti Sikkim Village Houses
www.shaktihimalaya.com

Available from October to April in Sikkim, village walks are at the heart of any Shakti experience, enabling you to enjoy the villages and rural life in remote mountain regions. Accompanied by local porters and guides, you step out of the modern world, walking between remote villages and staying in traditional village houses at Sandyang Lee, Hee and Radhu Khandu in the Rinchenpong region of West Sikkim, which Shakti has spruced up to provide proper comfort without compromising their authenticity, while still giving you a taste of the spartan Buddhist aesthetic. Visits to local schools, monasteries and colourful markets are arranged to enable you to get a full understanding of the culture of each region, its people, religion and customs. At the table, it is usual to find rice, corn, lentils, wheat, vegetables and meat throughout each meal. A basic, everyday meal would consist of the holy trinity – steamed rice, dal and a vegetable preparation, whilst a typical dinner might include a vegetable or lentil soup, two or more vegetable and meat preparations, an *achar* or chutney, *roti* (flat wheat bread), steamed rice or rice pilaf, served with *mahai*, a diluted version of *lassi*, finishing with a local dessert and tea. Staples such as *momo*s (steamed dumplings filled with meat or vegetables) and *shafta* (salted dried beef) appear often, sometimes cooked with spinach or radish, other times with onion, tomato and chilli. Watching as eggs were cooked in a banana leaf cup over hot coals for breakfast reminded me of childhood days as a girl guide. In the markets, I tasted *chow chow*, a soupy Himalayan dish with stir-fried noodles and *shafta* – smoked dried beef strips spiced with turmeric and dried chilli, cooked with onion, tomato, fresh chilli and salt. The flavours are simple and robust. This is an authentic mountain experience.

Eastern Himalayas
NAGALAND

ONE OF THE SMALLER HILL STATES OF INDIA, THIS REMOTE
eastern corner beyond Assam that borders Myanmar is starting to gain attention
from adventure-savvy travellers, and has become the most recent hotspot for
Indiaphiles like me. This part of the world is off the beaten track, where the
rich heritage and customs of the Nagas from the fourteen officially recognised
tribes becomes immediately apparent during their annual Hornbill Festival in
early December, the best time to visit. It's an amazing spectacle of chilli and
pork eating contests, colour and movement, song and dance (and some of the
most extraordinary *a cappella* music I have ever heard), art and culture, entirely
intact and so utterly removed from our modern Western lifestyle. A stay here
will transport you to another plane altogether as you become absorbed in their
rich cultural traditions, experience its natural beauty and eat unusual food if
you're more game than me – expect rodents, frogs, roaches, silkworms stir fried
with young bamboo shoots, and the larvae from hornets' nests among them.
The festival is a food lover's dream. Nagaland is prized for its use of wild food;
the Nagas are known for their broad palates and a reputation for eating anything
and everything. It reminds me a lot of Laos and their food habits, cooking
whatever is to hand. Not that you will necessarily be served any of this where
you stay, unless you request it. I was quite taken by the smoked pork that had
been stir-fried with fermented bamboo shoots and sesame, *khorisa aru masala
paat murghi* (tender chunks of chicken flavoured with fermented bamboo
shoots and a herbal *masala* paste) and leafy wild greens or pumpkin vines
cooked with chilli and ginger and served with a dried beef pickle. Whatever
your choice, it will leave you in awe.

EAT & SLEEP: NAGALAND

The Ultimate Travelling Camp

Kohima Camp, Nagaland
www.tutc.com

Open for the first ten days of December to coincide with the annual Hornbill Festival, when the different tribes of Nagaland come together to celebrate their biggest festival of the year. This company is a newcomer to the region, bringing glam camping (the only way to go) to this largely undiscovered mountain region and its unique culture – it's like peeking into a world where time has stood still. The plush tent pavilions offer luxury and comfort; this is remote living at its best – this corner of India is a new frontier, totally off the beaten track, where brave hearts venture to explore the unique Naga culture, unlike any other. The food is spicy hot – this is where the hottest chillies in the world grow – *raja mirchi* or ghost chilli, so it pays to be respectful. Pork (*gahuri mungsu*) and beef (*guuru mangsu*) are the staple proteins, vegetables are often smoked, dried or fermented, and bamboo shoot (*baastinga*) and potatoes are mainstays. A cultural program is woven into your stay. You fly into Dimapur to be collected and driven to Kohima where the camp is situated; the road transfer takes about ninety minutes.

Northern Himalayas

UTTARAKHAND

The northern mountain state of Uttarakhand is stunning, with beautiful vistas of permanently snow-capped peaks. There's an openness to the spirit of mountain people that is charming, refreshing and special. Uttarakhand is home to the famous yoga and pilgrimage centre of Rishikesh in the west, and the little-known Kumaon region to the east.

EAT&SLEEP: UTTARAKHAND

Ananda in the Himalayas

The Palace Estate, Narendra Nagar,
Tehri Garhwal
www.anandaspa.com

Being in this region means immersing yourself in the spiritual heritage of India. Ananda is a destination unto itself. Located in the foothills north of Delhi in the Garwhal region – you fly into Dehradun, then drive for forty-five minutes through Rishikesh, the birthplace of yoga and meditation. It's also possible to arrange a private helicopter charter from Delhi; it's the most efficient, dramatic and expensive way to arrive. The former palace residence of the Maharaja of Tehri Garhwal (right), opened in 2000, this mountain retreat is considered India's premium wellness spa resort and has paved the way for others. The way of life here is holistic, following the Ayurvedic principles of the knowledge of life, an ancient Hindu science that encourages you to re-energise, rebalance and rejuvenate with Ayurveda,

aromatherapy treatments and advice that restores mind and body to its natural state. The main wing offers rooms with balconies, either with a palace view or valley view. For the ultimate indulgence, I book a garden villa (there are only three on the estate) overlooking Rishikesh and the Ganga, and spend a week. I love my secluded private

garden and pool, the ritual of my morning yoga and gentle exercise sessions, and the personal Ayurveda program that is given to me after my arrival consultation. To follow a prescribed wellness program, they recommend a stay of fifteen days as ideal; some stay for a shorter period, but approximately one-third of guests stay for twenty-one days. Some guests come to simply relax and enjoy good food, others come to commit to a strict wellness detox program and others come for a bit of each – healthy food with some indulgences. The resort caters to all preferences and the fresh natural ingredients used in the Ayurveda-based detox dishes place the emphasis on whole grains, organic fresh fruits and vegetables (grown on their farm in the valley), lean proteins and dairy products. A choice of freshly squeezed vegetable juices, immune boosters, elixirs and tonics get the day under way in the best way possible. I can recommend any one of the Indian breakfasts – *masala dosa*, spinach *uttappam* (rice pancake) with coconut chutney, *pesaruttu* (thin crisp pancake made with a *moong dal* and rice batter) with chutneys or *poori bhaji* (fried whole wheat puffed bread) with a mild potato and tomato curry. They are equally delicious and light. Their house-made yoghurt in clay pots is fresh, tangy and creamy. If you adopt a prescribed wellness program, then meals are determined for you, with menus changing daily; aromatic spices are blended for their health properties but no chilli is used in any of the dishes. For the indulgent, the a la carte menu offers a choice of popular western, Asian and Indian dishes. This is some of the best food you will taste in the mountains. The Ananda chefs are happy to show you how to make quick and easy dishes at home, to encourage healthy food as a way of life. The place exudes a serene atmosphere, conducive

to appreciating what this mountain retreat has to offer. Take a late-afternoon drive (one hour) to nearby Haridwar, a sacred city considered the gateway to the gods, where the mighty Ganga emerges from the mountains to flow through the plains, and witness the daily *aarti* prayer ritual on the ghats by the river – illuminating and magical after the sun has disappeared beyond the horizon.

Mary Budden Estate

Binsar Wildlife Sanctuary,
Ayarpani District, Kumaon
www.marybuddenestate.in

A private estate located in the cosy corner of Kumaon, a four-hour drive from Kathgodam station. There are two cottages set deep in the pine forest – the original Mary Budden Cottage dating back to the mid-nineteenth century, lovingly restored with three bedrooms, and the more recently constructed Rhododendron Cottage with four bedrooms, each with en suite. The property is as charming as its owner Serena Chopra (who happens to make some of the best chilli pickle I have tasted). Both houses enjoy privacy and are designed for comfortable, elegant living; an ideal mountain nest, open all year round, that makes a perfect base for a yoga retreat (hosted by Samara, Serena's daughter), mountain trekking, village walks and exploring the virgin beauty of the Binsar Wildlife Sanctuary – home to leopards, Himalayan black bears and many species of migratory birds. In keeping with its colonial heritage, the food has a focus on health and home-style comfort cooking – sometimes it's classic roast chicken and potatoes; other times it might include local Kumaoni dishes like *maduae ki roti* (a local bread), *kumaoni raita* (yoghurt with turmeric and cucumber) and *lai ka saag* (sauteed mountain spinach).

Shakti 360° Leti

Leti Village, Bageshwar District, Uttarakhand
www.shaktihimalaya.com

This is an idyllic Himalayan retreat, far from the madding crowd and off the beaten track, where contemporary design meets authentic tradition (above). With only four spacious pavilions, it offers exclusivity and privacy, and the food cooked by house chef Yeshi is beyond compare. Situated on a stunning mountain spur close to where Nepal, Tibet and India meet and with mind-blowing views of the Great Himalayan Range, this luxury lodge is one of a kind. Getting there is all part of the journey; a unique experience. Walks from the house through oak forests reveal magnificent views of the Ramganga Valley, Heeramani Glacier and Nanda Kot to the majestic Nanda Devi, the highest mountain in India. The food is as much a part of the experience as the views.

A primitive wood-fired camp oven sits out in the shed behind the kitchen and works a treat; Yeshi bakes bread, biscuits and cakes every day in this modest contraption. The garden produces many of the vegetables and all the herbs used in cooking, chickens are killed as required in the nearest village down the track, and small trout are fished from the ice-cold waters of the nearby river. Samosas with tamarind chutney are served with sundowners (so civilised), and the repertoire from the kitchen for lunch and dinner treats is simply astounding; no indulgence is overlooked. To avoid a very long day of travel getting there, it pays to spend a couple of days at the Kumaon village houses before the five-hour drive further up into the mountains to Leti Village.

Shakti Kumaon Village Walks

Kumaon

www.shaktihimalaya.com

In the less-known, remote Kumaon mountain region, which lies in the northern hill state of Uttarakhand, Shakti has pioneered the concept of village walks. It offers some of the most stunning mountain scenery imaginable, from the perennially snow-capped peaks of the Great Himalayan range in the north to the pretty hill stations at the foothills. Getting here has been made easier with the early-morning Shabdati Express train from Delhi, which arrives in Kathgodam around noon. The Shakti team will have a snappy car waiting to whisk you off for a three-hour drive through dense forests and the Himalayan foothills, with spectacular scenery all the way. The village houses are located in the Almora district and we arrive at Deora to the first of the village

houses and base camp for the Kumaon village walks to Jwalabanj and Kana. The walks incorporate hiking between villages, sleeping at a different house each night, taking you through fields of herbs, following streams and waterfalls, and watching the friendly local farmers at work in the terraced fields. You can walk to the Binsar bird sanctuary or head to Panchachuli and visit the enterprisingly successful women's cooperative, where more than a thousand women are employed to weave pashminas, scarves and shawls. Settle into the sensitively renovated village houses where healthy delicious food is perfectly attuned to its mountain environment. Breakfast includes house-made muesli, fresh fruit, flaky *parathas* with herb omelette, and pots of steaming tea served in the garden looking straight across to white peaked mountains. Bliss.

Northern Himalayas
HIMACHAL PRADESH

THE NATURALLY BEAUTIFUL REGION OF HIMACHAL PRADESH, nestled in the lap of the Himalayas and considered the Switzerland of India, is perhaps best known for its two major cities. Shimla has long been referred to as the Queen of the Hill Stations, once the summer playground of the Raj and its official summer capital and the most important British hill resort prior to Independence, now the capital of Himachal Pradesh. Dharmsala is home to the Dalai Lama and the exiled Tibetan government. Both states have distinctive food cultures and offer rewarding and diverse travel experiences.

I've always been intrigued by the allure of Shimla and by the intriguing food culture of Himachal Pradesh, with its blend of Punjabi and Tibetan influences (they are its neighbours) that varies from region to region; this diversity is reflected in the regional variations of its food culture. Non-vegetarian food, with a generous dose of spices such as cardamom, cinnamon, cloves and red chillies, is very much the norm. The average Himachal kitchen churns out all sorts of meat, lentil and cereal preparations. In the barren regions of Kinnaur and Lahaul-Spiti, there is more emphasis on locally grown, indigenous grains such as buckwheat, millet and barley. In areas with a pastoral tradition, milk products are used liberally in food preparation.

To the west of the state lies the Kangra Valley and the well-known town of Dharmsala, made famous since becoming the residence of the Dalai Lama and Tibetans in exile. The easiest and most direct way to get there is to fly to nearby Gaggan. The food in this region is different again: vegetables play a starring role, and milk and curd are used extensively. One of my enduring food memories is tasting *kheru*, where whisked yoghurt is cooked with chickpea flour and flavoured with ginger, garlic, cumin and *methi* (fenugreek leaves). It has a smooth, gravy-like consistency and is utterly delicious.

Further east lies Shimla, perhaps the best-known hill station of India. To get there, take the early-morning train from Delhi to Chandigarh then transfer to the novelty toy train that runs from from Kalka to Shimla. You can get off half-way at Dharampur and drive the rest of the way if you prefer (it's quicker).

The climb into the hills is dramatic and breathtaking, and Shimla is a bustling city that sprawls down either side of the mountain ridge, the most densely populated hill slopes of India. Surrounded by forests of oak, deodar (cedar), pine and rhododendron, with the lofty peaks of the great Himalayan range on both sides, it has an interesting core of colonial Victorian buildings around the Mall and the Promenade and colourful local bazaars that wind down the narrow lanes off the Mall. Stop off at Krishna Misthan Bhandar on Lower Bazar Road to taste a few sweets and the best housemade *paneer* (local cottage cheese) in town. These days, the typical diet is changing to include more vegetables. Once it was predominantly potatoes and turnips; now leafy greens and a wide variety of vegetables have found their way into Himachali kitchens. The markets during summer provide a veritable feast of various types of eggplant, tomatoes, okra, radish, pumpkin, kohlrabi, gourds and fiddlehead ferns. They appear in many dishes I taste during my visit. A meal is called *dham* and *dham* places (like *dhabas*) serve local food, usually specialising in just a few dishes. An everyday *dham* is the usual *dal-chawal-subzi-roti* (the common north Indian combination of rice, lentil broth, a dish of vegetables and bread). Have a taste of *sidu*, a type of bread made from wheat flour that is kneaded with yeast and left to rise for a few hours. With a stuffing of fat and *urad* (black gram), it is first browned over a slow fire and then steamed. It is normally eaten with ghee, *dal* or mutton, and is quite heavy, typical of mountain food.

EAT & SLEEP: SHIMLA

Oberoi Cecil

Chaura Maidan, Shimla
www.oberoihotels.com

With an imposing presence at one end of
the Mall, this grand colonial hotel comes
with distinctive heritage status, a family
hotel (read – lots of children) that is packed
to the rafters during summer when the
locals escape the heat of the plains and
head north into the mountains – a quieter
and better time to visit is November or
December. With its central location, it
makes a good base to explore the immediate
city sights – Rashtrapati Niwas, State
Museum, St Michael's Cathedral and the
Gaiety Theatre. From their dining room
menu I chose dishes that were typically
Himachali – *sepu vadi*, mashed white lentils
spiced with fennel seeds and black pepper
and rolled into small balls then steamed and
fried and served in a smooth spinach gravy;
chha gosht, a rich mutton dish with a creamy
sauce of mustard oil, buttermilk and *masala*
spices, a hot favourite of Himachal (where
the absence of onion and garlic is the
norm); and *channa madrah*, a mild chickpea
and yoghurt curry.

Spars Lodge

Museum Road, Chaura Maidan, Shimla
Tel: 0177 265 7908
www.sparslodge.com

Don't miss the opportunity to have
lunch here to experience the warmth and
charm of Joey, the owner of this modest
guesthouse, and gain a real sense of Shimla
hospitality. The food in his dining room is
wonderfully authentic: home cooking at its

best, his passion for what he does shining
through in every detail. For lunch, he
prepared a perfectly balanced, aromatic
goat curry slow-braised in spices and
buttermilk; stir-fried *lungru*, fiddlehead ferns
with a texture and similar to asparagus;
a mushroom rice *pulao* seasoned with
cumin, and *kaddu kesar kheer*, a dessert
of white pumpkin and creamed rice
with saffron – comfort food at its best.

Wildflower Hall

Mashobra
www.oberoihotels.com

With spectacular views of the cedar (*deodar*)
and pine (*chir*) forests and mountains,
the former estate of Lord Kitchener, now
converted into a grand luxury hotel, is
a 45-minute drive along winding mountain
roads further on from Shimla, an ideal base
from which to explore the foothills and rural
life of this fascinating region. Of the two
Oberoi hotel properties in Shimla, this one
is for grown-ups – no children under twelve
allowed (families with children stay at the
Cecil) so the tone is more relaxed and laid
back. Early-morning walks through the
forests are bracing and invigorating (watch
out for those pesky monkeys), the mountain
air pure and clear, and the food truly
wonderful. Chef Mohan and his kitchen
team cooked us a sublime Himachali *thali*
for dinner one night – a hit parade of small

dishes served with a wonderfully fragrant Himachali rice *pulao* (basmati rice with raisins, cashews and almonds); *kheru*, a hot yoghurt soup tempered with *methi* (chopped fenugreek leaves) and asafoetida and served with succulent kebabs; *sepuwadi ka madra*, poached lentil dumplings and spinach; *chaa gosht*, lamb simmered with a thin yoghurt and onion gravy that was delicate and flavoursome; trout fished from the Kullu River cooked in a tomato, onion and mustard gravy; and *murgh dhauladhari* – a typical chicken preparation from the mountain region bathed in aromatic spices and a black pepper tomato gravy.

EAT & SLEEP: DHARMSALA

Raas Kangra

www.raaskangra.com

Just as these pages go to print, this welcome addition to Dharmsala is opening its doors. I have included it for two reasons. It is sister property to the Raas Jodphur (one of my favourites in Rajasthan), so trust their integrity and ability to deliver, and this beautifully designed hotel has finally given Dharmsala somewhere luxurious and sophisticated for visitors to stay – more than enough reason to make a visit worthwhile. Its position out in the remote Kangra Valley, away from town, is also a drawcard. It makes a great base for exploring the Tibetan and Buddhist pilgrimage sites, hill stations, spiritual relics and the rolling slopes of the tea gardens in the region, and each generously proportioned room has a private balcony with uninterrupted views of the Himalayan peaks – the perfect dramatic backdrop. The restaurant includes an *al fresco* dining area, the best place to hang out and take in the pure mountain air. Take an early-morning dip in the heated indoor pool before a leisurely breakfast. The food promises to be of the same exacting standards as Raas Jodphur's, with a focus on regional specialities, Indian staples and Western comfort food. Staying here and at places like this reinforces just how incredible India really is.

Western Himalayas
LADAKH

Ladakh is the epitome of a Buddhist way of life, its food reflected by its extreme climate and remoteness. Distinctly different because of its strong Buddhist heritage and culture, this place feels more like Tibet than India; the region is known as Little Tibet, or the rooftop of the world. Buddhist *gompas* (monasteries) dominate the landscape and prayer flags flutter in the breeze wherever you look. Because of its rugged geography, it was protected from the ravages of the Chinese and contains one of the most intact Tantric Buddhist societies left on earth. Ladakh is a deeply spiritual place and come summer, there are many festivals to celebrate, so it's a wonderful time to visit. Physically different from any other part of India, with its high-altitude desert dominated by rugged snow-capped mountains and deep turquoise lakes, this has to be one of the most picturesque places on earth.

Like the terrain, the food is unlike anywhere else in India. Flavours are simple, spicing is minimal, and everything is preserved after the summer harvest for the long harsh winter months, the diet supplemented by tinned food. Peek into a village house and watch as an old woman prepares *sque* – little chunks of dough cooked in a large copper pot of boiling stock until softened, with strips of yak meat added for flavour. I've found a couple of small cafes in Leh with acceptable food: short menus offering vegetable salads, noodles and sandwiches. Penguin Cafe seems to be everyone's pit stop; the bakery beneath the palace, next to the old tree, sells the best bread, like a Turkish-style flatbread; the Tibetan Kitchen serves hearty mountain food, and I like the *samosa* stall at the end of the main street. Another place made great *lassi*, the ubiquitous, refreshing yoghurt drink. Ladakh is prized for its apricots, apples, barley and wheat, and the food shops of Leh specialise in apricot products of all manner and variety.

EAT&SLEEP: LADAKH

Give Back Adventures

www.lillefro.org

Tamara Cannon is an Australian woman living and working in Ladakh who launched the Lille Fro Foundation in 2008 and has recently launched Give Back Adventures – fundraising adventure trips that are designed to give the intrepid traveller a unique opportunity to get up close and personal to the foundation's philanthropic projects, and experience first-hand the places in which they work, as well as offering a holiday of a lifetime to one of the most amazing parts of the world. With a travel philosophy of 'do something that matters and give back', you can choose between an ice river expedition up the Zanskar, a biking adventure through the Himalayas, or participating in a hands-on experience with the Lille Fro team at a local school while exploring the region. These bespoke journeys will give you a chance to explore Ladakh off the beaten track and to witness for yourself the difference Lille Fro is making in one of the most extreme corners of the world. Included in the cost of each trip is a direct donation to Lille Fro.

Shakti Ladakh Village Houses

www.shaktihimalaya.com

Shakti opened up the region for the luxury vagabond traveller, and offers access to the unique cultural life of Ladakh. They have designed an amazing village house experience without parallel that avoids over-commercialisation and takes you out, off the beaten track to these untouched villages in the Indus Valley. The traditional village

houses have been given the Shakti makeover and are situated in Stok, Nimmu, Taru, Sakti, Likhir and Shey, affording every luxury imaginable. Spend a week or so in this most remote rural region of the Indian Himalayas, moving from house to house. The season is open for summer only, from mid-June to September, and Shakti will tailor-make an itinerary to suit you. Days are spent absorbing everything the mountains have to offer – from leisurely walks to trekking or rafting, museum and monastery visits to taking tea with the locals to just chilling out on the roof terrace of the house. Shakti chef Yeshi oversees the menus and food preparation, and his gift with clean and simple flavours is evident with every bite. His pastries, cakes and biscuits compete with the best I have tasted anywhere. He cooks with the purity of a Buddhist's heart. Divine picnic lunches

1) Main street, Leh, Ladakh
2) Shey valley, Ladakh
3) Buddhist stupas near
   Stok Palace, Ladakh
4) Monks at Thiksey Monastery
5) Yak herds, Ladakh
6) Srinigar Old Town, Kashmir

enhance the experience, whether it's in an apricot orchard or on the banks of the river under willow trees; our table is set with salads of lettuce, walnuts, beetroot, couscous or quinoa and pomegranate, and baked tomato and onion tarts. I call it our picnic in the sky. Cold towels and chilled glasses of *nimbu pani* (sweet lime soda) miraculously appear at the end of a long walk and dinners – maybe a vegetarian *thali* or a fragrant *biryani* – in the cosy living rooms leave you wanting for nothing. No indulgence is overlooked. This is a unique, very special mountain experience. If you wish to explore the remote Nubra Valley, Shakti can arrange a camping expedition, moving your tents as you head further up the valley. This is for serious outdoor adventurists.

The Ultimate Travelling Camp

Chamba Camp, Thiksey
www.tutc.com

A glamorous newcomer that brings glamping to the remote, varying and dramatic landscapes of the Land of the Lamas, open from late June to September. Set up in the fields below Thiksey Monastery (referred to as Little Potala – Potala is Lhasa's iconic monastery), the twelve plush tent pavilions with private decks offer homestyle comfort and make an ideal base for exploring myriad cultural activities and adventures that are woven into your stay – a visit to the extraordinary Alchi Monastery and ancient Hemis Monastery, wandering the main streets of Leh, river rafting on the Zanskar, watching Ladakhi polo and early-morning prayers with the monks at Thiksey Monastery. The camp kitchen rustles up anything from delicious *dosa*s to healthy stir-fries and steamed fish.

Western Himalayas
KASHMIR

THE MUGHALS GAVE IT THE NAME OF PARADISE ON EARTH – a magical wonderland among the high Himalayas. Although the region has long been fraught with political tension, it's easy to be smitten by far-flung Kashmir with its mysterious allure, compelling beauty, turbulent history, verdant valleys, alpine grasslands and a sense of serenity – a paradise on earth and a paradise for savvy travellers. Abundant crops of walnuts, apricots, almonds, saffron, morel mushrooms, lotus root, apples, rice and the prized Kashmiri chillies are grown in the orchards and sold at the bustling bazaars and define the food of Kashmir. Extravagantly beautiful in every season, the luminous landscape underlies the Kashmiri spirituality and their love of soulful Sufi music – Sufism (mystic Islam) is the predominant religion of Kashmir. The royal house of the Dogra family once ruled the entire Jammu and Kashmir region. Kashmiri Pandits are the Brahmins (priestly class) and the Dogras are Rajputs (warrior class): two different castes with different cultures. Collectively they make an amazing tapestry of culinary traditions.

Come in April when the tulip gardens are ablaze with colour. The Mughals established Srinagar's many formal pleasure gardens, now collectively known as the Mughal Gardens (Pari Mahal, Shalimar and Nishat) with great love and care. They also supported the development of art and craft among the people of Kashmir, leaving a heritage of exquisite artisanship, while the British legacy left behind the thousands of wooden houseboats on Dal Lake. The best shopping for Kashmiri handicrafts, pashminas, papier mache, Dogra jewellery, dried fruits and walnuts, lacquer ware and embroidery can be found along Residency Road, near Lal Chowk or Polo View Market and Boulevard Road. Best times to visit are either September, after the summer crowds have left, or in April to witness the beauty of the tulip gardens. Make time to escape Srinigar into rural Kashmir and explore the nearby districts of Gulmarg to the west, or spend a day trout fishing in either Yusmarg to the south east or Mansabal, on the lake just to the north. All are within a manageable two-hour drive of the city – easy for a day tripper.

When you visit, it's essential to take a *shikhara* at sunrise to visit the early-morning floating markets on Dal Lake, taste *kehwa* (Kashmiri green tea flavoured with saffron, almond and cardamom), stay on a houseboat, experience authentic home cooking by arranging to have lunch or dinner in a private Kashmiri home, cruise along Jehlum River through the old town to see the crumbling riverfront palaces and early architecture, lose yourself meandering through the laneways of the Old Town and see the artisans applying tin coating to copper plates in the copper bazaar, and watch the local bakeries making morning bread *chout* (like a thick *roti*) then *chuhworo*, the afternoon bread (small rounds with a hole in the centre, baked with either sesame seeds or *khus khus* (white poppy seeds) on the crust). To get an insight into everyday life, explore the roadside food vendors and market around the beautiful white Hazratbal Mosque to taste myriad fried snacks such as *samosas*, *pakoras* (especially the ones made with lotus stem) and *mutthi* (bread slices fried in ghee or oil). One section sells all manner of mutton offal, from head meat, liver, brains and *paaya* (trotters) – not for the faint-hearted. Kashmir was once peacefully shared between Muslim and Pandit (Hindu) communities, but most Pandits now live in exile since Partition; the politics of a divided state has turned everything topsy-turvy. Both have a love of meat and it features prominently in both diets. The details of how they cook and the spices they use for the same dish is different, and it's these subtleties that make for an intriguing taste discovery. Kashmir is also renowned for its Wazawan celebratory feasts, whether they be Kashmiri Muslim or Pandit (Hindu Brahmin), influenced by its rich Persian and Afghan ancestry.

EAT: SRINIGAR

14th Avenue Cafe

Lal Mandi, Rajbagh (near footbridge)
Tel: 231 0472

This modern, Western-style cafe with river
views is a welcome newcomer, has the
cool factor and serves consistently good
espresso, tea and cakes throughout the day,
as well as decent savoury snacks such as *peri
peri* chicken or hummus with pita bread.

Ahdoo's Hotel

Regency Road, Regal Chowk, Munshi Bagh
Tel: 0194 247 2593

A typical restaurant that's always packed
with locals and family groups, serving
authentic Kashmiri Muslim food – come
with an appetite and order their Wazawan
feast of sixteen or so different dishes; this is
one of my favourite food hangouts in town.
It's no-frills dining at its best; lamb and
chicken are the proteins of choice. Chicken
korma is damn fine and the *shahi* chicken,
boneless chicken slow braised in a yoghurt
gravy and given a tangy edge with lemon
juice, is a standout. This is the best place
to try *tabakmazz* – roasted lamb ribs,
a must-have. Finish with a slice of their
walnut crumble tart from their bakery
on street level. Open for lunch and dinner.

Coffea Arabica

Moulana Azad Road, near Broadway Hotel
Tel: 245 9002

Another place in town that serves very
good coffee, cakes and *shwarmas* (sandwich
wraps); the doner kebab also passes muster.
More fun when you are taken by a local.

The Harisa Shope

Aail Kadal (near the Nawakadel Bridge),
Old Town

Open for breakfast, and only during winter
from November to March. I became a fan
of the hearty breakfast dish *harisa* with the
first mouthful. It bears no resemblance to
the north African chilli condiment; lamb
rib meat is slow-cooked overnight in a large
handi pot over hot coals with lamb fat, rice,
herbs, saffron, cardamom and a few other
aromatic spices until it becomes like a paste.
Rich and unctuous, it is slathered with hot
ghee and served with *chout* – like a dense
roti flatbread that is only baked and served
in the morning. Bring an appetite.

Imran's Cafeteria

Khayam Chowk, Nowpora
Tel: 990 645 8081

Famous for its kebabs – muttton *tikka* is chunks of meat threaded on to a long skewer and roasted over hot coals roadside at the front of the shop, and mutton kebabs are the minced meat variety (as in *sheekh* kebabs) pressed into a sausage shape along the skewer, also cooked over hot coals. Equally famous are their ten or so different types of chutneys served with the kebabs: tomato, onion, kohlrabi, radish and carrot among them. A plate of plain *lavas* (roti-type soft flatbread) accompanies the meat and chutneys. Khayam Chowk has several other little kebab places along this street, but it's Imran's that has the queues. Owner Mohsin Hameed (Imran's son) cooks with gusto over the hot coals, working at a furious pace to keep up with demand, especially after 3 p.m., when the place is constantly packed.

Krishna Vishnu Dhaba

Ram Munshi Bagh, near Polo View
and Burnhall School

This is the most popular vegetarian restaurant in town and it's always full of people, so if you have an aversion to crowds, then this is not the place for you. It's popular because it serves Pandit vegetarian food, a welcome break sometimes from the meat onslaught of Kashmiri cooking. Keep it simple and go for *Rajma Chawan* (kidney beans cooked with ghee, spices and mixed with basmati rice), a plate of mixed vegetables with *chapatti* or *paneer bhurji*. Steamed *idlis* and crispy *masala dosas* are the breakfast staples served during the morning.

Lal Sheikh

Residency Rd, Polo View

This is the oldest tea stall in town, just down the road from Ahdoo's – so drop by for a *chai*, and if you fancy a snack, try the chicken patty sandwiched into a bun (like *pao bhaji*) – a Kashmiri-style burger.

Tao Cafe

Residency Rd, Polo View, Munshi Bagh

A charming little place that is a perfect pit stop after a spot of shopping in the area. Grab a table under the *chinar* (pine) tree in the garden and have a pot of tea and Kashmiri-style lamb kebabs.

SLEEP: SRINIGAR

Almond Villa

Boulevard Rd, near Zabarwan Park, opposite Jetty #3
Tel: 997 192 4583
www.almondvilla.in

A unique destination overlooking Dal Lake and facing the Zabarwan mountain range, this heritage family bungalow is a showcase for cultural heritage tourism and is set amongst spectacular orchards and lush gardens, a sought-after sanctuary where Jyoti Singh gives a warm welcome, perfect if you prefer to avoid the big-brand hotels and wish to relax in this pleasant homestay. The rooms are functional rather than plush, offering colonial charm and generous hospitality in spades. There are two houses on the estate – Almond Villa with six bedrooms and Walnut Cottage with two basic bedrooms and a separate living space.

Don't expect hotel-style a la carte menus – this is a more intimate and personal experience with authentic home cooking. Decide what you fancy for dinner before heading out for the day; the kitchen shops according to your preference (Indian or Western), but I would always recommend you stick with their Hindu Dogra food from the neighbouring Jammu region, with dishes such as *auriya* (potatoes in a mustard seed and turmeric yoghurt gravy), *khatta kaddu* (yellow pumpkin with tamarind and fennel seeds), *kadam saag* (turnip greens), *rajma* (red kidney beans simmered with chilli and tomato in a ginger and garlic sauce), and a fragrant tangy mutton number cooked with sour pomegranate seeds. Dessert often includes fruit from their orchard – you have lucked in if you visit during the cherry or strawberry season, or they may make *meetha chawal* (rice sweetened with *jaggery* (palm sugar)) if you ask. Much of the organic produce is sourced from their own farm and orchards, and they hold a farmers' market and craft bazaar every Sunday from 11 a.m. to 5 p.m. in the orchard, popular with locals and visitors in the know. Their delicious homemade jams and preserves are served at breakfast (you can also buy some to take home); the strawberry is a knockout.

One afternoon, Jyoti showed me a basket full of *waar* – Kashmiri *masala*: sun-dried, reddish-brown pats of garlic, dried Kashmiri chillies and spices that are stored in their dry state. Cooks break a piece off as needed and use them in sauces and gravies for depth of flavour, or mix them with eggs and onion and fry them together for people suffering from congestion or a cold.

Make the most of this natural sanctuary – take a brisk morning walk around the lake, wander through the orchards and relax in this delightful hub, which is often used for artists in residence. Almond Villa also hosts the *Dara Shikoh Festival* every August, a celebration of the cultural diversity and inclusiveness in Jammu and Kashmir – workshops with artists, reviving artistic culture and traditions with a strong message of inclusion, integration and acceptance – a broad representation of the various tribes throughout the state.

The Cottage Nigeen

Mirza Bagh Nigeen, near Nigeen Lake, Hazratbal
www.thecottagenigeen.com

Shakila Riyas is the most engaging and generous host, passionate about her Kashmiri heritage. She opened her house (and her heart) to me and I left with a deeper insight and understanding of Kashmir, particularly of its food traditions. Her house is as elegant and stylish as she is, and the food from her kitchen is refined with distinctive and perfectly balanced flavours, astute seasoning and contrasting textures. A home-cooked dinner is a sumptuous affair under Shakila's watchful eye and includes typical Kashmiri dishes such as succulent mutton and chicken kebabs, the best *rogan josh* imaginable, a sublime *haaq munji* – leafy greens and kohlrabi cooked in a light onion broth with fenugreek seeds and garlic, a divine rice *pulao* studded with apricots and cashews, and the most outstanding, meltingly tender lamb *korma* I have ever tasted. Another night, Khursheed, her house cook, makes the most sensational mutton *biryani*. Be sure to try Shakila's authentic version of *Phirni*, a dish of Persian origins: semolina cooked in lightly sweetened milk with saffron, green cardamom and cinnamon, then set

in small bowls and dusted with white poppy seeds and almonds. Her garden supplies many of the vegetables and herbs used in the cooking and the orchard provides fruit for breakfast. The house has four en suite rooms for guests to stay in, where you can experience first hand the hospitality Kashmir is famous for.

Qayaam Gah

www.abchaprigroup.com

To complement a stay on the Sukkoon Houseboat (see below), the same group are opening Qayaam Gah (a Sufi term meaning an abode for deep rest) in 2016, a new eco-lodge with seven state-of-the-art stone and wood cottages and a heated infinity swimming pool, built in a valley of cherry and apple groves with expansive mountain views, a fifteen-minute drive from Sukoon. Your car will drop you at the end of the road and you walk the last ten minutes to the property – bags are carried in by porters – offering a very special 'off the beaten track' experience. The food will have the same meticulous attention to detail as that of Sukoon. Together they will form a spiritual link to the majestic beauty of Kashmir. The food will be to the same stylish standards as Sukoon, with a menu of regional specialities that changes daily.

Sukoon Houseboat

Rani Mahal, Dal Lake, Srinigar
www.sukoonkashmir.com

The most luxurious houseboat on the lake and the first eco-stylish one, this has been a labour of love for A.B. Chapri Retreats, who have meticulously restored this floating residence with five en suite bedrooms into an essential place to stay when in Srinigar.

Moored in an enviable location on Dal Lake (opposite Almond Villa), a quick *shikhara* (wooden boat) ride directly across from Ghat Number 19(A), it has lovely hand-carved wooden interiors and the friendly staff invite you to lounge on the rooftop deck and take in the breathtaking vistas of the snow-capped mountains and unhurried serenity of the lake, preferably with a glass of wine in hand – sunrise and sunset are particularly spectacular.

A couple of nights on board will guarantee contentment and relaxation, and the excellent food prepared by chefs Deepak (from Sikkim) and Amin (from Srinigar) enhance the whole experience. These boys cook with a Western sensibility – portions are mercifully small, flavours are distinct and produce is local. Lunch is a chilled soup and a simple fresh salad, while dinner is a five-course tasting menu that changes each night. Request that they make saffron chicken consommé, lotus stem kebabs with a spicy smooth spinach sauce, *gushtaba* (pounded lamb formed into small round dumplings and cooked in yoghurt gravy with mint), *rogan josh* with lemon rice or a spicy hot grilled *masala* fish. Whatever you do, don't miss their papaya and ginger jam slathered on toast for breakfast. Make sure you take a *shikhara* (boat) just before sunrise to the floating vegetable market – it's a moment lost in

time, totally memorable. Hot tea and biscuits are served along the way, which is wonderfully indulgent. The Sukoon philosophy is that there is more to life than its apparent surface.

Vivanta by Taj Dal View

Kralsangri, Brein,
www.vivantabytaj.com

A spectacular location set high on Kralsangri Hill with commanding views of Dal Lake and the surrounding mountains, this contemporary design hotel offers an international standard of luxury, woven into the essence of Kashmiri traditions. The Deluxe rooms are the way to go – expansive and warm as toast in winter. Watch the snow falling over the lake and mountains from your cosy interior, then take advantage of the infinity pool, private outdoor terraces and balconies during summer.

The kitchen cooked up a few typical Kashmiri dishes for one of my visits – *kokkor kanti*, chunks of chicken marinated in a few spices with ginger garlic paste then sautéed with onion and tempered cumin seeds; it was a knockout, as was the *nadir haak* – lotus stem braised with spinach. *Zafrani Phirni* was chef Subash's take on a Kashmiri classic dessert, using coarsely ground basmati rice in place of the traditional semolina, cooked in fresh sweet milk with saffron (like a rice pudding) and set in little clay pots and garnished with flaked almonds, was sublime.

EAT&SLEEP: GULMARG

The Khyber

Himalayan Resort and Spa, Gulmarg
www.khyberhotels.com

A comfortable two-hour drive from Srinigar by road, this area is a popular ski resort during winter, with India's only heli-skiing and deep powder snow, attracting many Europeans who are drawn to this off-beat location. Gulmarg, known as the meadow of flowers, is popular with wildlife enthusiasts and in summer, when the locals flock here (especially on weekends) to go horse riding through the hills or trekking through the forests and mountains. It's an ideal place to chill out and take in the pure mountain air. I have visited in both seasons and each have their appeal. The luxury balcony rooms facing the mountains are the best option and there is no need to leave your suite at all; it's the kind of place that encourages you to just be. Chef Manish Sharma cooks traditional Kashmiri food with an expert hand, whether it *is paneer tikka* with *podina*, *chicken tikka lal mirch* (with Kashmiri chilli) or whole trout cooked on the grill for lunch, or a full-

blown Wazwan feast for dinner at Cloves, the main restaurant in the hotel. Served on a copper *tarami* (thali plate), *murgh kanti* (chunks of chicken grilled and tossed with red onions, sweet peppers and Kashmiri chilli), and crispy fried slices of lotus stem tossed in spices and served with a walnut and radish chutney make terrific snacks to start. *Rajhma*, a *dal*-like dish of kidney beans simmered in tomato cardamom gravy, and *haaq saag*, Indian spinach stewed with tempered whole dried chillies, are two of my favourites from the stream of dishes, served with a delicate apple and cashew rice *pulao*. It's worth noting that this is a dry hotel; no alcohol is available, so if you fancy a tipple, bring your own and enjoy it in the comfort of your private balcony.

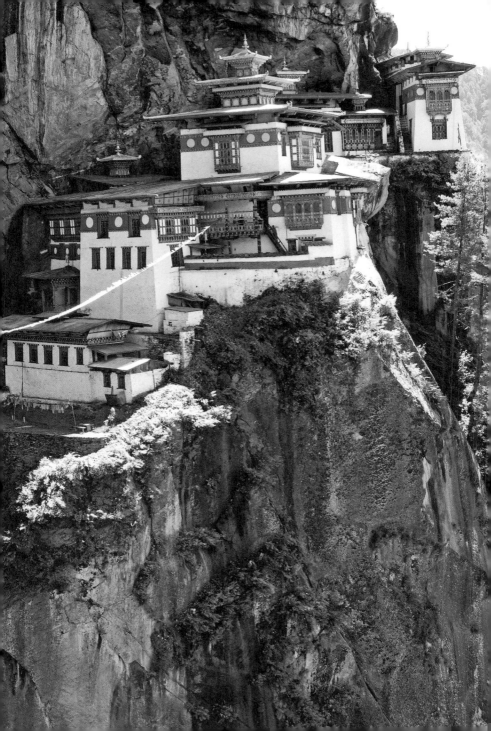

BHUTAN

Country

HAPPINESS IS THE MAGICAL, MYSTICAL KINGDOM OF Bhutan. Also known as Drukyul, the land of the thunder dragon, it's wedged into the Himalayan foothills; a richly textured landscape sandwiched between north-east India and Tibet. A small country, roughly the size of Switzerland, with a population of a mere 700 000, Bhutan is a paradise whose landscape is densely forested with blue pine, cedar and oak trees that cover more than 70 per cent of the country, giving it a distinctly alpine air. Much of the north is impenetrable, the exclusive habitat of nomadic shepherds with their yak herds. It is an idyllic Shangri-La that many people don't even know exists: one of the world's last frontiers; a time warp. Bhutan is a sanctuary of harmonious evolution whose history stretches back to the origins of Buddhism, with a population that is deeply spiritual, earthly, pragmatic and enterprising. The people live in harmony with nature and have evolved a unique identity derived from a rich cultural and religious heritage, in sharp contrast to the rest of the world. The national dress is worn by most of the population: the women wear *kira*, ankle-length skirts, while the men wear *kera,* long robes tied at the waist – compulsory for locals when visiting temples or *dzongs* (fortresses that are also religious and cultural centres), or for ceremonial occasions.

There are several main reasons to visit Bhutan – to immerse yourself in the spirituality of its Buddhist culture and visit its many monasteries and *dzongs*, and to trek through its valleys and mountains, whose national parks offer some of the best trekking experiences in the world. Its bucolic, dramatic landscapes are breathtaking in their beauty and magnitude. Archery and darts are national sports. Last but not least is its food, although it takes some fortunate encounters with food-loving locals to discover those secrets. The local diet includes *ema datse*, its national dish, a staple on any Bhutanese table. Whole chillies (either fresh green or dried red chillies) are cooked with butter and garlic and then simmered with the local cheese (*datse*, made with cows' milk, with a texture like a hard ricotta or feta, and which can develop into a strong fermented flavour when aged), creating a dynamic combination of heat and richness that everyone in the country is addicted to.

I fell in love with *zimsi*, an indigenous seed similar to pepita that is roasted with the local black pepper (like Sichuan), chilli and salt and pounded to a fine powder in an all-purpose seasoning, often added to potatoes and cucumbers, and introduced to me by my friend Chuni, one of the best home cooks in Bhutan – her knowledge of Bhutanese food culture is inimitable. She cooked dinner for me one night to prove how diverse and unknown the Bhutanese culinary repertoire really is. Her table included *jumbulay*, cold noodles seasoned with zimsi; roti bread stuffed with spiced beef and garlic chives; bible tripe cooked with green chillies; air-dried pork; salt-dried fish with tiny potatoes and green onions; pork slow braised with radishes, dried red chillies and spinach; fried chicken with shredded cabbage and dried red chilli; lamb trotters with Sichuan pepper and chives and two versions of *ema datse* – one spicy and one mild, one made with fresh cheese and the other with fermented cheese (think Roquefort in flavor) – both were sublime. What I noticed was how each dish was distinctive in its flavour and unlike anything else I had tasted in Bhutan – it was an epiphany. This was certainly the real deal and I felt most fortunate to have befriended Chuni and her husband Palden through a shared love of food. Their parting gift was a bag of *zimsi* and some homemade chilli pickles to bring home with me.

Saffron-robed monks are part of the landscape, from elderly lamas to young men being trained for a life of religious devotion. Druk Air now operates regular domestic flights from Paro to Bumthang (Jakar) and Tashigang, except when the winds are not amenable (usually during the monsoon season), so this has started to open up those once-remote regions that could previously only be accessed via a long, gruelling road journey. Bhutan has two peak seasons – March to May and then September to November, but it is also wonderful to travel outside these times – there are fewer visitors and the place can seem even more serene. I have been here during the summer monsoon months (July and August), when the weather is punctuated with daily showers. It has not been hard to manage, though the low-lying cloud prevents you from seeing the best views of the mountains, and I have it on good authority that a visit in December and January offers spectacular weather – pleasantly cool during the day and a little colder at night, perfect for firing up the *bukhari* fireplaces. ✿

ESSENTIAL SIGHTS

Taktsang Monastery (Tiger's Nest; see page 262) demands a visit during your stay in the kingdom. It is one of Bhutan's most revered monuments, where legend has it that Guru Rinpoche, the founder of Tibetan Buddhism, flew on the back of a mythical tiger and landed to meditate in the cave before bringing Buddhism to Bhutan in the eighth century. The climb is about 900 metres up from Paro valley; the monastery is at 3000 metres, so the air can get a little thin. The monastery defies gravity and literally hangs from its rock edifice of the towering cliff face – the round-trip hike takes between four and five hours depending on your fitness level. Mules are available to ride up but I reckon it's more dangerous as they walk right at the edge of the sheer drop to the valley below; you'd need nerves of steel to do this. And besides, the pilgrimage demands you walk it. Go early to avoid the crowds, enjoy the calm before they arrive and spend time with the resident lama. Start your trek from the car park by 7 a.m. at the latest.

Visit the **dzongs** in each region – medieval administrative fortresses such as **Paro Dzong** (above) that are strategically positioned across the country. Each important town has one; as centres of spiritual and secular power they also function as focal points for the country's artistic and intellectual heritage. They are commanding, impressive buildings that represent traditional Bhutanese Buddhist architecture.

Visit the former fortresses and administration centres for each province; try to make your visit coincide with when the monks do their chanting. **Punakha Dzong** is the most lavish, the largest and the most important – the spiritual centre of the kingdom.

Walk up to **Cheri Goemba**, a beautiful seventeenth-century monastery at the northern end of Thimphu Valley – it's a 3–4-hour trek there and back from Amankora Lodge.

Attend a lecture on **Gross National Happiness**; it is possible to attend a seminar (by Dasho Karma Ura, director of Bhutanese studies and a foremost authority) at one of the Amankora lodges to learn about this unique philosophy and take some its spiritual wisdom away with you.

Book a morning **hot air balloon flight** over the **Phobjikha valley** during spring or autumn with Balloons over Bhutan, owners of Gangtey Goenpa Lodge and of Balloons over Bagan in Myanmar – a spectacular early-morning vista of the mighty Himalayas, this is one of life's essential travel experiences. www.easternsafaris.com

Visit **Kyichu Lhakhang**, one of the oldest and most sacred monasteries in the kingdom that dates back to the seventh century – it's a fifteen-minute drive from the centre of Paro town.

Listen to the monks performing their morning or evening prayers at any one of the monasteries across the country.

Visit the **Royal Textile Academy** of Bhutan (also a museum) in Thimphu. www.royaltextileacademy.org

For some adventure, go **river rafting** in **Punakha** – either Mo-Chu or Pho-Chu rivers, which meet at Punakha Dzong.

Visit the **Haa Valley** – known as the hidden land rice valley, one of the least visited parts of the country. Drive from Paro over the Chele La Pass – the highest road in Bhutan, with uninterrupted views of the snow-capped Himalayas and home to the blue, white and pink poppy flowers – the blue poppy is the national flower. Trek through fields of wildflowers, rich pastoral land with buckwheat, barley, millet, wheat and potato crops – *momo*s (dumplings) from this region use the more dense buckwheat flour for the pastry and are stuffed with mustard greens or turnip tops and garlic. You can take a either a day excursion (about a two-

hour drive each way from the lodge to the valley), or it is possible to arrange a four-day / three-night trek through this region through the Amankora lodge at Paro.

There are small farmers' markets scattered across the kingdom of Bhutan as well as many makeshift stands along the road that offer organic fruits and vegetables, grilled corn on the cob and handmade cheese (*datse*). The **Centenary Market** (commonly referred to as the Weekend Market) in Thimphu is the biggest and most intriguing market in the country and is open on Friday, Saturday and Sunday. You will find fresh imported fish, huge amounts of dehydrated fish, and a wide variety of fruits and vegetables, as well as grains (mainly rice), specialty teas, and an entire area dedicated to incense, an important trade for the Bhutanese. The **Khuruthang market** in Punakha is open every Saturday, then on Sundays at nearby Wangdue, while **Paro** has a large market in the town centre every Sunday morning. Expect a flurry of activity and lively trade. In Bhutan, a mainly Buddhist country, it's common practice not to kill animals (they leave that to others), but there are butcher shops and stands that sell bacon and blood sausage as well as butter and cheese. These shops and stands are kept separate from all other produce, and meat (pork, beef, yak and chicken) is hugely popular.

Sample *ara*, the local rice wine served warm, made with corn and butter and flavoured with wild herbs.

The drive over the **Pele Le Pass** from Gangtey to Bumthang (regarded as the cultural heart of Bhutan) is breathtaking, passing through the virgin Black Forest and stopping off at Trongsa en route to visit **Chotse Dzong**, which houses a museum dedicated to the history of Bhutan's monarchy.

Visit the **Himalayan Chefs Garden**, next to the National Food Testing Laboratory in Yusipang on the outskirts of Thimphu, managed under the astute care of Wangchuk Kuenga, a passionate farmer and keen cook who spent years working at The Chef's Garden in Ohio, where he got the inspiration to return to his homeland and set up this incredibly valuable sustainable food resource for chefs in Bhutan – look up his Facebook page: Himalayan Chef's Garden.

Explore the four wide glacial valleys of **Bumthang** – lots of day walks, where you'll see gorgeous local houses with their bright colourful facades, home to some of the kingdom's most auspicious and highly revered houses of worship.

Buckwheat, millet and honey are regional specialities of Bumthang, a region that is also home to the **Swiss Cheese Factory**, which produces excellent Gouda and Emmental and the **Red Panda beer brewery** next door – they both offer tastings.

Potatoes and fiddlehead fern are staples in Gangtey; for me the potatoes were the most

surprising ingredient, because the variety there has a minimal amount of starch and tastes light and delicious.

Buy some fiery *dallay* chilli paste from one of the many food shops in Thimphu to take home with you – a flavoursome reminder of your Bhutanese travels.

Walk up to the **Khamsum Yuelley Namgyel Chorten** in the Punakha Valley – a Tantric Buddhist temple built by the Queen Mother to honour K5 (fifth king) in 2000. You walk through farmyards and rice paddies from Amankora Lodge; in the early morning is best – have a picnic breakfast in the gardens of the *chorten* (monument to a distinguished Buddhist). The views from the rooftop on the third level are spectacular.

Visit **Talo**, the family home of the Queen Mothers, and **Talo Goemba**, further uphill from the **Sangchhen Dorji Lhuendrup Lhakhang Nunnery**, a centre for higher learning and meditation for Buddhist nuns. This is a stunning temple perched on a mountain ridge overlooking the Punakha valley, about an hour's drive from Punakha town.

Try your hand at **archery**, the national sport, and realise it takes enormous effort and many years of practice to perfect the skill. Locals can shoot an arrow into a target at 140 metres, the standard competition distance.

Tashigang in the easternmost province on the border of NE India now has accommodation and is starting to open up, and Lingkhar Lodge has been recommended as the best place to stay. www.lingkhar.com

1) Making butter lamps, Paro monastery
2) Prayer flags, Thimphu Valley
3) School kids creating kitchen garden
4) Traffic director, central intersection, Thimphu

PLANNING YOUR PILGRIMAGE

To best experience all that Bhutan has to offer and for an unparalleled experience of pampering and immersion in Bhutanese culture, the Aman Resorts team offer bespoke journeys that include each of their five Amankora lodges, located in the valleys of Paro, Thimphu, Punakha, Gangtey and Bumthang. These are intimate retreats *par excellence* that set the benchmark. A rich cultural program is woven into your itinerary, making for an unforgettable experience. www.amanresorts.com/amankora/home.aspx

Transcend Travellers

www.bhutantranscend.com
toby@bhutantranscend.com

I can highly recommend this Thimphu-based travel company, where vivacious Tshewang (Toby) Namgayl is managing director. Luxury, adventure and memorable experiences are his trademark and he can arrange accommodation to suit your budget from various five-star properties to Bhutanese hotels and more rustic farmhouses, or a mix of each, whatever you prefer. His company specialises in trekking and adventure holidays.

FOOD IN BHUTAN

Trusted local friends tell me that most of the standard Bhutanese food served in the local restaurants and bar is pretty ordinary and basic (sometimes tragic), and doesn't do justice to their true culture, so be wise with your decisions on where to eat. If you're lucky enough to score an invitation for a home-cooked dinner by an enthusiastic and passionate local foodie, accept it – it will be a revelation. The following are all places I have tried personally and recommend.

EAT: THIMPHU

Ama

Karma Khangzang Building, Norzim Lam
Tel: 02 335 817

A modest local haunt with a Himalayan menu of Indian and Bhutanese dishes, their *sikam datse* (pork, bacon and cheese) and the fried beef and vegetable *momos* (dumplings) are the pick. They have a large lounge bar out the back that turns into a karaoke bar at night – popular with locals who like beer and *ara* (local rice wine).

Art Cafe

Doebum Lam, near Main Traffic Circle

Try the *totshe* (Bhutanese fried rice) or one of their pastries, baked inhouse. Coffee is good and the service is friendly.

Cloud 9 Gourmet Burger & Milk Bar

Ground floor, Ghaden Khanzang, Building 42, Phendey Lam
Thimphu, Bhutan
Tel: 02 331 417 | www.cloud9burgers.com

Australian chef Stana Johnson and her Bhutanese husband Toby Namgayl opened this terrific casual diner in 2014. The ingredients are all made inhouse, from the various breads used for the different burgers, to pickles and cured meats, to cakes and pastries. Open for breakfast, lunch and dinner as well as take-away, this has quickly become a favourite haunt for locals and visitors alike.

San Maru Restaurant

Norzim Lam, Thimpha
Tel: 77 342 451

Tashi and his Korean wife Eun Ji own this terrific Korean barbecue place in the centre of town; it's been a welcome addition, bringing a little diversity to the growing restaurant scene. The food is deliciously authentic, with Korean staples such as pickles, *kim chi*, *bibimbap* and *kimbap*, and little morsels that are cooked on the barbecue at the table.

Seasons Pizzeria

Hong Kong Market, Doendrup Lam
(a short block from Norzim Lam)
Tel: 02 327 413

Italian food cooked by Sanday, a Bhutanese woman who has learnt the craft and authentic flavours of Italian cooking. This is a small cafe with a sunny terrace that seats about thirty – there are often queues, so be prepared to wait. Local advice is to only go when Sanday is cooking. The menu has good pizzas (especially the one liberally doused with chilli) and pasta – the spaghetti with chilli and garlic oil hits the spot. Beer and soft drinks are also served.

Zombala

Pendey Lam, Hong Kong Market (one block behind Norzim Lam, the main street), Thimphu

This is the best place in town for *momos* (dumplings; I like the pork and vegetable ones the most), rice and noodle dishes. Their chilli sauce is an essential condiment. Try the *thupka*, a traditional dense noodle soup, if it's cold or if you're after something hearty.

EAT: PARO

Brioche Cafe

Main street (next to Bhutan Made store), Tshongdue, Paro
Tel: 17 741 231

A modest cafe with take-away pastries, cakes, biscuits, sandwiches and coffee. Everything is cooked by Amankora pastry chefs Rupa and Ruki.

Bukhari Restaurant

Uma Paro hotel Como
Tel: 8271 597
uma.paro@comohotels.com

Relaxed dining in this glass-walled circular restaurant, with wonderful views of Paro town and the valley beyond. The menu features contemporary, healthy dishes showcasing local produce. I love their selection of fresh fruit and vegetable juices.

Bhutanese, Indian and Western food is on offer; the yak burger is legendary and lives up to its reputation – perfectly formed and utterly delicious. The chicken *masala biryani* that comes in a brass *handi* pot with a *naan* bread lid to seal in the aromas during cooking is perfectly cooked with just the right amount of spicing. The potato and pea samosas with a tangy tamarind chutney make a great starter snack.

Sonam Trophel Restaurant

Paro Tshongdue

The best *momo* dumplings in Paro (some say in Bhutan) are to be had at this modest authentic Bhutanese restaurant. It's on the right side of the main street as you drive into Paro town from the airport or the dzong – don't confuse it with the hotel of the same name. Look out for its big blue and white sign on the side of the building.

EAT: BUMTHANG

Sunny Restaurant

Chamkhar Town, Jakar
Tel: 17 254 212

Typical Bhutanese dishes – I came here to try *datse*, the local cheese, and the menu has various cheese dishes – chilli cheese (*ema datse*), potato (*kewa datse*), mushroom (*shamo datse*) or cauliflower with chilli and cheese (*meto copi ema datse*) where the vegetables and fresh chillies are slow braised with the local white cheese.

SLEEP: PARO

Amankora Paro Lodge

www.amanresorts.com
amankora@amanresorts.com

Start the day with yoga each morning, with views through the pine forest. This is the largest of the Amankora lodges, with twenty-four suites (above). Every suite has uninterrupted views of Bhutan's most sacred mountain, Mount Jumolhari (except during monsoon season in July and August, when cloud cover prevents clear views), and the nearby ruins of Drukgyel Dzong –

an easy fifteen-minute walk from the lodge. Lounge around the outdoor fire pit in the late afternoon for a sunset drink (weather permitting). Dinner offers either a set Indian menu or a la carte Western bistro-style dishes – the tomato and chive salad and the wild mushroom and spinach ravioli are both good healthy options.

Hotel Gangtey Palace

Gangtey, Paro, Bhutan
www.gangteypalace.net
Tel: 8271 301

The former ancestral home of owners Genzing and Tobgye Dorji (above) is set amidst the scenic beauty of the Paro Valley with spectacular views across to the imposing Dzong on the opposite hill. The decor is traditional Bhutanese, full of charming heritage character. Of the nineteen rooms available, suite 301 is the pick, with excellent of the town and valley beyond. Their Glass House Bar offers the best views and is ideal for lounging with a late-afternoon drink even if you aren't staying here. The home-style food prepared in their kitchen is deliciously authentic, with dishes such as *ema datse* (naturally), *shamday* (rice fried with chilli, ginger, egg and coriander) and *shamu datse* (mushrooms and cheese). When I had lunch there with the family, they served a freshly baked apple pie from Brioche Cafe in Paro town.

Uma Paro

www.comohotels.com/umaparo
uma.paro@comohotels.com

Operated by the Singapore-based Como Hotel group, who have key properties throughout Asia and the Caribbean, this hotel is situated on the hill overlooking the airport and town with expansive views of the Paro Valley. The rooms are of various sizes and standards (many are quite small), and there's a terrific yoga centre and serene spa facility. The food at their inhouse restaurant Bukhari is exemplary.

Zhiwa Ling Hotel

Satsam Chorten, Paro
www.zhiwaling.com

This enchanting hotel (above) is built on the grand scale of Bhutanese traditional design and was the first large-scale, five-star Bhutanese-owned hotel property to open in Bhutan, with forty-two spacious and comfortable suites. Their Royal Raven Suite has an altar in the lounge room and is pretty spectacular. The kitchen produces delicious *momos* (dumplings). It's a couple of kilometres out of town on the road to Taktshang Monastery and caters to larger groups as well as busloads of visitors. The hotel's name is pronounced 'Shorling'.

SLEEP: THIMPHU

Amankora Thimphu Lodge

www.amanresorts.com

amankora@amanresorts.com

Although there are many other options in Thimphu, none can match the pampering hospitality and exceptional service of the Amankora lodges; their deep commitment to local culture is unparalleled. The lodge, which offers sixteen spacious suites, is situated in a pine forest about fifteen minutes' drive from the city centre, and the style is elegant yet casual, and respectful of Bhutanese heritage. Dinner offers either a set Thai menu or a la carte Western dishes. The *pad thai* on the lunch menu is my firm favourite and the fried rice with egg is total comfort food.

SLEEP: PUNAKHA

Amankora Punakha Lodge

Punakha Valley

www.amanresorts.com

amankora@amanresorts.com

This lodge includes a traditional Bhutanese farmhouse (below) that serves as the common area for guests with a main dining room, private rooms for dining or a meeting, an altar room (where you can make a water offering with a local monk to start the day), a sitting room and a library. With only eight suites, this lodge feels like a luxurious and intimate country house. Dinner offers either a set menu with southern-style Bhutanese dishes or a la carte Western – light, clean flavours using local produce. The cooking here is astute

and utterly authentic, with dishes typical of southern Bhutan such as *churu om jaju* (river weeds and milk soup), *jasha maru* (chicken cooked with ginger, onion and tomato), *kewa tshem* (potato simmered with green chilli, ginger and onion), and *langphu rou ngo ngo* (fried fiddlehead fern with tomato). Dinner is always served with local red rice.

Uma Punakha

Punakha Valley
www.comohotels.com/umapunakha

At the western end of the valley, with expansive views of the river towards Khamsum Yuelley Namgyel Chorten, this sister property to Uma Paro (above) has eleven rooms and small suites and two villas for family groups. A stylish country lodge, half an hour's drive from Punakha town, although for me it lacks the attention to detail of the Amankora lodges. The outdoor terrace is stunning.

SLEEP: GANGTEY

Amankora Gangtey Lodge

Phobjika Valley
www.amanresorts.com
amankora@amanresorts.com

Nestled into the pine forest hills, with scenic views across the less-visited Probjika Valley, this area was once a glacier, home to the black-necked crane and a wide variety of bird life. This is the wetlands of the country and one of its most important wildlife sanctuaries. Gangtey is the ideal place to stay if you are a keen birdwatcher or into botany. There is so much to see and there are plenty of relatively easy hikes through some of the most picturesque parts of the region. The altitude is high enough that the landscape is often shrouded in clouds, giving a mystical aura. The valley is part of the Black Mountains National Park, one of Bhutan's most important wildlife sanctuaries and home to flocks of endangered black-necked cranes who migrate here every winter from Russia. A morning walk through the forest and across the valley floor is invigorating.

This intimate lodge has eight suites and the food is perfect for its location: honest, hearty country-style dishes like *kakur thingye jaju* (pumpkin soup seasoned with ginger and local Bhutanese black pepper) or *jasha hensey maru* (a light curry of minced chicken and spinach). Their *ema datse* (green chillies cooked with the local cheese) is among the best I have tasted. A standout on the lunch menu is the yak chilli con carne with locally made Emmentaler cheese and corn bread, served in the small cast-iron pot in which it was cooked, one of the most delicious dishes imaginable, cooked to perfection by chef Sha and his ▶

kitchen team. Arrange to luxuriate in a hot stone bath (using stones from the river bed) in an old stone hut out in the fields in the late afternoon, watching the sun sink over the vast valley, with totally uninterrupted views of forests and mountains, and feel the therapeutic effects of the mineral-laden water and the medicinal fresh wormwood floating on the surface.

Gangtey Goenpa Lodge

Phobjika Valley

A wonderful new addition to the valley, set high on a hill behind Gantey Goenpa, the local monastery, this stunning and beautifully designed country lodge has twelve spacious suites with expansive uninterrupted views across the whole valley, giving the impression of glamorous farmhouse life.

Chef Sara (a Swede who has taken up residence here and cooks like an angel) makes the breakfast table very seductive with treats such as scrambled eggs with *azze* (the most divine chilli coriander and *datse* condiment imaginable), *kule* (buckwheat pancakes with bacon), and *azze* and *shamday* – butter-fried rice with boiled egg and *azze*. Pastry chef Tracey bakes the best pastries in Bhutan, and don't miss her condensed milk bread, perfect with one of Sara's house-made jams – either wild strawberry or orange marmalade, or the local Bumthang honey. For dinner, choose from either the Indian, Western, Asian or Bhutanese set menus. Flavours are refined and precise.

SLEEP: BUMTHANG

Amankora Bumthang Lodge

Jakar Town, Bumthang
amankora@amanresorts.com
www.amanresorts.com

In central Bhutan, this lodge is the furthermost from Paro and Thimphu as you travel east through the spectacular Black Mountains. Bumthang is the spiritual hub of the country, home to many temples and monasteries, the centre for Bhutan's art and painting traditions and consists of four valleys – Choekhor, Tang, Ura and Chhume. As the roads are not great and are currently being upgraded (a painstakingly slow process), the drive is very long if you do it in both directions, so I strongly recommend that you drive one way and fly the other – arrange your itinerary around these sometimes infrequent domestic flight times. Druk Air are now operating domestic flights but their timetable is irregular, so it's best to check beforehand to avoid disappointment. This lodge has sixteen suites and is surrounded by apple orchards. It's neighbour to the royal Wangdichholing Palace (home to the first and second kings of Bhutan). Dinner offers either a set Bhutanese menu or an a la carte continental menu, and for lunch there are some terrific salads and nourishing broths on the menu. Try the *puta* – buckwheat noodles tossed with fresh chilli, mustard oil and green

onions, or the *nay kha chung tshem* (asparagus cooked with local cheese). This is a great place to borrow one of the lodge's bikes and ride through Jakar town and the valley beyond. The lodge can also arrange for you to have a private lunch with a family in their farmhouse in nearby Dorjibee village, or you can learn to make *khabzey* (Bhutanese biscuits), with a local expert in the lodge kitchen. Make time to visit Kurje Lhakhang, one of the oldest and most sacred temples in Bhutan, surrounded by 108 stupas (the number is symbolic of *Chig Ja Gye* – the 108 principal temptations in Buddhism).

ACKNOWLEDGEMENTS

Over the past two decades of travelling through India, I have had the good fortune to meet some incredible like-minded souls and kindred spirits who have opened their hearts and homes, shared their food secrets and taken me out to eat whenever I have visited. I have been lucky enough to have developed an enviable network of friends, colleagues and ground support throughout India, which I share with guests who travel with me on any one of my bespoke Tasting India tours. These have been life-changing experiences. My deepest gratitude goes to the following people – thank you for sharing these travel and culinary adventures and pointing my tastebuds in the right direction; every mouthful has been a revelation, and my horizons expanded because of your generosity, which resonates through these pages.

To the extraordinary teams of travel experts who magically arrange my ground support in India, no visit would be the same without your exacting expertise. Thank you all so much: Jamshyd Sethna and Lucy Davidson at Banyan Tours + Travel and Shakti Himalaya, Alok Singh at Enriching Journeys and Jennifer Wilkinson at Epicurious Travel.

My eternal gratitude to the expert city guides who have afforded me generous and warm hospitality, and to the home cooks and chefs who have cooked for me and shared culinary secrets and treasured family heirloom recipes so generously.

In Bombay: Anjali Tolani, Lizzie Chapman, Saket Khanna, Tejaswi Gupte, Harsh Tanwar, Yamini Oja. In Delhi: Navina Jafa, William Dalrymple, Manjeet Singh Ghumman, Rachna Sharma, Puja Sahu, Robyn Bickford, Manish Mehrotra, Marut Sikka, Ritesh Negi, Prem Singh, Tejas Sovani, Sameer Himalian, Atul Soni, Karen Yepthomi, Natalie Daalder, Mohammad Saleem, Serena Chopra and Tamara Cannon. In Goa: Jonas Cotinho, Neville Proenca, Oscar d'Chuna, Siddharth Savkur, Anita and Sarika Satakr. In Madhya Pradesh: Aimee Junker and Shyamanand Choudhary. In Varanasi: Indrajeet Kumar,

Mr Shashank and Sumalya Sarkar. In Amritsar: Ahbimanyu and Gayatri Mehru, Gagan Khanna. In Gujarat: Gautam Popat. Across Rajasthan: Dumisani Sakuinje, Jai Singh Rathore and family, Vasundhra and Nandi Singh, Harsh and Shrinidri Singh, Siddharth and Rashmi Singh, Abhay Singh, Durga Singh, Richard Hanlon, Vimal Dhar, Vishal Gautam, Nikkitesh Bhati, Satish Dhole, Prateek Kumar, Hajra Ahmad, Naresh Bharghava, Ramkesh Saini and Adiraj Rathore. In Kolkata: Seema and Mohan Chandran, Sunil and Marina Gandhi, Abhijit (Bhaiya) Bose, Arun Lal, Sanjay Kapur, Husna-Tara Prakesh and Rakhi Dasgupta. In Hyderabad: Jonti Rajagopalan, Manisha Gadhalay, Heartz Desirez, Mohit Agarwal, Girish Sehgal and Arun Sundararaj. Fiona Caulfield in Bangalore and Mini Chandran in Karnataka. In Kerala: Nimmy Paul, Faisa Moosa, Ajita Skaria, Manoj Nair, Sabu Joseph, Anish Kumar, Sasi K.K., Sujith K.K., Jayan K.V., and Anu and Anaissa Philip. In Tamil Nadu: Praveen Anand, Meenakshi Meyyappan, Malavika and Vijiya. Across the Himalayas: Yeshi Lama, Altaf Chapri, Siddharth Pradhan, Manzoor Dar, Jyoti Singh, Shakila Riyas, Nikhil Kapur, Dr Mathew, Raaja Bhasin, Deepak Kumar Rai, Amin Lone and Narendra Sharma.

In Bhutan: John Reed, Palden and Chuni Tshering, Tobije and Genzing Dorji, Stana Johnson and Tshewang Toby Namgayl, Carolyn Hamer-Smith, Khin Omar Win, Sara Rezgui, Glenn Monk, Sha Bdr Pradhan and Wangchuk Kuenga.

Your collective voices have given resonance, depth and clarity to this comprehensive, erudite guide.

My writing is always made possible by the enduring love and support of my partner Margie Harris, who shares travel adventures and exploring new frontiers with me; the vision, wisdom and implicit trust of my publisher Julie Gibbs, who shares my love affair with India and Bhutan and breathes life into my written work; the painstaking care and eagle eye of editor Jocelyn Hungerford, and the cleverness and brilliant attention to detail by designer Daniel New.

GLOSSARY

While definitions have been given wherever possible for specific dishes, these are some of the more commonly used food terms.

chaat – a general description for fried savoury snacks

dal – a general term for lentil dishes

dosa – a pancake made from ground rice and white lentils that are soaked and left to ferment overnight then made into a batter; the thickness of the dosa varies in each region: some are steamed, some are cooked on a flat pan until crisp

falooda – transparent vermicelli (sev) threads and basil seeds in sweet syrup with a jelly consistency

halwa – can refer to many types of fudgy sweet, and also a pudding made from carrots, nuts, sultanas, sugar and sometimes a cereal (whole wheat), depending on its region

kokum – a fruit native to south-west India, used as a souring agent in dishes (mostly coconut-based), rather like tamarind, known for its cooling properties

kulfi – ice-cream made with reduced milk, sweetened and flavoured with saffron, cardamom, pistachio or almonds and frozen in small conical moulds

lassi – a yoghurt drink, or a thinner version made with buttermilk, served either sweetened or unsweetened (with salt)

masala – refers to many different types of spice mix

mishti doi – a fermented sweetened yoghurt or curd; a Bengali staple

naan – an oval-shaped, leavened flatbread (made with yeast), baked in a tandoor oven

paan – a combination of areca nut, lime paste, aromatic spices and sometimes tobacco wrapped in a betel leaf and folded into a triangle, chewed for its mildly stimulating effect; a mouth freshener that also aids digestion

paratha – a fried, unleavened flatbread, enriched with ghee, the dough rolled and folded to create layers that yield a flaky character

puri – a deep-fried unleavened flatbread that puffs up as it cooks, hollow in the centre; sometimes called balloon bread

rasgulla – sweetened milk balls made from soft cheese and semolina, soaked in rosewater syrup, a Bengali speciality

roti – an unleavened flatbread made with whole wheat flour

sandeesh – a sweet milk dessert with a melt-in-the-mouth texture, a speciality of the Durga Puja festival

shrikhand – strained, sweetened yoghurt flavoured with saffron, typical of Gujarat

thali – a meal consisting of a selection of different dishes served in small bowls arranged on one plate; also refers to the name of the plate it is served on, which is round with raised edges

INDEX

INDEX

LANTERN

UK | USA | Canada | Ireland | Australia
India | New Zealand | South Africa | China

Penguin Books is part of the Penguin Random House group of companies
whose addresses can be found at global.penguinrandomhouse.com.

Penguin
Random House
Australia

First published by Penguin Group (Australia), 2015

1 3 5 7 9 10 8 6 4 2

Text copyright © Christine Manfield 2015
Photographs copyright © Christine Manfield 2015

The moral right of the author has been asserted.

Cover and text design by Daniel New © Penguin Group (Australia)
Author photograph © Margie Sixel
All photography by Christine Manfield except for p. 10 © Pawel Pietraszewski / Shutterstock,
p. 40 © Evgeny Baranov / Shutterstock, p. 52 © Vivek (Bobby) Bhargawa,
p. 115 and p. 118 © Margie Sixel, p. 133 © Jennifer Wilkinson, p. 166 © Arteki / Shutterstock,
p.176 © Markus Gebauer / Shutterstock, p. 242 © Peter Thornhill, p. 220 © f9photos / Shutterstock,
p. 232 © Sihasakprachum / Shutterstock, p. 262 and p. 268 © Fritz 16 / Shutterstock
Typeset in Dante by Post Pre-press Group, Brisbane, Queensland
Colour separation by Splitting Image Colour Studio, Clayton, Victoria
Printed and bound in China by 1010 Printing International Ltd

National Library of Australia
Cataloguing-in-Publication data:

Manfield, Christine, author, photographer.
Christine Manfield's guide to India and Bhutan / Christine Manfield.
ISBN: 9781921383922 (paperback)
Includes index.
India – Guidebooks.
India – Description and travel.
Bhutan – Guidebooks.
Bhutan – Description and travel
Dewey Number: 915.4

penguin.com.au/lantern